TWO SUITCASES

AND A DOG

Finnbar Mac Eoin

ORIGINAL WRITING

Cover photo 'Bono Bono and Finn'
By Ward Price
Savannah College of Art and Design,
Savannah South Georgia and Lacoste, Provence France.

Two suitcases and a Dog and Table illustrations by stevenweekes@gmail.com

978-1-906018-87-0

A CIP catalogue for this book is available from the National Library.

Published by ORIGINAL WRITING LTD., Dublin, 2009.

Printed by Cahills, Dublin.

DEDICATIONS

Not to my wife, who said that it would never be published and if it was, it's only purpose would be for leveling tables

And to my friends Harper Collins, who not only agreed with my wife, but also said that the company had decided not to return my original manuscript in an effort to save money.

Caron and Finn

ABOUT THE AUTHOR

Finbarr Mac Eoin continues to work as a gardener and when he is not writing best sellers, he has taken up a hobby which he developed when he was at sea. That is, the manufacturing of furniture for uneven surfaces. Tables are his speciality and he is currently trying to convince IKEA, that not only his furniture, but also his book is worth looking at.

Mossy

ACKNOWLEDGEMENTS

Recognition, admission, confession, thanks, an imitation of receipt ! This is what my Chambers tells me. I am particularly interested in the latter, "An imitation of receipt". Sounds like forgery or even plagiarism ! Yes indeed it does and we all at sometime in our lives, are impressed by the achievement of other people. To the point of wanting to mimic them. They can be heroes or villains, it makes no difference to us, we are smitten by them.

I met Eugene Carey, a solicitor, at my nephews wedding and he said to me, "Finn, when I was a young lad you were my hero". Has anyone ever asked, who's the heroes hero ? We finally get to the acknowledgment.

Finbarr Rubens (Molloy) from Mallow was my hero and I never thought the day would come for me to let him know.

To my brother Patrick Owens of the Hibernian Hotel in Mallow and to my sister Jacqueline, thanks for all your support.

HIBERNIA

Haunted by a Celtic shroud

Like a snow blanket

That envelopes the hiber-nation

As leaky taps announce

The nightly frost by silence

I return to the Motherland

And there,

Untouched by life's anomalies

My wisdom's understood

Chapter 1

We never meant to go to France. It was all because of the dog.

After ten years in New Zealand, we arrived at Amsterdam's Schiphol airport. It was 7 a.m. on a damp and foggy October morning and Mossy, our wire-haired fox terrier, had been retained by the customs awaiting clearance.

Had it not been for the quarantine regulations in Britain and Ireland, we would have flown directly home to Cork, but we decided on the smuggling option because neither of us was prepared to put Mossy through six months in some dingy English holding bay and besides, she was too old for that.

Schiphol can prove a bit of a maze for first-timers, especially after a 32-hour flight, but we finally tracked Mossy down. The sight of her in a cage was enough to reinforce our resolve to accept exile on the continent until we found a way to foil the customs authorities.

The airfreight cage, which was built in New Zealand, was about twice the size of her and we noticed that the self-feeding water trough hadn't been touched. On closer inspection, we saw that she had neither wet nor soiled the straw.

After we finally cleared up all the details, which in Schiphol are easy and after we had explained our reason for coming to Holland, we were given Mossy and she made straight for the grass and relieved herself, in what could only be described as a marathon piss, with neither the thunder of the airliners nor the spitting rain bothering her.

We had made no further plans beyond arriving in Europe, so there we were, with two suitcases and a dog, no continental language and approximately £400 to our names. It was my side of the globe and my responsibility and as I was accompanied by my New Zealand-born wife who hadn't yet learned how to complain, my bohemian lifestyle was allowed to flourish and my strong belief in Irish luck gave me the confidence I needed to deal with the next phase of our adventure.

Amsterdam seemed like a good place to base ourselves, but because of the country's drug reputation we thought that smuggling a dog from Holland to England might prove difficult, so at seven o'clock in the morning with no onward plans, we made a spontaneous decision to give France a go, and bought two train tickets to Boulogne-sur-Mer.

Although it was an offence for a dog to travel without a ticket, Mossy had already cost us enough and we simply could not afford it, besides she was small enough to hide under a seat.

As we left Schiphol, I tried to imagine what Caron was thinking as she gazed out of the window at the gloom of the low lands. Was she questioning the wisdom of my decision to quit New Zealand? Did she know that in Ireland, where these clouds were manufactured, the weather would be worse?

Perhaps she was missing the blue skies of Wanaka, the open spaces of home. I wished that it were night as we passed endless condominiums, motorways, and what appeared even to me, to be the gates of hell. Luckily they had both fallen asleep and I could easily have joined them, but I had to keep an eye out for the ticket collector, in case Mossy got sprung. As I peered out of the window, I looked at my reflection in the glass and although I detected a degree of uncertainty, I knew that my continuous ill-health and depression in New Zealand had shown no signs of abating and George Bernard Shaw's saying about the place:

'I would hate to live there, but it would be a great place to die!' led me to think, well Mr Shaw, I could always go back to accommodate the latter.

Sitting there, I think I experienced the meaning of responsibility for the first time in my life, past and future becoming strange bedfellows as I permutated a lifetime of running away yet never finding contentment. Questions and doubts kept my long overdue sleep at bay.

How wise was it going back to Ireland after thirty years? Where would we live? Would I be accepted back? Ireland had become affluent since my time there. Would I be seen as a failed disciple of the Commonwealth, returning to pluck a golden hair from the Celtic Tiger?

We were somewhere in Belgium and there was a brief stop, enough for Mossy to honour the Mannequin Pis in one of the flower boxes on the station platform. People sitting opposite were amused by my antics as I hid Mossy in my jacket under the seat every time the ticket man came by.

Caron was still sleeping. I was glad, because Belgium seemed even more sombre than what she'd already missed in Holland. Our next stop was Lille, where we had to change for Boulogne-sur-Mer.

It reminded me of a stopover at Sydney for Auckland where almost everyone left the plane and those of us that remained gave the impression that we were characters in a Bram Stoker novel on our way to some sinister destination.

After Lille, the almost empty train certainly did not bode well and I got the frighteners. Caron was falling in and out of sleep and despite all my efforts to hold the fort until Boulogne-sur-Mer, I finally conceded defeat and dropped off. Mossy must have had her sleep quota and had taken herself off for a walk through the carriages to return with a French ticket inspector in tow. He gently tapped us awake and we think he asked if the chienne was ours. He checked our tickets, patted the dog, smiled and perhaps said, (as we had no french at the time)

"Bienvenue en France!" and permitted the dog to travel free.

CHAPTER 2

Arriving at Boulogne Ville, almost twelve hours since our landing at Schiphol, I found a cell phone that someone had left behind on the seat. This looked like another good omen for our first day in France and I made a quick call to a friend in London to advise him of our arrival, and of course to tell him of my good fortune at finding the phone.

As we set off with our two suitcases and the dog for the centre ville, the phone rang, with a French voice on the line making no sense to us. He hung up and called back a few minutes later. This time, a young girl who spoke schoolgirl English explained that it was her father's phone and could we rendezvous somewhere to return it? For us, the only somewhere we knew was the station - so back we went. We met and I admitted that I had made a call to London, which didn't seem to bother him. He gave us a 50 FF tip for our troubles and suddenly things were looking up.

En route once more to the centre ville, we found a bar that had rooms for 120FF a night (about £10 at the time). Dogs were welcome at no extra charge. We had a shower and hit the town. Arriving in a square where fish restaurants were as plentiful as pubs at home we discovered that vegetarianism was not a concept readily understood by the French, so we settled for moules marinières (without the moules), pommes frites, lashings of baguette and Normandy butter plus a glass of red or white wine. The total cost was 50 FF. Our first meal in France, and it had been paid for by a Frenchman!

We tied Mossy outside, but the restaurant owner came into the by then, almost full restaurant, asking something about a chien which he had untied and she came directly up to us, wagging her tail. Our naivety of the French custom of allowing dogs in restaurants brought a smile from other diners. They began to call her Milou, Milou, which we discovered was the name of Tintin's dog, also a fox terrier.

One of the waiters brought a bowl of water and a few pieces of biscuit so Mossy was not being overlooked inside either. How civilised it all seemed, and such a far cry from what we had expected. New Zealand practice was to keep dogs tied up outside for the entire meal, like horses in Western movies. But then New Zealand would not win any prizes for sensitivity or indeed anything cultural either.

How wonderful everything felt in France and how exciting it was to be amongst such difference. Tomorrow had suddenly lost all importance and despite being filled with doubt initially, a holiday feeling had come over us, giving procrastination its rightful place.

I browsed through the restaurant's Visitor's Book and found an entry that had been made the previous evening. I'm sure it would have made no sense if I'd read it a day earlier, because I was unaccustomed to the French traditional greeting practised by everyone arriving in the restaurant.

The entry read:

'There's only one thing wrong with this damn country, you can't choose who you can kiss".

signed, Amanda Fry.

As evening closed on our first day in France, this did not seem such a bad complaint and we hoped one day to run into Amanda Fry in order to express our delight on reading her complimentary quote which gave us so much encouragement at the beginning of our epic tale in France.

Our bedroom window was just opposite a set of traffic lights and under normal circumstances, the revving of engines and changing colours would have made it impossible to sleep, but as soon as we hit the pillows, all three of us slept like sedated babies with a spoonful of whiskey in our bottles.

My first recollection of waking up in France, wasn't the hustle and bustle of morning traffic, it was the aroma of fresh brewed coffee from downstairs.

While Mossy and Caron continued in slumber, I went and got le petit dejeuner for everyone, and all three of us breakfasted in bed. Equipped with a pocket Larousse and an innocent ignorance of France, we embarked on an incredible adventure which, in hindsight, seemed an impossibility and I'm not sure I would choose to relive it.

We vacated the room, leaving our suitcases in the care of the proprietor and made our way back into town to look for the Tourist Information Centre and someone who spoke English. Just opposite the post office, was a little bus shelter type building that looked like a converted toilet and it was here we met Boy Lingus, a bi-lingual young Frenchman who gave real meaning to the term 'entente cordiale'.

I remember once in New Zealand a doctor saying to me:

"I'm only as good as my secretary."

It's true. The first person you meet can set the precedent and Boy Lingus had us off to a great start in France.

We weren't the average tourists looking for Chateau Napoleon or some fancy restaurant to dine in, no, we were looking for the social security office, because we wanted to go on the dole and Larousse didn't seem to have a word for that!

Boy Lingus gave us a gift of a 2FF city map, which had everything important in colour and he penned in the non-tourist route.

CHAPTER 3

It was then that we discovered that the French agencies dealing with work and no work were ASSEDIC, CAF, ANPE and DSS. Boy Lingus thought it better to start with CAF (Caisse d'Allocations Familiales) so we asked him to write us a letter in French explaining our predicament, that we had just arrived from New Zealand, but could not continue on to Ireland due to rabies control and of course that we spoke no French and had very little money.

The French love affair with dogs is far more genuine than that of the British and though we weren't yet to know it, Mossy was to become our saviour.

We were about to receive our first lesson on the workings of the French system and as we arrived at the CAF bureau just before noon, I approached the reception with my note from Boy Lingus and was promptly shown the clock. It was clear that the exodus for the midday lunch rush had already commenced.

The sudden mayhem caught us by surprise; cars were rushing in all directions as though some major catastrophe was imminent. Traffic lights became victims of hypoglycaemic colour blindness, proving that le petit dejeuner hasn't the staying power of bacon, eggs, sausage, tomatoes and a fried slice. We calculated that our chances of being fatally injured in France could only occur at this time of day. For us, it was to be a baguette au fromage de chevre, Badoit and a long wait.

Fortunately, Mossy had always eaten the same food as us and she was quite content as we sat there watching the fishing boats return. Boulogne-sur-Mer is the biggest fishing port in France, and the fresh fish on the pier would be well within our budget - had we not been vegetarians (true vegetarians).

Back at the CAF Bureau, Caron waited in the garden with Mossy as I was much more experienced at that sort of thing, I was deputised to do the business. After presenting my letter from Boy Lingus, I was taken in to an interrogation room where a Lady Lingus was brought in to ascertain why I had left Ireland thirty years ago and why more recently I had left New Zealand. The line of questioning amazed me and I couldn't see any relevance to our impending dilemma, but anyone familiar with France will be aware that the French don't move about in their own country other than on holidays and they are very suspicious of nomads.

After a half hour of confusion, she told me that I was in the wrong office. Cases of homelessness were dealt with by the DASS (Department of d'Action Sanitaire et Sociale). I asked her for my introduction note back, but she insisted on writing her own note. To this day, one of my regrets is that I did not keep a copy of what Boy Lingus wrote, because we have no idea what he actually said in it.

On our way back to the DASS, Mossy developed what we called the sits, she refused to walk and despite all sorts of coaxing and pulling, she had had enough. We had never encountered anything like it before, but then it dawned on us that dogs suffer from jet lag just as humans do and she had obviously not slept during the flight, due to fright I imagine.

We had to carry her in our arms as she was out for the count.

At the DASS office, we again wondered if we were in the right place, because the Sanitaire bit seemed particularly dodgy. We found ourselves in the company of the worst misfortunates we'd ever seen, real destitutes, probably drug addicts, alcoholics, homeless and abused, and some just wanting to get out of the rain and cold.

To Caron it looked like a precursor of what we would have to go through in Ireland. It was all so dismal, and enough to drive anyone to drink. My own feelings of despair had descended like a low cloud as the reality of County Cork entered my consciousness. I too felt like reaching for the rescue remedy.

'What the hell am I doing here with this lot,' I thought miserably, 'I'm better than that!'

Some weather-beaten Frenchman asked me for a cigarette, I don't know why he bothered - the room was already like a

Chinese opium den with a thick haze of Gitanes and Gauloise smoke. Then came the wine bottle, which was being passed around and partial as I am to a drop, I was rather hoping we'd be excluded. But after Caron refused, I felt it would not be polite for me to do likewise. I had no alternative but to partake and it was the worst gut rot I had ever tasted and believe me, I have drank some shite in my day, but this was as close to vinegar, as the salt is to the fish, in chips.

Mossy was still asleep, or off duty as those people in our midst would have seen it. We were not to know, but a dog is a status symbol for beggars and hoboes in France. The only difference was that we were slightly better dressed than everyone around us and we also had wonderful suntans after ten years in the Antipodes. But it made no difference, we were, in their eyes, just as much failures as they were.

Despite everything going on, it was imperative that the receptionist got her lipstick straight before she attended to us and when we were finally called, I approached like Oliver with my introduction note. The only thing I could say to assist our case was "Bonjour Mademoiselle!"

It was virtually the same procedure as at the CAF. An interpreter was called in and so commenced another interrogation while Caron and Mossy stayed outside with the Gitane smokers.

"But why France?" I was asked. I couldn't tell them that I was only here until I smuggled the dog to England or that I had seen Jean de Florette four times or that I read as far as the April section of Peter Mayle's book, 'A Year in Provence'.

I was about to say all this, but when I thought about it seriously, I decided to tell them the truth - that I was a victim of draconian Anglo-Saxon rules and that I loved my dog and was prepared to exile myself in France rather than put her through six months of quarantine in England.

Bingo! I hit the jackpot as the English came in for a right ear bashing and I was immediately asked to produce the pauvre chien.

9

Fortunately for us, Mossy's New Zealand tags were still on her collar.

"Ah, Milou!" they exclaimed as they crowded around her.

"Comme elle est belle!" and all sorts of affectionate utterings.

Mossy was in, now only Caron and I had to pass muster.

The famous French clip folder was produced and this was a good sign. We were asked to furnish all documentation, passports, airline tickets and Mossy's papers. They photocopied everything and filed it neatly like the white linen over the Eucharist at Mass.

Because we had been away from Europe for so many years, we had no idea of the problems with asylum seekers from Eastern Europe and that was why, despite our Irish passports, the authorities were taking no chances.

What came next amazed us. The woman rang the Irish Embassy in Paris and spoke to someone for a little while before passing me the phone.

"Ar bfuil aon gaelge agat?" (Do you speak Irish?) the familiar accent of a fellow countryman enquired.

"Ta alan gaelge agamsa," (I speak it well) I replied, and was asked to pass the phone back to the woman. What a cunning bit of French manoeuvring that was! She was simply ascertaining the validity of my claim that I was indeed Irish and she had got my own Embassy to verify it by listening to my accent.

We were asked to take a seat outside while our case was being assessed and since we had satisfied them that I was indeed Irish, I felt confident that something positive was going to happen.

All this sort of stuff was new to Caron, as indeed it would be to white (Pakeha) New Zealanders, but of course it would not have been unfamiliar to the Maori, who are still an underclass in their own country.

We were called into the office again and later handed our third introductory letter of the day, this time it was for the manager of Hotel Hamot, overlooking Bassin Napoleon on the waterfront. Our status of homelessness had been accepted so we were given an apartment for one week, compliments of the state, after that, we were on our own.

We went to fetch our suitcases, and called to see Boy Lingus to thank him then proceeded to settle in and to prepare for the next stage, whatever that was to be.

CHAPTER 4

The pressure was off, we had time to look around for work and to seek a cheap room to rent after our sojourn at Hamot expired.

It was the weekend, a good time to explore the city. At the bottom of the Hotel Hamot was a large outdoor eating area, which seemed to be well frequented despite the unsightly views of the Basse Ville, as it was known.

Unfortunately, Boulogne-sur-Mer had been massacred twice in the last century, first by the Allied Forces' bombing of German U-boat bases on the Liane River and then again by the government-appointed architect who was employed to rebuild it.

There were rows of London-style tenement blocks along the waterfront, most of them facing the wrong direction and all blocking each other's view.

Further down the river at the mouth of the Channel, or La Manche as it is known in France, you find the two greatest architectural contradictions of all times.

There is Nausicaa, an aquarium, sea-life and marine environment centre, which with a bit of imagination looks a little like the Sydney Opera House, white and pure on the isthmus that protrudes into the sea. Then, on the opposite side of the river is the fish and ore factory. It requires no imagination at all to see the marked resemblance to Chernobyl and it smells just as dangerous twice a week when the offal is burned.

Walking up the Grand Rue, which links the old town or Haute Ville with the Basse Ville, one passes the Place Dalton, a wonderful square where a market is held twice-weekly regardless of weather. Overlooking the square is the 12th century Chapel of St Nicolas which fortunately for Boulogne-sur-Mer, miraculously escaped the blitz.

In 1870 the chapel was totally restored, and an English sculptor called Hopkins fashioned the new Saint and it is rumoured that he set an English sovereign on the head of St Nicholas, which by all accounts is still there. Henry VIII, who had difficulty holding Boulogne-sur-Mer after besieging it in the 15th century, would be delighted to know that the chapel remains to this day, because the Sovereign's head on the coin is reputed to be that of Henri VIII, lui meme.

The old town is quite spectacular with its well-preserved ramparts encircling the equally impressive Cathedral and Chateau. Rue de Lille is the main commercial area, and at the Cathedral end one finds what could well be the smallest pub in the world, the Mole Hole. It reminded me of a flat I had in Earl's Court once, where I could draw the curtains, close the door and turn off the light without getting out of bed!

The Mole Hole is run by an Englishman and if you ever go there, try the famous Angelus beer, which is half price while the bells are ringing, provided you are a Catholic!

We found the evenings rather strange in France, the closing of volets or shutters seemed like a self-imposed curfew and for us who knew no one, it was almost a snub. Someone later described it as a siege mentality.

Our week of job and flat hunting had not proved fruitful and the term was almost up at the hotel. We had good reason to panic as our funds were disappearing fast. There was only one solution for it, Boy Lingus, so back to the Tourist Office we went.

Ever dependable, he gave us a list of addresses and phone numbers of cheap student accommodation that would be empty coming into winter and he asked us to contact them. How he expected us to do this, I don't know. If we couldn't speak French last week, we'd hardly have improved much since!

We didn't want to bother him anymore, so we did a bit of 'Laroussing' before telephoning, but the phone itself had to be mastered first. This we did by practising on a man who sat by a window in an insurance office opposite the coin box - seeing the phone number on the glass, I tried calling him. I waited until he reached for the receiver, then I'd hang up. After a few practice runs, we had it figured.

I called the first number. The lady I spoke to must have thought I was a psychiatric case, or had the wrong number, because she hung up as soon as I said:

"Bonjour, je suis Irish!"

Undeterred, I dialled another number. After using the same format, I was given time to elaborate, making good use of our selection from Larousse although I didn't know what she said in response, it sounded favourable. We went back to Boy Lingus, who rang on our behalf and we were given a room with the use of a shared kitchen in a student house.

It was our first real insight into how a French family works and boy do they have a love affair with aspirateurs! There was one for every floor!

Madame Douzy was the lady's name and she made us most welcome and again, Mossy was no problem despite there being two cats in the house. It just meant that she had to be brought through the house on a leash. Fox Terriers and cats don't hit it off!

There was a green carpet on the floor and Mossy who had never seen a carpet in her life, assumed it was grass, and promptly shat on it. Fortunately, Madame didn't see, or we might have been out on our ears on the first night!

There was a Dutch girl called Helene staying in the house and her English was perfect. She was on a French language course at Nausicaa and she did all the initial introductions for Madame Douzy and relayed the house rules to us.

She helped us with translations and began to give us our first French lessons by putting stickers on all the items in the kitchen with the French equivalent. It was her first time out of Holland and the hills around Boulogne-sur-Mer seemed horribly foreign to her and in fact the bus ride from Haute to Basse Ville still frightened her.

Through Helene, we were introduced to Emmanuelle Laga who was the Advertising and Promotions Manager at Nausicaa. She spoke five European languages and when she heard that we'd opted for exile in France rather than put Mossy in quarantine, she adopted us and was to become almost our Fairy Godmother.

Unlike England, New Zealand or Ireland, it is impossible to go on the dole in France unless you have already worked and in order to work, you must have a Carte de Sejour. To be eligible for a Carte de Sejour, you must have a job! Sounds Irish, I know, but these are the sort of inexplicable anomalies that exist in France. This must be one of the reasons why asylum seekers risk life and limb to get to England. There's nothing here for them and perhaps why those people at the Department thought I truly was a nutter to be trying to stay in Boulogne-sur-Mer.

Anyway, Emmanuelle said she'd try and find a way round the impasse for us, as she knew the system inside out. So she took us to register at the ASSEDIC (Associations Pour L'emploi dans L'industrie et la commerce) which is compulsory before going to the ANPE (Agence National pour Emploi) or Job Centre.

The documentation you have to provide in France for any simple transaction is enormous. They seem to keep asking you for stuff until they find something you haven't got. That was certainly our experience.

We had no birth certificates, which in France is a big no-no. The whole business was driving me crazy, but I expect a foreigner in any country not speaking the language is likely to receive the same run around and even the French find their own system tiresome.

Our money was rapidly diminishing and with no job prospects on the horizon, I considered going to London to work in order to subsidise us, but I had lots of reasons for not wanting to do this, the most obvious being my poor health. Ten years in New Zealand had taken its toll as whilst out there I had developed an illness that could not be cured, at least not there. I became extremely allergic to pesticides, herbicides and fungicides, of which I assure you New Zealand uses its fair share - it's one gigantic farm. A book entitled "The Poisoning of New Zealand" by Merril Watts makes reference to my case, and exposes the misconception of NZ being a clean green country. Most people are not aware, but the last country in the world to ban DDT was NZ and the sixty million litres of Agent Orange which was used by the American forces in Vietnam, were made in Taranaki, an area which is now full of birth defects and psychopaths. Traces of chemicals used in NZ by crop dusters, can be found as far away as Antartica and the water table in New Zealand is laden with all sorts of impurities. This I can attest to, as I once had the occasion to have a well drilled on a property in Wanaka which is in the sparsely populated South Island and the water had visible traces of chemicals.

My health suffered the entire time that I was there and no doubt I had developed some serious defects which were going to affect me in later life. At least now I was in France and could try and forget the privations of the Antipodes.

Fortunately I came up with a money-making idea which would keep the wolf from the door and would mean that I didn't have to go to London to work, although I made one last visit to meet my old friends and it was as a result of this trip that my life was to change forever.

CHAPTER 5

Christopher (Chris) Beresford, with whom I shared a house some twenty years previously at Britannia Road in Fulham had received a letter from Italy addressed to me. It came from Brindisi and had been sent by the brother of Lucianna Giannini a girl I knew very well before I met my wife and went to New Zealand.

Every night for the three months while she studied English in London, Lucianna visited me at my local pub, the White Hart on Fulham Broadway, where the publican Ignatius Dunphy once told me:

"Finn, you have not missed a day in this pub for 7 years!"

Well, Ignatus, you might have wondered where the brass door handle dissappeard to ! I had to take some momento to New Zealand and I promised Caron that one day when we would truly settle somewhere, I would fit the handle to signify that we had finally settled down.

As it wasn't to be New Zealand, the handle arrived back in Europe with us and who knows, I might just slip it back one night when the White Hart is closed.

Lucianna tried everything to get me out of there but wild horses would have had no more success. At the time I knew her, I was living rent free at Britannia Road in a house without a bath and with an outside toilet. The roof was leaking and my bed had a chalk circle around it, as it was the only location on the floor that did not get wet when it rained.

I was drawing Social Security in several different offices under bogus names and doing the occasional bit of work with Paddy Feely and his under-pinning gang who met up on Fulham Broadway every morning at 7 a.m.

Lucianna became very close to me, especially after an accident I had on St Patricks Day when I got into a fight with two Englishmen and I punched a reinforced-glass door with my fist ending up in St Stephen's hospital (now Chelsea & Westminster) with a serious injury which was to affect me for the rest of my life. My right hand was unusable for months and it was Lucianna who wrote all my letters, even to my mother back in Ireland. My drinking had got completely out of hand and nothing else in life interested me, not even women or sex, much to Lucianna's disappointment. She eventually gave up on me and returned to Italy, but not without one last attempt to bring me with her.

Chris handed me the large brown envelope from Lucianna's brother when I arrived in London and the contents are to haunt me for the rest of my days.

Lucianna had just died and she had been looking for me to help her through her last days, but just as I was unavailable for her while she was living, neither was I there when she was dying.

I was devastated. In the envelope, there was also a book which Lucianna had been writing while we were together. It was titled Le Ore Laschiate, The Final Hour.

She wrote of my alcoholism and of the nights she had brought me back to her apartment which to this day I have absolutely no idea where it was.

News of her death and the contents of the book sent me on the worst drinking spree of my life, despite my pledge to give it up when I read the letter initially. Suddenly London seemed an inappropriate place to be and as soon as the fog lifted I returned, a changed man, to France.

Going back to Boulogne-sur-Mer did little to ease the torment of self-loathing which enveloped me, as I reflected on those selfish months when a beautiful Italian girl had fallen in love with me.

Luciana Giannini

LE ORE LASCIATE

Perugia, 1994

I had an empty feeling and said nothing to Caron about what had transpired in London. I tried to get myself back into the survival mode which I had had before leaving and hoped someday I could come to terms with Lucianna and even forgive myself.

Back in Boulogne-sur-Mer, the money-making idea that was to sustain us was conceived from the campaign in Britain being waged by Lady Fretwell and Elizabeth Hurley against the quarantine laws.

I had noticed lots of people begging on the streets of Boulogne-sur-Mer, but unlike the buskers one sees elsewhere, they offered nothing by way of entertainment, other than badly written placards. These signs weren't meant to amuse, but occasionally they did. One by an old hobo whom we later christened Marlboro Man, read as follows:

'Sans emploi, sans abri, j'accepterai argent, cigarettes et nourriture.'

We watched a concerned lady who went and asked him which was his favourite brand before she made a donation of 20 Marlboro. I was shocked by this especially as the man did not even get off his behind to thank her.

Most of these guys around the streets of Boulogne-sur-Mer attract sympathy by using dogs, just as the Tinker women in Ireland use babies. There was another bloke who used to stand outside the Post Office, using the top of an aerosol can as his receptacle for money which encouraged people to put in something decent as the last coin was always visible.

Then there was George, who everyone knew did the streets from nine to five with a 2 hour lunchbreak of course and treated his profession as a normal job. In fact, Emmanuelle overheard him say one day that he was going to retire in a couple of years. Of all the beggars on the street, George was my favourite. He had quite a sophisticated face, he was sallow and reminded me of Orson Wells. George had no actual patch, but would meander around the Centre Ville, intimidating people by poking his hand at them and crying like a well-rehearsed Shakespearian actor. He fascinated me and I promised myself to try and gain his confidence as soon as my French permitted.

My idea for raising money in Boulogne-sur-Mer was totally different to anything we had seen and with Lady Fretwell's aid and with Mossy, plus a little capital to get it off the ground, I was sure that our stay while waiting to smuggle the dog was going to be made easier and I envisaged our sejour being subsidised by a percentage of the 12 million visitors from Britain, who crossed the Channel every year.

Lady Fretwell, wife of Sir John Fretwell who had been British Ambassador to France 1982-87, had begun a campaign in Britain to abolish quarantine. It was known as Passports for Pets. Sir John was also chairman of the Anglo-British society, an organisation founded in 1904 (the Entente Cordiale) which was meant to improve relations between the two countries. Lady Fretwell had a country house in Normandy, not far from Boulogne-sur-Mer and I wrote to her regarding my plight and to ask her approval for my Post Cards for Pets venture.

Postcards for Pets was to be my first entrepreneurial concept in France.

I designed a story using Mossy as the main character and I took the idea to a few different printers before getting an incredible quote of 150 FF (£15) for five hundred black and white double-sided cards.

The text went as follows:

POSTCARDS FOR PETS

Jock offered to help Paddy smuggle his dog into England.
"We'll hide her in the bagpipes" he said.
But the alert English Customs officer noticed the bag was moving.
"They're automatic pipes for Asthmatics." Jock explained.
"Can you give us a tune then?" asked the Englishman.
"We can't," said Paddy, "it will wake the dog...."

The other side of the card had the usual space for the address, as well as:
Postcards for Pets is for the welfare of Mossy.

Not all pets are in quarantine, some are in exile.

On the top right hand corner there was a square the size of a stamp and in it the words:

"Stamp out Quarantine".

I bought some coloured felt-tip pens and put a border on each card to make the black and white look less bland, then equipped with the dog and my harmonica, I headed for the waterfront, to Nausicaa the maritime museum where the English tour buses parked. The price of the cards was 50 pence or five francs, with an option to buy a stamp which I pre-bought for their convenience.

With Mossy perched on a stool looking as cute as a chocolate box advertisement, I commenced to play 'Red Sails in the Sunset'. A crowd quickly gathered around us as Mossy howled away in harmony.

The cardboard poster explaining our predicament very soon produced the first of many sales and after reading the text, one elderly English lady enquired:

"Do you think you'll fit 'im in the bagpipes, luv?"

She went on to say:

"It's terrible you know, all these young men sitting on the streets of France with their dogs, I wish Tony Blair was 'ere' to see it."

The poor old dear thought that all the hoboes were here with their dogs because of the quarantine laws in Britain.

The morning went fine and as well as wishing for Tony Blair to come to see the poor misfortunates in France, I also wished that Caron had come to see how we were doing. An Englishman gave me a hundred francs for one card and said:

"The refugees are coming over 'ere by the thousand with far worse than rabies, and you, Pat, with your little dog, stuck 'ere in this tip!"

He was one of the away-day shoppers who came over for the cheap booze and cigarettes, a europhobe who detested the French.

On my way back to lunch with Mossy, we passed a rather famous Boulogne-sur-Mer bar known as 'The Finest Dog'. This well known watering-hole was frequented by English lager louts who come over on the Quick Cat to show the Froggies 'ow to drink. They even brought their own yard glasses with them and gave demonstrations on how it's done in Blighty. The French, with their more civilised approach, looked on with a mixture of ridicule and disgust at these beer-bellied hooligans bulging like toads whom often as not ended up vomiting on the streets before going back on the Quick Cat for Folkestone.

Baffled by the French menus, the majority of the English lager louts went the whole day without food and by the time the Quick Cat came back to collect them, almost to a man they would have become violent. Regardless, Mossy and I decided to give it a go and in we went. I placed Mossy on a stool and proceeded to play a few tunes. I began with 'The Wild Rover', a song that almost every Englishman can sing along to, it's a great icebreaker.

While I was playing, I thought back to the last time I had played in a pub. It was before Mossy's time, about 15 years earlier, in a little tavern on the island of Naxos, a charming little bar and shop combination of the type we used to have in Ireland long ago.

It was full of old antiques, who sat around all day with worry beads and walking sticks that were rarely used for anything except occasionally pointing at something or tapping the floor when they wanted the next Ouzo. They all seemed to be dressed in the same morgo material of black and grey, with an air of suspicion about the lot of them.

I played a few Irish jigs and reels to the Greeks and before long I had them all tapping away on the floor as they do on the pubs at home. This went on for a few days, until one afternoon when we visited, there was a silence that no amount of coaxing would get them to break. They simply refused to participate and we could not understand what had come over them.

'Maybe it's because no Greek music has been played!' I thought, so I immediately got into the Zorba dance and a Nana Mouskouri number. But no, it made no difference. What the fuck could be the matter with them? Buy a round of drinks for the house, perhaps. But again to no avail. Just then, we noticed four sombre-faced men descending the stairs with a coffin. A Greek funeral!

I had no such experience with the English boys at 'The Finest Dog'. By now they were on the tables, as a crowd assembled in the street to witness what began to look like a riot. Mossy and I were centre stage and an excellent opportunity arose to make my move and sell some postcards. I got talking to the most intellectual looking of the bunch and explained our case regarding quarantine. After reading the story on the card, he called for silence and made the following announcement:

"Paddy 'ere and 'ees fucking dog is stuck over 'ere with these Froggies, because 'ees dog 'as rabies, that right, Pat?"

Well, it wasn't quite the story, but it made little difference. One of the others came up to me later and enquired:

"'Ow many babies did he 'ave, Pat?"

The post cards ended up as beer mats, as I doubt if many of them could read.

I thanked them for their generosity, which came to 12 pounds sterling. Mossy and I left 'The Finest Dog', after a most enjoyable launch to our joint enterprise.

From that encounter, the idea of leaving cards in the bars around the town seemed the obvious thing to do. Boy Lingus also agreed to promote them for us at the Tourist Office. Suddenly, I felt confident that our survival in France, despite being without job or social security, was going to be possible. Meanwhile, I would continue to plan our smuggling effort.

DOG AND OWNER IN EXILE BECAUSE OF QUARANTINE. NO FRENCH, NO FRANCS, NO FOOD 5ᶠ POSTCARDS 50ᵖ "MAY YOUR DOG GO WITH YOU"

Sign

POSTCARDS FOR PETS

PASSPORTS FOR PETS

Jock offered to help Paddy smuggle his dog into England. "We'll hide her in the Bag Pipes." He said.
But the alert English Customs officer noticed the bag was moving.
Jock explained 'They're automatic pipes for asthmatics."
"Can you give us a tune then" asked the Englishman.
"We can't", said Paddy, "it will wake the dog...."

Postcards for Pets

CHAPTER 6

Mossy, with the pride of a Cruft's champion, had picked up my confidence and we strode up the Grand Rue to the old town to announce our success to Caron.

We now had some money for the finer things in life and we could indulge in a bottle of wine and some cheese. We were fully vegetarian and the students with whom we shared our house did little to encourage us back to eating meat. One of the girls had a passion for steak tartare, using all of the raw egg, which looked like a vampire's dinner or jelly meat Whiskas for cats - and she thought we were odd because of our eating habits! I recall one evening when we were eating a Chinese meal using chopsticks, we were quickly handed knives and forks. The French, despite their 70 million tourists a year, are still quite parochial, especially when it comes to foreign food. Our teapot, which had built up a reasonable amount of tanin, became a victim of the bleach brigade and no amount of explaining would educate these jeune filles the benefits of what they deemed a dirty pot.

Tea in France is another story. In the cafés, tea varies from place to place, but with one common denominator, cold. It can be called a host of different names, such as 'thay ole' or 'thay anglais', which is serviced with a menagerie of silverware; a teapot full of tepid water, a jug full of warm powdered liquid milk, a little pot of almost hot water for which I have yet to find a use, a chocolate and the least important player of all, the tea bag. When you try and infuse the tea, it gives the impression that it has been round the block before. You end up with an anaemic-looking liquid, wishing you had ordered a Perrier.

Our days in Boulogne-sur-Mer rarely passed without a visit to some bureau or other and although we were not eligible to take a job from the ANPE, we could avail ourselves of any courses that came up from time to time. In order to remain in the system, we were obliged to visit the office at least twice a week and apply for a minimum of two jobs a month (which we could not take) sounds Irish again, but that's how it works in France.

Occasionally, we would see a position that one of us could easily have filled, but it would invariably be accompanied by "Il faut avoir entre 18-26 ans" and even if it was 18 plus 26 ans, we would still have been out-numbered and not eligible.

All jobs as a matter of course required a CV. I didn't even know what a CV was prior to coming here. Every construction job I ever got was found in the pub and the distance between your shoulders was the only CV you'd have to produce. Besides, if I wrote to any of my past employers, they would most likely come looking for me.

As for listing all the jobs I had done since I was expelled from school, I'm sure the computer would fuse. So, to simplify everything, I always said that I had been a busker all of my life and although this was not entirely true, there were periods in my life when I survived solely by playing the harmonica on the streets in various countries around the world. One example was in Sicily, when my wife and I were mugged at gunpoint and everything with the exception of the harmonica was taken. It happened in Palermo, on the same day that a Government Minister who came down from Rome to open an enquiry into the Mafia activities, was shot dead on the runway!

So there we were, on the first day of a two-week holiday with no passports and no money. The American Embassy bought us two return tickets to Rome in order to get two new passports, but the rest was up to us.

After we were issued with our new passports, we had to return to Sicily and wait for our flight home. It was during this ten-day period that we discovered an aspect of Italian life that would have otherwise been hidden from us.

One day, while I was playing in the centre of Palermo, an American man called John Morrici got talking to us and he asked me if I could sing Danny Boy. No better man I replied. A conversation ensued in which we explained our current predicament - John adopted us for the remaining days of our holiday.

He bought us to his family in the middle of the island and so began the holiday of a lifetime. It was tomato time in Italy, which is like the potato in Ireland. The old ladies were preserving the precious fruit while the menfolk collected them from the plants. We became involved and worked for our food and board whilst enjoying some of the best home-cooked meals you could imagine. The whole incident certainly gave meaning to the expression: 'Every cloud has a silver lining!'

Chapter 7

Busking in Boulogne-sur-Mer looked like my destiny until one day a course finally became available at a Government run school called Gretta and even though it was not a job, it could lead to something. It was a French language course for beginners held twice a week and we were accepted. The class was quite mixed, eleven of us in all, with a lady teacher, whose curriculum had probably been in use since Roman times. There was a Lebanese woman, whose husband was a gynaecologist and everyone got to know about it on the first day. Then we had a Turk who had been kidnapped by a local girl while she was on holiday in Istanbul. There was a Moroccan who looked like Omar Sharif - naturally, all the women and some of the men, had the hots for him! We also had a psychopath who was French and under some sort of police supervision. We were all afraid of him, especially the Moroccan.

There was a woman from the Philippines who was only there to improve her accent and another French lady who spoke perfect French and nobody knew why she was there, except perhaps the Moroccan!

There were two illiterate French brothers, one wanted to learn how to read and the other to write. They obviously had something up their sleeves!

There was an Englishman who although he had been in France for eight years, had suddenly realised that Europe was not going to make the English language compulsory for all member states, so he was forced to do something about his limited vocabulary of Bonjour!

Caron and I, although we had no intention of staying in France, were availing ourselves of the course in order to get some work.

Madame, the professor at the college, had a particular interest in verbal eloquence. Our first word in French was 'coccinelle' which by the way is a feminine noun meaning 'ladybird', and she pronounced it 'una cock-si-nelle-eh'. Much of our first day was devoted to this word and by the afternoon we had it off so pat we thought we would be fluent by the end of the week and maybe Boy Lingus was right in assuming we could conduct our own phone calls after just one week in Boulogne-sur-Mer!!!

From Gretta, the language college, to Rue Marignan where we lived was a long haul and uphill at that. We had to make the trip at lunchtime, as Mossy wasn't allowed in the class (one of the few places in France which prohibited dogs.) Ever since she had been speyed in New Zealand, she had developed a kidney problem and the two-hour break gave us ample time to do the round trip, cook a meal and take her for walk around the ramparts.

When we weren't at school, Mossy and I spent the other five days on postcard duty and it wasn't long before we were on our second edition of the Postcards for Pets.

Now that we had an income, I decided to take a day-return trip to Folkestone to see how the Customs operated, plus it gave me an opportunity to sell cards on the boat. The fare was only twelve pounds return and with a bit of luck I would make that with the cards.

There was a very seedy element on one side of the boat, they were known as 'Flyers,' who made their living out of collecting and selling duty-free goods, in addition, I suspect, to drawing the dole. They did all five crossings a day and were usually well pissed by the last. On the other side of the boat were the more well-heeled, the car owners club. These were the ones who suffered from claustrophobia or who simply wouldn't risk the Channel Tunnel because them Froggies had built half of it!

"I'd never trust them French", one man told me.

"If that tunnel 'ad bin 'ere during the War, the collaborators would 'ave let the entire German army through while we was sleepin', no, while England had water all round us we were much safer, Pat."

Coming from the other island, I suppose I should have been in agreement but my hesitation to comment gave him reason to believe we were synonymous.

I met an Irishman on the boat who had been reduced to 'Flying' as a result of his alcoholism, induced by ten years of excess during the construction of the tunnel.

"If I'd known them bastards were going to charge so much to use it, I would never have dug it out!" he used to say.

When I told him of our predicament with the dog in Boulogne-sur-Mer he said he knew one of the Customs officers and that he was a sound man and trustworthy. He'd find out the days he was on and this officer would wave us through with Mossy. As we walked towards the declaration zone, I was tapped on the shoulder.

"I'm an officer of Her Majesty's Customs, would you mind stepping this way please sir!"

My Irish friend deserted me, but I knew at least that this officer was not the sound bloke. A search of my bag produced nothing except the postcards. When he read the text, he seemed quite amused to see the Englishman coming off so well in the story. He asked me if he could have one to show to his colleagues and I was sure that my attempt to smuggle Mossy had been ruined, as the card had given the game away, but there was always the Calais - Dover route.

Folkestone itself was a bit like the Yukon after the gold rush. They lamented the artificial economy generated by the tunnel workers and the remnants of Irish Pubs, like Scott's tractors decaying in the snow after his polar expedition, were the only traces of change on the landscape.

I had a productive day there and discovered a little about how the Customs operated as well as selling enough cards to cover my expenses.

Getting the dog through might not have been as easy as I thought and waiting in France until she died was beginning to seem a real possibility.

One day at Gretta we met a Russian girl who was learning English who offered us an hour of French in exchange for conversational English twice a week in her flat. Her husband was quite fond of the Vodka, so it was an incentive for me.

Something that always amazed us about them was that they would never open the volets (shutters) even on a bright day and we assumed that this must have been as a result of their time under the communist regime. It was through meeting them that we discovered Travaille Partage, an organisation which found work for all sorts of people without the red tape encountered in other French institutions.

We simply had to show up every morning to check the day's listings, which were often just short-term contracts for a few days. Our first assignment was addressing six thousand envelopes for Nausicaa, which earned us five hundred francs. Next came a weeks contract of leaflet deliveries around the town and two neighbouring catchment areas. The money was not good, as we had to pay tax and all the other charges that France is renowned for but at least we were now in the system and this made us eligible for the elusive Carte De Sejour, thus permitting us to take advantage of what was on offer at the ANPE (job centre).

CHAPTER 8

Our three-month term at the student accommodation was soon to end and it was necessary to find an apartment of our own. Madame Douzy had only permitted us to stay until the new students arrived. Renting is reasonable in France, but finding an apartment is a tedious affair, as a track record is necessary and also a job and guarantor are obligatory. French landlords are a rarified breed and they care as little for their property as they do for their tenants.

We eventually found a one-bedroom flat and our new friend Emmanuelle acted as our guarantor, although she was unaware of this, as I had forged her signature. A rather strange thing occurs in France when one rents property. A pre-inspection is made by a Hussier who is a bailiff or court usher. The Hussier works both for the landlord and tenant, in the event of disputes over the state of the property on departure. Unfortunately, these bureaucratic professionals have absolutely no practical experience, as we discovered to our cost.

A problem arose after we moved into the apartment. We were situated on the fourth floor of a free standing building which had exposed stonework, or pierre apparente as they say here, and the walls were permanently damp. The landlord had some plasterboard fitted just before we moved in, but a couple of weeks later, we noticed furry black stains coming through. The windows which were made of steel were totally rusted and had broken hinges. On opening one of them, it fell into the room. Complaining to the landlord was a waste of time as the Hussier had made no such observations in his written report. What was I to do? I went to La Forêt the letting agency, with some photographs of both the dampness and the broken windows but I may as well have gone to George the beggar man, for all the reaction I got.

For anyone who is unfamiliar with France, allow me to explain. There is no standard here when dealing with government institutions as each have either a different or their own agenda, which is a principle that seems to run through the fabric of all French society.

Helpless, I took my case to the Droits de l'Homme, a modern French equivalent of the Magna Carta. I didn't know whether there was any clause in their charter pertaining to broken hinges and dampness, but I did know one thing for sure - they found the whole incident rather odd and ushered me along to yet another government agency, this time the Department of Health and Safety. All of this was being conducted with only a few weeks of 'coccinelle' French, but in northern France, they are far more accommodating with the language than they are in Paris and if you throw them a bag of words they don't mind sifting through them. My efforts at the Department of Health were futile and I didn't think it could be attributed to my nationality or indeed to my lack of French, they simply put it in the famous lost file department marked 'Attention Urgent!' and sent me away happy, or so they assumed.

It was now mid-winter and in Boulogne-sur-Mer it can be quite as miserable as Dunedin in New Zealand, where people are known to stay in bed all day just to save on electricity bills. Our flat was impossible to heat, it was many the day we had to take three showers to warm up and Mossy would pass the day curled up in a chair with her teeth chattering.

With no response from the Health Department, I decided on drastic measures. I removed the windows, and walked into the manager's office of La Foret. I told him that if something wasn't done about the dampness and the broken hinges in three days, I was going to the newspapers. Furthermore, I said, if anyone fell out of the window in the meantime, I was holding them personally responsible. The French are not nearly as gullible as the English, but I had no choice and as I was an étranger they just might take notice. Foreigners often fare better than the locals as a sign on the door of our parish church back in Mallow (Ireland) written by a famous author, Canon Sheehan, attested;

'Mallow is the home of the stranger and the grave of the native.'

Emmanuelle, who had helped us since we came to Boulogne-sur-Mer, had been lending us her car for the leaflet deliveries but she occasionally had to go to Holland and Belgium to promote her company, which left us more often than not without a car, so we decided to look out for one.

Just around the corner from where we lived was a Renault 4L for sale. The price interested me, 1000 Francs, (£100.) I had had one back in Ireland and they are indestructible. This one had a current CT, controle technique, what we would call the MOT. When I saw the car it appeared that an exception had been made in this case. It was painted a tricolour of pink, brown and white which looked like it had been done by someone who had a few cans of old paint in the garage that they wanted to use up. There was a hole in the floor that was big enough to go through in the event of locking oneself out. It had only one wiper, no spare wheel and the hand brake was non-existent. One advantage of owning this fine specimen was that no one would ever be stupid enough to steal it, so we took the punt and bought it.

At school, the class was thinning out, with the psychopath being the first to go. He threw a wobbler in the class one day and the boys in white uniforms were called in to take him away. The Turk got a job at a local restaurant in Place Dalton and we often saw him on the street opening oysters and practicing his French on the customers. The wife of the gynaecologist applied for a teaching position, anatomy I expect. The two illiterates decided to stay on and repeat the course only this time, the one who was learning to read changed places with his brother and decided he wanted to learn to write, and vice versa. This must have caused some confusion to Madame so she took sick leave. Nobody knows where the Moroccan went, but the English chap by all accounts ended up in Casablanca! The Phillipino lady got a job in the library and Caron got a job as a serveuse at the Hotel du Centre in Wimereux, a few miles out of Boulogne-sur-Mer on the waterfront. Mossy and I continued with the leaflets and postcards for pets.

Before the three-day deadline to go to the newspaper over the windows, I had a phone call from La Forêt offering us a months rent holiday and a promise that the problems would be rectified in the near future. It was a good response, but it came too late. We had found a different apartment in a much nicer house, so we tendered our notice. Our new abode was on Boulevard Daunou, a first-floor flat close to the city centre, sandwiched between two octogenarians, one of whom had been renting the top floor for the previous fifty years.

We were the first non-French people to have ever darkened their door and their initial reaction to us was bizarre to say the least. The lady on the ground floor, Madame Delanois, was so distraught that she called the Social Services to come and interview us to make sure we weren't German spies.

Above us was Madame Bienfait (which means 'well done') who had apparently raised twelve children in her small appartment - I wondered if her name was just un jeu de mot! She was quick to introduce herself and to let us know that her husband, although dead some ten years, had been a Gendarme and that he visited her every night. In other words, if the social worker didn't put the frighteners on us, the sleeping policeman surely would!

Madame Delanois had a dog for her protection and every time we passed down the hall Mossy did her piranha impressions at the door. This resulted in another visit from the French 'secret service', forcing us henceforth to transport Mossy through the house under our arm.

As time passed, the xenophobia abated and we got to know our neighbours rather well, including the Gendarme. We were surprised to learn that Madame Bienfait had lived the entire time in that flat without a bathroom. There is only so much one can do in a bidet and she must have bathed in the kitchen sink.

CHAPTER 9

We were situated almost opposite the ANPE office, so I was able to make regular visits. One day I saw a great job which I felt I had a good chance of securing.

'Homme, avec son propre chien pour monter la garde.'

(Mature man wanted with own dog for night security.)

The rate was 40 francs an hour, which was the minimum wage or SMIC, (Salaire Minimum Interprofessional de Croissance) plus 7 francs an hour for the dog. At the interview, I was asked if I'd mind working alone at night. The interviewer explained what was entailed and advised me that under no circumstances was I ever to engage an intruder. It made me wonder why I was necessary at all. Then he asked me :

"Oh, une petite question monsieur, votre chien, il est de quelle race?"

«Fox Terrier,» I replied as I turned to give Mossy a pat.

"Ah oui, je sais, mais pour le poste, quelle sorte de chien allez-vous utiliser?"

It then transpired that Mossy had failed the interview and was discriminated against because of her height. We were forced to continue with the Postcards for Pets and I kept looking for a day job.

Meanwhile, Caron was doing rather well at the Hotel du Centre, making a pile of money in tips. Our food repertoire also improved, as there was a policy in the hotel of no re-cycling. I'm sure this was a major contributing factor in its success as du Centre was then in its fifth generation and a large percentage of its customers seemed old enough to be likewise.

Madame dans la cuisine, was a demon for quality control. The last customer complaint had been some thirty years earlier and she still spoke it about as though it had happened only yesterday.

As well as the little hamper that Caron brought home every night, we were allowed wine at the in-house price and this was just up my street. Caron's French improved, while mine was still at the same level as the two illiterates whom I met occasionally while Moss and I followed in George the beggar-man's footsteps. My drinking became more frequent and a large proportion of Mossy's hard-earned money started going back in over the counter at 'The Finest Dog', but my pledge which I made in London to Lucianna Giannini to stop was ever present in my head.

I continued my job hunt and was finally rewarded with a wonderful opportunity that almost seemed like divine intervention.

'Wanted: 14 people to put together a museum of Boulogne-sur-Mer's 2000 years history since the Roman occupation.'

They were looking for woodworkers, leather workers, researchers, typists, model makers, seamstresses and artists. The only position they had failed to fill at the time I noticed the advertisement, was an ironworker and I had some knowledge in this field. After one of my escapades in Ireland when I was released from a psychiatric centre, I was sent for an aptitude test for a government sponsored course. It was there, that some genius of an Irish civil servant decided that I was perfectly suited to becoming a welder, so that I could spend the rest of my life in a Ned Kelly style helmet, like a goat looking at lightning through a dark glass the size of a cigarette packet. Not me at all, but as I had no mind of my own, I was volunteered.

I did the course, but never really pursued welding as a profession, if one could call it that. Right then in France, my training came in handy and I was called for an interview. I feel in some strange way that this job was the work of my Higher Power, because only weeks earlier, for no reason other than my own curiosity, I went to the library in the Boulogne-sur-Mer old town to find out why the main square in the city was called Place Dalton. It transpired that Dalton was a very well thought of General in Napoleon's army, the son of an Irishman who had come to France with the famous Wild Geese, which was the nickname for the 40,000 Irishmen who fled to the continent in the troublesome years between 1600 and 1750, many of them ending up in the French army. At the battle of Fontenoy, it was the Clare Dragoons who took the laurels for the French victory and George II of England exclaimed after his defeat:

'Cursed be the laws which deprive me of such subjects!'

Patrick Sarsfield was another Wild Goose, who turned the tables on his former enemy William of Orange at the Battle of Landen. Sarsfield died with the words:

'Oh but were this for Ireland!'

The term Wild Geese comes from those Irish noblemen who stowed away in crates marked 'Wild Geese' which at the time Ireland was exporting for the Parisian markets.

In the library, I made photocopies of my findings about General Dalton and by pure co-incidence or Irish luck, I had them in my pocket the day I went for the interview. The interviewer was one Monsieur Vigneron who fortunately spoke English and he said that he found it rather odd that an Irishman should be looking for the position, as all the other applicants were French.

"Do you know anything about the history of our city?" he enquired.

When I showed him my findings, he was quite taken aback. He had lived all his life in Boulogne-sur-Mer and was not aware that Dalton was Irish. He asked if I had any interest in research. I said I had, although I did not think much of my chances due to my still rather appalling French. He told me I would be notified forthwith with the details of the start-up date, in the event that my application was successful.

While I was waiting for Monsieur Vigneron's response, Emmanuelle found me a job painting a house on Rue Blanzy Pourre, where the house next door was for sale privately. It had been empty for ten years since the old lady died and because one member of the family could not be located, the sale could never go through. Under French law, property has to be divided equally between all children, even if they are the biggest bastards under the sun. The Notaire from Desvres dealing with the transaction told us that four years after the old lady died, he had managed to track down one of the missing heirs in Paris and left a message for him to ring. Shortly afterwards, he received a call from a coin box and he explained to this man that he had co-inherited a house in Boulogne-sur-Mer. The Notaire said that the man ran out of coins and it took six years for him to call back! The house was on the market for 140,000 Francs, about £14,000 and as we potentially had two jobs, we could get a mortgage. The Notaire told us to be prepared for a wait, as the Parisian was liable to do anything.

CHAPTER 10

I was called to an induction day for the start-up of the museum project, situated in Wimille, five miles from Boulogne-sur-Mer, in a tastefully restored old farmhouse overlooking the sea. In the distance was a monument of the great Emperor Napoleon himself, with his back turned to England and some would say that his fingers were in a Harvey Smith position!

During a grand banquet, we were told about the city's colourful history. I had no idea that it had been graced by so many royals and ruffians. Monsieur Vigneron introduced me as a soudeur (welder) extraordinaire. I'm sure that if the geniuses back in Ireland, the ones who deduced from my aptitude test that I was to be a welder, heard me being described thus, they would most certainly have been flabbergastered. I had got the job as welder/ researcher on condition that I teach an apprentice how to appreciate the joys of sparks.

A letter arrived from the Notaire regarding the house which was for sale on 8 Rue Blanzy Pourre and it appeared that the elusive Parisian brother was in agreement to sell. A site meeting was arranged with one of the owners who lived in Boulogne-sur-Mer, a typical Gaul with an accent like Lee Marvin and buttresses under the eyes. The smell of pastis could be detected at ten paces despite the billowing of his Gitane smoke in our faces.

The first thing he told us about the house was his total contempt for it and he went on to add how sombre and cold it was:

"Je deteste cette maison!"

An amazing sales pitch, we thought, but an honest one at least.

The house was sombre, but that was because it had been painted from top to bottom in a brown colour which was used a lot around the turn of the century. There were also three coal fireplaces which functioned right up to the time the old lady died and the coal dust had left a residue in every nook and cranny. Nothing except the corpse had been moved for ten years and it had the feeling as though a homicide enquiry was on-going. What misery those people had lived in and so recently at that. There was no bathroom and the toilet was outside beside the coal bunker which was full to the brim, suggesting that the old lady must have died in the summer. The kitchen sink was of the shallow type one still sees a lot here in France was just 60 centimetres from the floor. Admittedly, the French are low in stature and the Dickens observation that the further south you go, the smaller they get, had me wondering about the Petit Provencals. The sink did not just serve as a culinary convenience, it was also a douche, a bidet, and who knows - maybe even as an inside toilet for pissing in during those freezing winter nights when the outside toilet was frozen solid!

Despite the paltry 65 square metres, it was a charming little house with all the original features still intact. Old fireplaces, proper doors, ornate ceilings and a most amazing staircase which had the same pitch as a barn ladder, or like the stairs one sees in the old houses of Amsterdam. It was obviously far too dangerous for Madame to use, and Patrice, her nephew, told us that she had not been up there for the last twenty years. Anyone over fifty would find it difficult to negotiate and even Mossy, who was after mastering a spiral staircase in a previous house, didn't like this one one bit. As for ladies first, unless they were true exhibitionists, they would have to wait their turn on this particular stair, it was so vertical.

"Suivez-moi," croaked Patrice, and like pot-holers out of a cave, we followed our guide. When we arrived at the top, we were abruptly told that if we didn't buy it, he wasn't going to bother himself with it anymore. I must say that we thought it a bit different from the usual sales talk of:

'There's someone else extremely interested in it and if you hang about it will be snapped up.'

Clearly Patrice was past his pastis time and just wanted to get it over with.

A wooden ladder which looked as though it had been used as a target at the world's dart championships, suggested that there may be a grenier.

"What's up there?" we enquired.

"Sais pas, j'ai jamais monté." From where we stood, it looked like the setting for a Spiderman movie, with hundred-year-old cobwebs playing with the beacons of northern lights trying to gain entry through the misplaced tiles. Patrice told us that we had seen enough, the tour was over and we were invited back to his house to discuss our intentions. A bottle of pastis plus a bottle of whisky sat side by side on a waiting table. Reaching a gentlemen's agreement was cause to open the bottles and to toast with our national drinks, as he described it. I felt misrepresented by the Glenfiddich, so I decided that when in France, do as the Romans and opted for the pastis while the women looked on like witnesses at a UN summit.

Unlike the UK or its subsidiaries, buying property in France has a lot of suspense attached to it, even after you have negotiated a price and signed at the Notaire.

Just as in feudal times, when the lord of the manor took the first poke at all newly-weds, the Mairie had an option on all properties for the community and they had two months in which to make up their minds. In some ways it is rather a good law - unless it affects you that is.

CHAPTER 11

Word from Monsieur Vigneron advising me of my successful application gave me a great boost. Before I commenced the job, I decided to make one more trip to England. This time on the Duo Line, or as the locals call it the Duo Lives, a bus and tunnel service via Calais, Dover, Folkestone and Canterbury. The reason I expect it is called the Duo Lives, is because of the English people who live along the northern coast. It is said that they could not afford to go further south because they were still on Social Security and needed to go over and back every two weeks to cash their giros. One can frequently see them at La Poste in Boulogne-sur-Mer, cashing sterling. The staff I'm sure are amazed at the regularity of these familiar English visitors.

"Ils doivent adorer La France!"

My French coccinelle teacher had told me to avoid the English like the plague until I had mastered French, but I did make a few acquaintances on the way over and back, as well as those I had met in the Finest Dog and other watering holes around the town. Perhaps they thought I too was on the dole in Blighty. Thomas, a Yorkshireman who was quite adamant that he was not English, was one of the few who spoke French despite some who had been there up to sixteen years. Most of these people socialised together and spent their time complaining about how arrogant and chauvinistic the French were. Their main gripe was the French resistance to the European Union. How could they not accept British beef and why are they still refusing to speak English.

"They understand it, but they just refuse, they just try to make it difficult for us!" is what they said to me.

There was Peter who although English was unlike the rest, perhaps due to his background, he was a sophisticated man who could well have been an aristocrat. The Jehovah Witnesses had been trying to convert him for years, without success. Peter had other ideas, such as the renovation of his house. This is where the Jehovah's came in handy:

43

"They don't accept money you know" Peter said to me cheer-fully.

Thomas the Yorkshireman was the most popular man in Boulogne-sur-Mer, even more so than the Maire- maybe this could be attributed to his linguist skills since he spoke six languages, including Esperanto. Thomas didn't get involved much with the English community, nor was he drawing the dole. He became French and looked all the happier for it.

I also encountered John, who though from the island, was from the other side of Hadrian's Wall, a published author and quite a learned man who was often embarrassed by his fellow Brits and their refusal to assimilate.

In amongst all these, was a German lady known as Anna Blanzy, who had spent part of her life in Blighty which gave her access to the English community, but only superficially. Anna once accused Peter of being a Nazi. Their lives in Boulogne-sur-Mer had a small town Irish feel about it and although my French was not yet at conversation level, I decided that I should maybe heed my teacher's advice and have nothing to do with the Brits or my French would go no further than theirs.

The work at the museum commenced and my first assignment was to make a model of a Roman soldier. I had just turned forty-nine and there I was, standing on a cold concrete floor, doing Ned Kelly impersonations with an icy wind from Siberia blowing across a sea of misery. Lucianna was haunting me, her spirit was whispering and eventually she took me away from the alcohol.

Suddenly I felt as though my life had no meaning or purpose. I was working for peanuts - I thought of all my friends back in Ireland, having a great time sitting around open fires and drinking lovely creamy pints of Guinness. The desire to walk off the job on the first day was overpowering me. Depression was slowly taking over, the black dog of winter had come to visit.

Fear, anxiety, guilt and fatigue were soon controlling my mind. Even though I had experienced it all before as a young man in Ireland, being practised was of no help. Depression had been a constant companion since childhood. I had been committed several times to psychiatric hospitals and on one occasion I had received electric shock treatment.

Thoughts of suicide came to haunt me and worst of all, my traditional ally, alcohol, had deserted me. I tried all the usual favourites, but this time the anaesthetic could not be found. After only a few days, I was forced to stop work completely. My mood, my personality, my appearance, went through a total change. When I passed people on the street, I could sense their fear. When I walked into shops, people stepped aside. I had developed a psychopathic look and could do nothing to change it. Paranoia set in and I had no desire to be seen in public.

CHAPTER 12

Word came from the Maire's office saying that they did not intend to buy the house on Blanzy Pourre and this meant that we were now obliged to purchase it. This made matters worse for me, I recalled the Oscar Wilde quote:

'The two greatest tragedies in life are not getting what you want - and getting what you want!'

My only sorties out of the house were the early morning walk with Mossy and to buy bread. I would take her for a couple of pees during the day, but only begrudgingly.

One morning, I met Madame Delanoy in the hall and her initial fears of xenophobia were well founded as she tried to engage me in a conversation about how miserable winter was but all I wanted to do was to tell her to fuck off and stop annoying me. The people in the bread shop also got a dose of my Celtic madness, when I discovered that they had sold me stale bread. Instead of going back to demand an exchange, as any normal person would, I walked as far as the front door and told them that they were a shower of French bastards and I then airmailed the 'pain de campagne' and virtually everyone in the shop got a slice.

The only safe place for me was at home and even there I was totally paranoid. Every time I heard footsteps on the stairs, I thought it was Monsieur Bienfait (the dead policeman) coming to get me. The only barrier I had between insanity and suicide was the telephone.

Phoning Ireland provided little solace. My mother, who came from a farming background, treated complaints with the same emotion as she would a hen gone off the lay.

"What could be wrong with you, aren't your two brothers doing fine and no nonsense from them?"

I even tried writing to my no-nonsense brothers, but I got no reply. My sister rang me and said that I should pull myself together. The only person, with the exception of my wife, who showed any sympathy was my Anglo-Irish friend Christopher Beresford in London. It was on his advice that I went to see a doctor who put me on Lithium, which is as big a national pastime as Boules in France, everyone is on it. The Lithium had an adverse effect so I discontinued it in favour of the whiskey in desperation.

Word came from the solicitor saying that the house on Rue Blanzy Pourre was finally ours. This happened when I least wanted it as it needed too much work before we could move in and I was in no fit state to do it. We had previously applied for a grant to renovate the house and we had engaged a local plumber to put in central heating. We chose the plumber because of his remarkable name, Constant Bigot. While we waited for him to start, I made an effort to tidy up the place, even though I totally regretted buying it.

Mossy, who had expressed some strange dislike for the house, stood there with her teeth chattering, it was so cold. The few rays of light from a weak winter sun attracted her attention and she hopped on the window sill to warm up. She fell asleep and rolled off, falling one floor down to the street onto a cobbled footpath. My already heavy heart sank as I looked over the side, fearing the worst. I felt like a careless parent whose child, just for a split second, has been neglected before a calamity.

Mossy's whole life scanned through my mind, from the time she was a pup sleeping in a wellington boot back in New Zealand. I'm sure that if she had died as a result of the fall, my mental state could easily have provoked me into harshly penalising myself. I rushed down and knelt beside her, crying at the innocence betrayed. She was breathing with faint moans, blood coming from her mouth. Just then a neighbour, who had seen her fall, came to our assistance. Fortunately, the Veterinary Surgeon was not far away and was open, so Mossy got immediate attention. She hadn't broken anything, and the blood was coming from a cut on her chin, which must have hit the ground first.

The whole affair made my depression worse so I went back to the doctor. This time he gave me anti-depressants which induced vomiting but I was told if I persisted for a few weeks I would overcome that sensation.

Can you imagine? You are in a state of acute depression, with constant thoughts of suicide and a few weeks of vomiting will put it all right! I couldn't go on with it, so I went to another doctor who sent me to the psychiatric hospital in Boulogne-sur-Mer for treatment as a day patient. Caron, who was still working at the Hotel du Centre, often went to work wondering if I would still be alive when she returned.

CHAPTER 13

I decided that I had had enough of France and only a week after we had taken possession of the house, I went to a real estate agent and put it back on the market. The agent obviously realised that it was a great bargain and said he knew of someone who would buy it straight away.

In any case, I wasn't looking for anything more than we had paid and I would be glad to get rid of it. Caron wasn't aware that I was even contemplating this. She was quite upset to lose such a charming house so soon, but she went along with it just for a quiet life.

I continued with my psychiatric treatment, and I was surprised when the doctor asked me if I had ever been to Alcoholics Anonymous as he was reluctant to prescribe antidepressants. He had obviously smelt the drink off me and no doubt spoken to my other doctor. The AA seemed a bit of a deviation from conventional medicine, but I took his advice and went along to my first meeting.

Oddly enough the Boulogne-sur-Mer reunion of Alcoholics Anonymous meets in the same building as the DSS where we first got housed when we were declared homeless. I was expecting once again to be sitting around with some junkie Gitane smokers sharing a bottle from a brown paper bag and for that reason I almost flunked it at the door.

My pre-conceived idea was pleasantly shattered when I found myself amongst a roomful of people who, although alcoholics, had not touched a drink for years. They described themselves as being in recovery, yet to me they all seemed as though they were totally cured of the problem and I wondered why it was necessary for them to be there at all. My French was still a bit on the rough side, but I did get the gist of what was going on. The feeling of being in a pub without beer was enough to keep my interest. It soon began to resemble my local bar back in Ireland, when I used to walk in on a Friday night and meet all my friends. Everyone was polite and turned out well. They all rallied around me like a mother round a sick child. I was a mess, yet it wasn't too long since, on the ground floor of the same building, I had looked at the misfortunate drug addicts and alcoholics and thought what a bunch of no-hope wasters that lot were.

Because I was struggling a little with my French, the Boulogne-sur-Mer group contacted an AA group on the South Coast of England to explain that they had an Irishman with little or no French who had recently joined them for help. The English group linked me with a man who acted as a sponsor he was known as Sugar Bill from Hythe in East Sussex and had been off the booze for forty years, which meant there was a lot of experience and knowledge available to me. The English group also arranged to send over two members once a week to speak with me. This was to be another turning point in my life. The meetings, together with regular talks with Sugar Bill, brought about a noticeable change in me. Soon the dark Irish cloud of depression began to lift.

Solace
As the periodic particles
Of light diminish,
Life takes on a deathly hue.
But beneath such earthly desolation,
Nature contemplates
And as often times before,
Renewed by a dormant vision,
Preconceives.
Then orchestrated by a single tap
Awakes its drowsy audience
To yet another grand encore.

CHAPTER 14

Constant Bigot arrived with all the copper pipes and boiler, ready to start installing the heating. I had totally forgotten to cancel him, he wasn't aware that the house had been put back on the market and just sold. This is the stuff that Irish jokes are made of and I must admit that I felt really thick, as well as regretting the sale, as I was beginning to feel better since I stopped drinking. But it was too late, the house had been sold and there was nothing I could do about it.

I rang my friend Chris in London, who advised me that if I sold the house while I was under psychiatric care, the contract could be annulled. On his advice, I went to see an Avocat (Maitre Brun) who transpired to be the French consul to Britain. Monsieur Brun who was of Irish ancestry, his family coming from Waterford in the 17th Century, was an interesting man, with a reputation of never charging anyone for their first visit. His advice was accurate and simple. Had I been the sole signature on the 'Compromis de Vente', my mental state of health would certainly have been a consideration. But because Caron was in a normal state of mind and body, this negated any possibility of voiding the sale.

But Maitre Brun didn't leave it at that. He rang the real estate agent on my behalf explaining the case and I was invited to their office to discuss the matter further. They told me that I did seem a little strange prior to the negotiations. The purchaser was contacted and a letter from my doctor was requested to verify my mental state. This resulted in the return of our house and I am quite sure that this sort of thing could only happen in France. The agents told me that I had created a national record for buying and selling a house in two weeks!

Constant Bigot, who despite having been given the run round, was happy to recommence as soon as possible, but first he enquired:

"*Vous êtes sûr cette fois-ci, c'est bien votre maison?*"

I was soon feeling well enough to go back to the museum, despite being on no other medication except my AA participation. My position of 'soudeur extraordinaire' had been filled and Monsieur Vigneron enquired if I would like to be a full time researcher. My immediate reaction was of obvious panic at my new role, but regardless of everything, I accepted the position.

My period of research was to be from 1500 to 2000 of the Anglo-Saxon and Celtic contribution to the city and region of Boulogne-sur-Mer.

My first character was Henry VIII who sacked the city in 1547 and was responsible for destroying what would now be one of the greatest Roman monuments of all time. Just on the isthmus above Nausicaa had stood Caligula's Tower, a sixty-metre brick lighthouse, octagonal in shape, which was a twin to the great tower of Alexandria in Egypt, destroyed by an earthquake. Henry, against the wishes of his engineer, ordered the construction of a wall around the tower in order to use it as a fortress. As the tower was close to a cliff edge, the engineer said the wall would be a cause of premature erosion, which was indeed what eventually happened. Henry's sojourn in Boulogne-sur-Mer was short lived as Charles II arrived four years later with a well-equipped army. This resulted in a cessation of hostilities at the famous meeting of the two kings, at the 'Field of the Cloth of Gold', not far from Boulogne-sur-Mer.

The brutality of the English during this conquest is as fresh in the memories of the Boulognais' as that of Oliver Cromwell's atrocities in Ireland and I was not surprised to hear them say that the biggest mistake Hitler made, was that he didn't arm the French and England could have been taken in a day.

During my research, I discovered some information in a book by Henri Malo entitled 'Petite Histoire de Boulogne-sur-Mer' which took me out of my allocated research zone back almost a thousand years.

Monsieur Malo stated that Saint Patrick, who was the son of Calfurnius the lighthouse keeper, was born in Caligula's Tower.

What a discovery! St Patrick's birthplace has always been disputed. When I researched Monsieur Malo further, I found his argument far more convincing than anything else I had previously heard.

Monsieur Vigneron was ecstatic at my findings.

"Quelle coïnçidence!" and he added, Trouvée par un Irlandais!"

It gave me an enormous personal boost, and I was soon living my job. Every available minute, I was either on the Internet or perusing some ancient manuscript at the bibliotheque. Chris in London became involved and sent me regular clippings on different characters he knew that were connected with the city. Thomas, the linguist Yorkshireman, looked after the translations that I was obliged to prepare for the typist. I loved it. I had finally found a job which I really liked. John Cunningham the Scottish author who lives in Boulogne-sur-Mer helped me find some interesting historical characters such as Doctor Edward Jenner, 1749-1823, the physician who discovered the cure for Vache Folle or smallpox. Despite the early ridicule Jenner suffered from sceptical cartoonists who depicted his patients as growing cow's heads after taking his vaccine, there is a wonderful monument to him in a very prominent part of Boulogne-sur-Mer. The Great Emperor Napoleon recognised Jenner's work by minting a medal in his honour in 1804.

In order to gain more insight into the work we were doing, Monsieur Vigneron sent us on visits to other museums in northern France, including the Joan of Arc Museum in Rouen. It was here my boyhood's fire was re-ignited when I read the story about the Maid of Orleans and of her death at the hands of our common enemy. I will never forget that day in Rouen. Even though the Joan of Arc Museum was memorable, what was far more memorable was the reaction of the rest of our team when they discovered we weren't going to be home in time for dinner. This was the second time I had encountered how attached the French actually are to their customs. There was a near mutiny when the driver suggested that we finish the tour with a visit to the Museum of Madame Bouverie. This would have meant arriving home at about nine o'clock and although for many of them, this may have been their first time out of Boulogne-sur-Mer, Madame Bouverie would have to wait for another time or there would have been a mutiny. Missing the midday meal at home was enough, but dinner as well!

CHAPTER 15

Every free moment I could afford, I was working on our house at Rue Blanzy Pourre. With the help of the woodworker at Monsieur Vigneron's museum I was making new windows at their workshop - all in strictest secrecy of course. Just around the corner from our Blanzy Pourre house there was a huge construction job going on at the Branly College. It was here that Mossy and I managed to get most of the materials we needed for the renovations. Mossy was always my excuse and if I was caught on the site by the security guards, I would simply say:

"J'ai perdu mon chien, monsieur."

The trick was always to carry a lead, as it gives credibility to the story. The neighbours on Blanzy Pourre I imagine, were keeping a close eye on the goings-on, especially every time I arrived with a load of wood from Branly at midnight. It was quite a narrow little street with alternate side weekly parking and there was never enough space for everyone, especially the man across the way who was a lorry driver. He had two mangy dogs that were only brought out three times a day, each time for a forty-foot walk, just the length of his truck and judging by the man's appearance, this was all he ever allowed himself too. The dogs, known as Depeche and Toi, were both ushered back inside as soon as they had discharged their loads,

"Dépêche-toi, vite, vite allez, allez dedans !"

Their owner was the Tuckin Futter (a German brand of dog food) delivery driver for northern France, one day he gave me a box for Mossy to try. She turned her nose up at the sight of them and judging by the smell, I would imagine that they were the dog equivalent of sauerkraut.

Up the street just a few houses away, there were two brothers who lived together like a pair of old Irish bachelors. They had survived on baguette and coffee since their mother died, they were both alcoholics and both on some form of state assistance. Virtually all the assistance went to the local wine shop.

One of the brothers whom we called Ghandi- came by one day as I was doing some work on the façade, he introduced himself asking if I had any work. He gave me his hand, which nearly came off when I shook it. Next to Ghandi's house was a drug and alcohol drop-in centre and my own recovery was helped by the daily misery I encountered on the street.

France has a strange attitude to alcoholism and the French find it difficult to understand that wine is alcohol. They see it as more of a dinner accompaniment and they do not accept any excuse for not drinking it, a bit like the Irish and the Guinness. For years, we were brought up under the illusion that 'Guinness is good for you'. If there was ever a case for a class action, that's got to be one, especially now that they have withdrawn the slogan!

Despite the long hours and the occasional awkward customers she encountered, Caron was enjoying the work at the Hotel du Centre where there was a regular flow of English day-trippers who came over for the cheap cigarettes and wine in the local Auchan Supermarche. One day in the hotel, she was asked by a group at a table:

"What is a New Zealander doing here working for the Frogs, there's plenty of work in England, you know, hope you are not married to one?"

"No," she replied, "I'm married to an Irishman."

"Oh, that's even worse!" one of them added.

My research for the museum was taking me on some wonderful excursions, probably the most fascinating of all was that of Marengo, Napoleon's famous charger. The Emperor called all his horses after his last battle and it was the campaign against the Austrians on 14 June 1800 at Marengo in Northern Italy, that lent the horse its name. It was also here that the famous French dish of Chicken Marengo, chicken sautéed with white wine, tomato and garlic, was born.

Chicken Marengo was created on the battlefield itself by Dumand, Napoleon's chef. Bonaparte, who on battle days ate nothing until the fight was over, had gone forward with his general staff and was a long way from his supply wagons.

Seeing his enemies put to flight, he asked Dumand to prepare dinner for him. The master chef at once sent men of the Quarter-master's staff and ordinance corps in search of provisions. All they could find were three eggs, four tomatoes, six crayfish, a small hen, a little garlic, some oil and a saucepan. Using his bread ration, Dumand first made a panada with oil and water. After drawing and jointing the chicken, he browned it in oil and fried the eggs in the same oil with a few cloves of garlic and the tomatoes. He poured some water laced with brandy borrowed from the General's flask over this mixture and put the crayfish on top to cook in the steam. The dish was served on a tin plate, the chicken surrounded by the eggs and crayfish, with the sauce poured over it. After Bonaparte had feasted upon his meal, he said to Dumand,

"You must feed me like this after every battle!"

As the French army was top heavy with an Irish regiment, it was quite common to buy their bloodstock from Ireland and the most loved of all Napoleon's horses, Marengo, was purchased a few miles from my hometown, in a village called Buttevant where the oldest horse fair in Europe is still held to this day. Incidentally, it was here that the first steeplechase was held in 1752, from the church steeple in Buttevant to the steeple in Doneraile, four miles away. This is definitely horse country. More recently, it has produced another equine phenomenon, the greatest trainer of all time, Vincent O'Brien, who himself was bred between the steeples.

Further research into the history of Marengo unearthed a startling revelation which got the museum people sitting up and paying attention. A friend of mine in Ireland was doing some research into the disappearance of another famous Irish horse called Shergar, who had been stolen from his stable in County Kildare. It was he who told me that the skeleton of Marengo was at the National Army Museum and that after Napoleon had fled from the battlefield of Waterloo, the English had stolen the horse. I contacted the National Army Museum and explained to Mr John Humphries, the public relations officer, that I was looking for an Irish candidate for the museum of Boulogne-sur-Mer but because of my nation's non-aggressive relationship with France, I was a little short on material. Mr Humphries replied as follows:

'I was interested to read your comments about Ireland's non-aggressive relationship with France. It should be remembered that the Duke of Wellington himself was born in Ireland, that even his English regiments contained a substantial percentage of Irishmen and that the Irish regiments played a crucial role in many of his victories, for example the 88th (Connaught Rangers) at Busaco, and the 27th (the Inniskillins) at Waterloo, where the regiment suffered a higher percentage of casualties than any other British unit.

I hope this information is of some help,

Yours sincerely,

Julian Humphries, National Army Museum"

'Well, Mr Humphries,' I felt like saying, 'The Duke of Wellington may have been Irish, but he disassociated himself from his Irishness by saying 'being born in a stable, does not make one a horse!'

And besides, the 27th Inniskillins were from Northern Ireland.

A trip was arranged for me to go to London and Ireland in an effort to track down all the relevant information I could secure on the life and death of Marengo. I went to Ireland first - how strange it was to be back at home after almost thirty years, doing research for France. During my childhood, I had seen a parade in Buttevant with a white stallion and a Napoleonic figure proudly prancing up the main street. On this visit I encountered a man on the street who helped me with my enquiry.

"Excuse me sir," says I, "I was wondering if you could help me, I'm doing some research on Napoleon's horse Marengo, do you know anything about him?"

"Marengo, sure, Napoleon came over himself and bought it off a Tinker from Kanturk and didn't he ride him back to France the same day, t'was fierce going, I couldn't tell you exactly when it was, but there's a man in the village and he could tell you, for I think he met him."

Well, I thought, how is Monsieur Vigneron going to like that on our information plaque when the Museum opens!

In London, I went to see the actual skeleton and sourced more information on the events which led to it being there. After the Battle of Waterloo, Marengo was put on display as a trophy of war until he was purchased by a General Angerstein who had a stud farm in Barnes. Marengo stayed there until his death in 1832 aged 38 - his skeleton was then articulated by a surgeon, Mr Wilmott of the London Hospital, and presented to the National Army Museum. Marengo's hooves were turned into snuff boxes and one is retained to this day in St.James' Palace.

*E*spoir

Un chercheur, Fionn Mac Eoin, veut rapatrier le squelette du cheval de Napoléon

Reviens-nous Marengo !

Après la bataille de Waterloo, en 1815, les Anglais ont capturé Marengo, le cheval de Napoléon qui a vécu dix ans de plus que son maître, mort en 1821 à l'île de Sainte-Hélène. Depuis Marengo n'a pas quitté les terres anglaises. Articulé et conservé par un docteur de l'hôpital de Londres, le squelette est d'abord transmis au Royal United Services Institution Museum. Puis, en 1963, il est transféré et exposé au National Army Museum situé dans le quartier de Chelsea à Londres. Aujourd'hui, Fionn Mac Eoin, un chercheur irlandais, domicilié à Boulogne, qui travaille à l'ABEP, voudrait que ce squelette soit rapatrier vers le musée du patrimoine de Boulogne.

Polémique d'origine

Les recherches de Fionn Mac Eoin sont habituellement orientées vers les hommes irlandais qui ont une histoire dans le secteur et dont le nom est souvent connu des Boulonnais.

Ainsi, alors qu'il travaillait au cas du général irlandais Dalton (comme la place bien sûr !), il est tombé sur une image du squelette Marengo. C'est à ce moment là que notre chercheur découvre, au hasard d'un article, que Marengo est un cheval irlandais. Napoléon aurait en effet acheté sa monture en Irlande, à Buttevant exac-

tement. Enfin, il aurait... car une autre école considère que ce cheval aurait été acquis en Égypte. Fionn Mac Eoin est donc à l'affût de documents et d'informations qui attesterait de sa version. Avis aux connaisseurs boulonnais.

Toujours est-il que Marengo - du moins ce qu'il en reste - est en Angleterre.

Fionn Mac Eoin s'est donc adressé directement au premier ministre britannique dans le but de faire rapatrier le squelette de Marengo à Boulogne. Tony Blair a répondu rapidement à notre défenseur du patrimoine : le National Army Museum n'est pas un musée public, et donc n'est pas sous le contrôle de l'État par l'intermédiaire du ministère de la défense. Il lui a donc conseillé de s'adresser au directeur du musée, M. Robertson. Et il y a à peine une semaine, Fionn Mac Eoin recevait une réponse du directeur. Hélas une réponse négative. Le directeur propose en revanche de réaliser une réplique du squelette qui pourrait ainsi trôner au musée du patrimoine de Boulogne. Mais Fionn Mac Eoin n'entend pas cette version là, bien décidé à réitérer sa requête. Il a même pensé se faire sponsoriser par une marque, celle d'une boisson gazeuse pour essayer de récupérer le squelette. C'est fou, n...on ?

D.D'H.

Le cheval de l'Empereur est-il d'origine irlandaise ou égyptienne ?
Ph. Repro « La Voix »

LA VOIX DU MARDI 11 JUILLET 2000

Newspaper article

With my newfound information, I decided to write to both Tony Blair and President Jacques Chirac to see if I could secure the return of Marengo for La France. Back in Boulogne-sur-Mer there was great excitement at the prospect and very soon the French newspapers got hold of the story, with such head-lines as:

"Rechercheur Irlandais veut rapatrier le squelette du cheval de Napoléon! ».

As it was out of the French government's control, Jacques Chirac was quite happy for me to go it alone rather than spark off an international incident. Tony Blair wrote back via the Ministry of Defence saying that I could gain access to the skel-eton and have a duplicate made up for the museum at Boulogne-sur-Mer.

Within days of the news coverage of Blair's response, I re-ceived hundreds of letters from all over France with offers of support for my quest. There were pledges of financial donations and haulage companies offered to collect and deliver the horse to the Museum.

CHAPTER 16

Following this I had a call from a descendant of one of the Wild Geese, who requested an interview with me. His name was Monsieur Gilbert Tierny and his family had been in France since the 17th Century at Pittefaux, not far from Boulogne-sur-Mer. On my way to the interview, I got lost in the countryside and enquired from an elderly lady who was attending her garden:

"Excusez-moi Madame, je cherche la maison de Monsieur Gilbert Tierny.'

"Ah oui, Monsieur Tierny, l'Irlandais!" came her reply.

How marvellous, I thought, after over three hundred years in France, and he was still known as the Irishman.

Arriving at the house, the horses in the paddock had a certain Irish feel about it . I must admit that I felt both honoured and indeed nervous about interviewing a Wild Goose in my coccinelle French. Monsieur Tierny was at the door to greet me:

"Je m'appelle Finn."

«Gilbert Tierny is ainm Dom agus caed mile failte agat, tar isteach agus lig de schin.»

(Gilbert Tierny is my name, you are most welcome, come on in and pull up a stool.)

He was speaking Irish like a native, yet he had never set foot there. I could see from the décor of the house why the old lady in the garden referred to him as l'Irlandais. Monsieur Tierny went on to say that he was 100% French and 100% Irish and I suppose one couldn't get much better than that, he said with smile.

He was a great source of information, as he himself had just published a book on the history of his family in France from 1600-1990. A line from his book which attracted my attention was:

'Our genealogy does not present any gaps or uncertainties.'

My sentiments as I had come up the avenue were well founded, these Wild Geese certainly were the cream of Ireland.

Today in France, you find many an Irish name which some assume are French established households. Take Hennessy of Cognac for instance, Richard Hennessey was born in Kilavullen, County Cork in 1720. He left for France in 1740 and joined the army following what had by then become a family tradition since 1691. After his successful career, he started the now world famous Hennessy Bras Arme distillery at Cognac where the Irish flag flies to this day. It was Gilbert Tierny who suggested that I try and track down a book which was published in 1949 entitled Biographical Dictionary of Irishmen in France M.H. Gill and Son, Dublin. This elusive book which I eventually found in Ballydehob was to become my Bible. But I discovered many more Irishmen and women who had been missed out in this edition.

One day, by complete accident, while Mossy and I were walking through the cemetery in Boulogne-sur-Mer, we found yet another great character who was well deserving of a place in the museum. It was Richard Martin, 1754-1834, born in Dublin, died in Boulogne-sur-Mer, one of the founding members of the RSPCA. Martin was a barrister and also a member of parliament for Galway in 1822.

It was Martin who introduced the legislation to the House of Commons for the protection of animals. He had brought many prosecutions before the courts, but the first and most famous was a case against Bill Burns for his mistreatment of a donkey. The magistrates were reluctant to charge Burns as the evidence was only hearsay, but Martin was having none of that, so he went and got the donkey and brought him into the courtroom to show the judges the scars. Burns was duly fined and this set the precedent for what is today an international law. At the head office of the RSPCA in Horsham, West Sussex, the original painting of Martin in court with the donkey by P.Mathews can be seen. I was rather interested to find out why Martin ended up in Boulogne-sur-Mer. I discovered that he got into financial trouble in Ireland, and fled his creditors for France.

He had a castle in Ballynahinch Lake where he gave refuge to the homeless and prison offenders. In France, he continued to work for the welfare of animals. What an anomaly, I thought, as Mossy and I sat on his gravestone in a cemetery where dogs are not allowed. It was I suppose an inadvertent tribute to him that Caron and I had chosen exile in Boulogne-sur-Mer rather than put our dog in quarantine. A gesture which everyone at home in Ireland thought insane, but Lady Fretwell had become my hero and at least she understood.

I had always been a sensitive person and perhaps this was why I became an alcoholic in the first place. Even my vegetarianism was a choice of reflection and those who ridiculed me for being soft simply had not the same nature. News of a policy change was soon to reward my sensitivities.

Tony Blair announced that the British Government was going to abolish the quarantine laws in the near future, but that all dogs would have to be micro-chipped before going to England. Now that we had the house almost finished, it was my cue to move on again. Caron, who certainly wasn't looking forward to the Boulogne-sur-Mer winter, had however, little desire to swap it for an Irish one. But one thing was for sure, she had had enough of the waitressing job with its unsociable hours. I contacted four real estate agents, all of whom said that the market value was no more than 300,000 Francs, so I asked them to advertise if for 350,000 Francs, regardless.

The first week, as often happens, there was an endless flow of visits, but it wasn't long before I was asked to reduce the price, as it was apparently a buyer's market, according to the agents. I took no notice of them and placed an advertisement in a local paper which cost me 60 francs, and two days after publication we had a full offer. In France, there is a great reluctance to buy from agencies as people feel they are paying more because of the fees, some 70% of properties are sold by individual treaty.

Anyway, despite what the agents said, I sold the house and it looked like it would be soon time again for the two suitcases and the dog.

Going back to Ireland was beginning to become a reality. I wondered was the passport for pets made a possibility because the then Governer of Hong Kong, Chris Patton, wished to return to England with his family dogs?.

Chapter 17

My job was coming to an end at the museum, so while the house transaction was in progress there was going to be a three-month wait for the Acte de Vente. Emmanuelle, the lady who worked at Nausicaa had friends in Haute Provence, who were looking for house-minders for a couple of months while they went on tour. Getting out of Boulogne-sur-Mer for the winter would be inducement enough and since neither of us had ever seen Provence, I took a train down to meet the owners, both French opera singers.

Their house was near the village of Cruis, about twenty minutes from Forcalquier, which is in the high country. It is doubtlessly the most beautiful area of Provence, but rarely written about. It was just the end of the lavender season and I was so overcome by the beauty and the scent that I picked a bunch to send to a Welsh friend of mine in the South Island of New Zealand. The Angelus bells were ringing as I wrote him a long letter telling all our news and inviting him to France. We had both suffered from depression and indeed alcoholism, but in his case he wasn't yet aware of the latter and believe me, New Zealand is no place to be waking up with the lonely disease. A strange feeling overcame me as I sealed the letter, it was somewhat spiritual and perhaps the saying that 'God spends six months a year in heaven and the rest in Provence' could explain it.

At the house in Cruis, called La Louvière (the she-wolf), I met Françoise and Marc who had just recently purchased it and planned to move there from Lake Annecy upon their retirement. The colline on which the house was perched had some inappropriate plantings, courtesy of the former owner who was Swiss. The pines which gradually made their way up the hill were topped by the apex of La Louviere in Provencal pink and the contrast of the evergreens amidst the reluctant oaks which refuse to part with their leaves, gave a distant impression of Toblerone.

The house was built on the site of an 11th century chapel and two of the original walls still existed. During the renovations they had found an extremely large stone with Latin inscriptions which came from a previous 6th century chapel on the same site. The stone can now been seen at the local church in Cruis.

I was in awe at the beauty and my mind was made up, we were coming south. Everyone was so friendly, a bit like the Irish with a che sera sera attitude, in the sun! Mark introduced me to an old berger who by all accounts was nearing ninety and had spent all his days wandering the hills with his troupeau of sheep and a couple of docile dogs.

The locals told me that he spent so much time on his own that he was constantly engaging people in conversation. The only way to avoid being trapped by him was to stop your car in the middle of the road and hopefully someone would come along and give you an excuse to drive on. For me, he wasn't a problem as I was a great talker and listener and besides I was fascinated at his almost biblical lifestyle in the hills. Monsieur Giraud the berger, with his four score years and ten, had only once left the hills of Provence, and that was for a day trip to Marseille, some forty years previously. It obviously didn't impress him that much, and he told me it was the first time in his life that he understood what it felt like to be a mouton!

How different it was to see the French treatment of their sheep, compared to what I had seen in New Zealand. When we were in the South Island, I saw a local farmer taking what I thought were dead sheep to a dump on his land. I was later shocked to find two sheep still moving and baa-ing down the hole. It's strictly money in New Zealand, while here in France there is still a lot of pleasure in being a shepherd.

Le Berger
Then, I wondered
What this solitude really meant.
Amidst such passive beasts,
Walking, stopping, waiting,
There must be more,
The hills no longer guard their secrets,
Aromatic flavours wafting in the breeze
Or repetitious bird song,
Surely hold attention
Not eternal.
Be what the mystery then?

Imagination needs no reason to exist !

CHAPTER 18

In the afternoon, I explored the village. A visit to the thousand-year-old church could not be missed and there I met a lady who was the official tourist greeter appointed by the Mairie. She said she had seen me earlier in the day picking lavender and that she had had a premonition I would visit her. She also said that I had a sense of spiritualism about me and this wasn't the first time that I had heard that, so I related a story which occurred during my time in New Zealand.

It was in a place called Wanaka and we were in the final stages of a chapel renovation we had undertaken almost a year previously. A lot of controversy was aroused by the sory that we were going to move into this old stone building and as in any parochial society we were the subjects of discussion. The concept of living in an old chapel was truly novel to New Zealanders. We were visited by the regional newspaper which was interested in doing an article on us and our motives for buying St Patrick's Chapel. When the photographs were being developed at the laboratory of the Otago Daily Times, a strange phenomenon was discovered which was a cause of concern for me.

I had a phone call from the reporter saying that in all the shots they had taken, there was a halo type aura all around me but nothing around Caron or Mossy. This would not have worried me under normal circumstances, but some time previously a Fantail, a small native bird, had flown into the chapel and a man who had come to visit told us that in Maori tradition this meant that someone in the building was going to die. Well, to be honest, for most of the time I lived in New Zealand I felt dead anyway, but I didn't feel like going just yet. As regards the Maori 'tapu' (curse) I couldn't very well ask the local Catholic priest to come and exorcise their own building. I had no alternative but to get a local Maori woman in to lift the tapu. Whatever she did certainly made me feel better, but whether it was Irish superstition or a genuine tapu, I had no idea. A week later we received a telephone call from Auckland with some bad news. Juliet Nesbeth, the woman we bought the chapel from, had died and this was the only reason we could find which explained the aura picked up by the photographer of the Otago Daily Times. It must have been that of Juliet Nesbeth, because she died the same day the photographs were taken.

CHAPTER 19

Marc and Francoise, the opera singers, were happy for us to have the house right through to the spring with only one request. That was that we try to track down the maçon who had repaired the roof and left it in a worse state than when he started. So I returned to Boulogne-sur-Mer with the good news. All we had to do now was wait for the final signature to sell the house on Blanzy Pourre.

We had a lot to do prior to our next move. By now, we were as professional as Pickford's, due to the rolling stone lifestyle to which we had become accustomed. This was to be our twelfth move in fifteen years, some across continents. Mossy, as usual, could sense that we were soon to be off again on another adventure. For some, our 'two suitcases and a dog' philosophy of travelling light might seem like a nightmare, but to us it was a breeze and the only way to travel. Mossy was prepared for any eventuality and if necessary she could always be packed away in bagpipes like a babushka.

Now that we were about to make a handsome profit on the house, we decided to get rid of the Renault 4L and look for something more substantial for the long drive south. We drove the Renault to Marie Rose, the local scrap dealers and although I had put a hundred francs of fuel in the tank the day before, they would not compensate me for it. All they were prepared to give was a hundred francs for the lot, fuel, car and all. But first, as in all French transactions, I needed a scrapping declaration from the Prefecture. This was a right pain the neck. Only because our next car was going to be a diesel, I would have siphoned out the 100 francs of petrol and left the 4L on the side of the road for the crows to nest in.

It was ironic, as only three weeks previously, The Gendarmes at Boulogne sur Mer left a note on my windscreen asking me to come along to The Gendarmerie. During the night whilst on patrol, they caught two young men stealing the car radio. At the

Police Station, I was asked to identify the radio in the presence of the two lads. As there was no way I was going to give them a criminal record for stealing something that I never listened to anyway, I told the Gendarmes that there was no radio in the car when I bought it and that it must be a mistake. The two lads looked at me as if I was some sort of a nutter when the Gendarme asked me if I would like the radio as it might improve my French. On our way out, I asked the two boy-os, "Why didn't you take the car as you were at it ?" and they responded,

" It wasn't worth the risk."

The house sale went through with the usual 'see you in the café before the signature for the tax evasion share, known as the 'sous table', when a portion of the sale amount is given to the seller supposedly unbeknownst to the Notaire. This was a potentially risky business for the purchaser, but we had already handed over the keys and besides this was northern France where people are far more honest than their southern brothers. We were only too glad to be rid of the house and they were unlikely to run off with our cash before signing at the Notaire's office which was in Desvres. I heard afterwards that before we actually signed, the whole family had moved in and if we had reneged on the deal we would have had a siege on our hands. After we had said our goodbyes to Boulogne, I recall thinking of a line from the Lee Marvin song, Wandering Star... I never saw a sight that didn't look better looking back. But unlike Lot's wife, we didn't turn around.

CHAPTER 20

On our way south, we stopped in Champagne, in an area where the sugar beet was being harvested and how reminiscent of Ireland it seemed. Caron remarked how dismal it was and how she couldn't live in a place like that. I kept quiet, as I knew that after our sejour in Haute Provence, she was in for a taste of it, because in Mallow where I came from, there was a sugar factory and the whole town smelt of it for most of the year.

Mallow.
The crows caw-cawing is such
Sentimental sound to me.
Dark days and the mist.
The houses seemed as though
A puppeteer in the heavens was
Toying with the smoke lines of
Carbon monoxide and mixed with
The stench from the beet factory,
Was enough to send sanity looking
For an excuse to rehearse for a lesser role.
We slept in the foetal position and
Never moved from the imprinted
Birth marks on the blankets.
Not a bark was to be heard after midnight.
Shunting, clack-clack-clack at the station.
The window panes were always wet inside
And our dog was never allowed to sleep in
The house. Rules ! I hated the alarm clock,
And O' Connors rooster must have had one.

It was cold when we arrived at Cruis, but the blue sky held a promise that was different from the clouds of the north. Our first task was to look for the missing maçon, who by all accounts had vanished after the last rains of winter past. His previous address was in a little village called Pierre Rue, so we decided to use the local café as our enquiry centre. If one is looking for information in Ireland, you frequent the pub for some days, before asking one of the locals "Excuse me, do you know where the maçon is living?" An enquiry on your first visit is likely to bring on the silent brigade and from what I had heard, these Provencaux were none too different to our lot, so I knew how to play them. There was an old man at the bar who looked like he had Parkinson's, but all he needed was the homeopathic remedy known as the hair of the dog. I had often experienced the same feeling myself and at home they were known as Shakin' Stevens fans. A large cat sitting on the counter was briskly whisked away when we approached with Mossy, despite my assurances that Mossy would not cause any trouble and the cat was most welcome to stay. The barman said:

"Non monsieur, c'est pas ça, c'est mon chat, il est agressif envers les chiens".

Come to think of it, I had heard that Provencal cats would take no messing from the anaemic looking fluffs brought down there in summer by the Parisians and although Mossy resembled a poodle, she was a Foxie and I had yet to see a tom stand his ground for her.

Now that I wasn't drinking, I found it difficult hanging round bars, in the circles I frequented before going dry, sipping coffee would be associated with homosexuality. Fortunately in France they are a bit more mature and no such peer pressure existed. Spending an hour or two over un petit café and La Provence doesn't provoke any suspicions whereas in Ireland, there would almost be a steward's enquiry!

To have asked the patron the whereabouts of the maçon at this early stage would have been suicide and like the barmen in Ireland who know more than the priests, they would tell you nothing but lies. Our best bet was Shakin' Stevens, but first the coffee and a beer for Caron. Over against the wall, we noticed a soccer table and I asked the patron if we could pull it out from the wall and have a game.

"Mais pourquoi?!" he exclaimed.

Pourquoi indeed, could you believe it, there were only handles on the one side, because the table was too big for the room! They modified it and both players to stand on the same side. Another typical piece of French manoeuvring if ever there was one!

I couldn't really laugh at it, because back in Ireland there was a craze some years back when all the pubs were getting pool tables but in most cases the rooms were too small, so we had to play with short cues and sometimes with the table against the wall.

Caron's beer arrived followed by the coffee, which looked and tasted like treacle. It must have been sitting in the pot all night, especially for tourists, just like the first pint of Guinness out of the tubes at home and if you were stupid enough to get it, you'd be shitting through the eye of a needle for days. A local would never be served it.

It was time to put the hard word on Shakin Stevens, who by now was calming down a bit. The pastis was beginning to take effect.

"Monsieur, je vais acheter une maison pas loin d'ici et je cherche un maçon, pour faire quelques travaux."

I got the same response as I got when I went looking for an IRA man in a pub back in Ireland years ago. Shakin' Stevens was just about to impart some details on the maçon when the proprietor intervened and put the lid on it. At least we knew we were in the right village. It's like that here in Provence, there's a sort of Mafia attitude and we would have to employ other means to source the phantom. We went into the local Tabac and placed an advertisement requesting the services of a maçon for a renovation job in the region and we put Christopher Beresford's London phone number as a deviation tactic. Christopher received more than one response, but our man was one of them and an arrangement was made to meet the maçon next time we came to France, supposedly !

Meanwhile Provence was ours to explore. Although it was coming up to mid winter, there was plenty to do and see as it was Fête de la Truffe time in many of the surrounding towns and villages. Apt in the Vaucluse, was our first major tourist venture. I liked it immensely, but I must say that we were apprehensive when we viewed it from the distance. The sky line had two phallic high rises which seemed so out of keeping with everything else in the area, but this I later discovered was due to Apt having a communist mayor. Apparently any town in France which has had a longterm communist mayor ends up ruined. Aubagne is another a prime example.

It was our first visit to a southern market and was it ever different from the produce one finds in Boulogne-sur-Mer! Apt has a large Arab influence, which certainly brings a lot more colour and variety, even on winter days. The truffles at fifty francs for a few flecks in scrambled eggs got me wondering what the pigs see in them.

On our way back to Cruis through Malfougasse which got its name from a 16th century baker who was renowned for making the worst fougasse (a type of bread) in Haute Provence, I ran over a young wild boar. The dogs and hunters were hot on his heels, but we managed to get him in the boot of the car before they laid claim to him. Mossy needed a bit of counselling as she thought we had adopted another dog. The nearest veterinary surgeon was only a couple of miles away and he was quite taken aback when we pulled up with an injured wild pig and asked for his assistance. It was a bit like taking Adolf Hitler to a Jewish synagogue to be circumcised! But despite it being open game season and we two silly vegetarian tourists with coccinelle French, he respected his Hippocratic Oath and set about repairing the razor back.

The following day, when we went to collect our pig, we were greeted by a crowd of hunters outside the surgery, demanding its immediate release. The French have no respect for anything which is edible and our cochon was not going to fall victim to their barbarism. It was looking like we were going to adopt the wild pig and when we eventually got round to going to Ireland, he would be joining our two suitcases and the dog.

CHAPTER 21

Because I was on chomage (the dole) I was obliged to go to the regional office in Forcalquier once a month and pretend I was looking for work. But I was quite safe, as I was registered 'Museum Researcher' and finding a job like that around Cruis was highly unlikely. I was on 500 francs a week which was just enough to keep us in food but little else. Caron unfortunately wasn't eligible, because in France if you give up your job for no reason, your rights are severed. This is obviously another one of the reasons the French tend not to move around as other nationalities do. Most people seem destined to stay in the same place for life- another thing one notices is that the majority of French people holiday in France perhaps this is what keeps them so parochial.

At the ANPE office in Manosque I met my case manager, an Englishwoman called Madame Collis who was living permanently in France and like the good socialist she was, she tried to hook me up with a job right away, despite my telling her that we were going back to Ireland as soon as Tony Blair lifted the quarantine laws and when the pig had improved. Madame Collis introduced me to an Irishman called Eddie Fitzgerald, who was living in the same village as herself, Dauphin, also in Haute Provence. Eddie was a bit of a wanderer like myself, and once, while en route to Romania, he stopped in Paris and was kidnapped by a French girl, who brought him south. Mind you, he wasn't exactly complaining.

Without realising it, Eddie was going to be instrumental in the next phase of my life. He had just recently been home and he related his impressions of what Ireland had become since the advance of the Celtic Tiger. The weather of course, always a favourite topic for Irish discontent, had gotten much worse and the Irish who could afford it were buying houses on the continent to get away from the rain. The price of a pint of Guinness, another important factor in Irish life, had seemingly gone out of all proportion and although this was no longer of any consequence to me, it was still sad to hear. Alcohol consumption had gone up forty percent but that, said Eddie, could be attributed to the national discontent at the soaring price of drink! The term ne'er do well, an Irishism which has a certain poetic softness about it, had been replaced by an American import of loser, as had the drinking out of bottles. Racism was rife, and for a nation which itself had been down all its days, Ireland had no right to become a beggar on horseback. Eddie was a true green Irishman and I was beginning to have reservations about returning to my motherland, but what was the alternative now that we had sold our house in Boulogne. For the time being, we would have to leave it in the lap of the Gods and live for the day. We went on a tour of Dauphin with Eddie, who introduced us to Patrick, the French baker, who was operating a 450-year-old oven and was producing manna from heaven. He was famous for his onion fougasse, which Eddie described as worth leaving Ireland for. After tasting it, I could but agree and I recalled what Sir Reginald Blomfield said, "There are only two things one has to be careful of in France, the bread and the butter!" Perhaps I should have heeded him, because I had been overdosing on both since coming and had developed Candida Albicans, which is a yeast infection of the intestine. My diagnosis came from a book I bought in a health food shop, titled 'Je Me Sens Mal Mais Je Ne Sais Pas Pourquoi'. When I translated it, it advised the patient to cut out all lactose, fructose and sucrose, including all products with gluten. Thus came to an end all the delights of France for me for the foreseeable future. There I was, a vegetarian and alcoholic dry and now no bread, cheese or desserts. Whatever would the French think of me!

My symptoms of Candida were depression, chronic fatigue and severe muscle pain. This was too much to cope with, so I made an appointment to see a doctor in a nearby village called St Etienne les Orgues. I was asked to come along to the surgery at 2p.m. assuming, as one would, that this was my allocated time slot. Not at all. When I arrived punctually, I was the first at the door, which was closed and remained that way until 2.15. Three old ladies came along and, being the gentleman that I am, I let them in before me and when the doctor finally arrived, it transpired that I was now fourth in the queue. The marathon wait which ensued was enough to try my Irish patience, so I upped and left, only to be followed down the street by the doctor, calling:

"L'Irlandais,l'Irlandais, attendez attendez un peu, vous êtes le prochain!"

What could I do but return.

Finally I was on the bench and the first question he asked me was had I read Ulysees. He then embarked on a literary voyage of what he deemed to be the greatest work of all time. I told him that I was a friend of the first Irishman to sail around the world solo in a boat, which he named 'The Molly Bloom' and that was like opening another sluice gate, because sailing was the doctor's second passion. Caron was summoned from the waiting room and she had to give an update on how the New Zealand team was doing in the America's Cup. Meanwhile, I lay there virtually fully exposed, in an under-heated room where the Mistral could be felt coming in through the badly fitted windows and doors of the ancient maison de village, which if it had been in Ireland would have come under the developer's hammer years back.

Half an hour later we established that he was also interested in medicine and when I told him that I had Candida, he said:

"Bupp, bupp, c'est une maladie pas connue en France, monsieur, c'est une maladie très Anglo-Saxon!"

After pressing my stomach like a veterinary surgeon would a horse in foal, he enquired:

"Etes-vous six heures et demi ou midi?"

This took me a little time to compute, but what he was asking was whether I was still getting erections. I deduced from this, that he reckoned there couldn't be much the matter with me if I could get an erection. Midi was his medical term for an erection (that is straight up, midday) and six heures demi, (pointing down to half past six) the brewer's droop. He sent me for blood tests, but prescribed nothing other than to go back to eating meat, fish and chicken. I revealed nothing about the pig.

CHAPTER 22

We woke to our first Provencal snowfall and Mossy who had never seen snow before, got a right drop when she went to do her morning business in the garden. Her normal meander around the trees to investigate the intruders of the night was cancelled and she was quite happy to hold her pee and return to the warmth of our bed. The mailbox was frozen - we had to heat the key in order to defrost the lock, but what I found there would have been better left unread, or at least better waited for a sunny day. The first letter I opened was from the Assedic, to tell me that my chomage money was to be stopped in two weeks. A second letter from New Zealand brought details of the suicide of my friend Griff to whom I had sent the lavender when I first came to Cruis to meet Mark and Francoise regarding the house minding. Griff had hung himself and when I reflected on it, I knew well that had I stayed on in New Zealand myself, we could have shared the rope. The lavender I had sent from Cruis earlier in the year had been buried with Griff. If only he had left with me or at least took heed of my letter, he might not have terminated his life. But as I have said many a time, New Zealand is no place for sensitive people. It is a Calvinist Presbyterian Scots enclave where isolation is their idea of passion and is it any wonder that it took a New Zealander to scale Everest. Calvinists thrive on misery and see it as an earthly punishment and passport for a guaranteed entry to the heavenly kingdom. About New Zealand it is said, " Never make love standing up, because the neighbours might think you are dancing"

The third letter was from Ireland, with an early Christmas card from my mother with a 20 euro note in the envelope and an account of how well all my friends were doing since the Celtic Tiger. Everything was suddenly bleak and as I looked across the valley, it reminded me of a scene from Joyce's 'The Dead'.

On top of all that, I had to go to Forcalquier to collect the results of my blood tests that the doctor had requested and on the way up the avenue from La Louviere, we got a puncture. This meant we had to drive all the way on one of those wheelbarrow type tyres that have become fashionable with some car manufacturers as the spare. It was starting out to be a day from hell.

While in Forcalquier, I popped into the magnificent old church to say a prayer for my friend Griff in New Zealand and as I was leaving I noticed a visitor's book on the table in the foyer. I am not one for commenting on how nice the architecture is, or how tranquil I found the place, but I looked through the pages to see if anyone from Ireland had passed through in the last few days. Just then, a man came up to me and handed me a pen, so I felt obliged to write something. I quickly wrote "c'est fantastique!" and put our address at La Louviere.

Caron was doing a bit of shopping at the bio market, so I waited in the grand square and whilst there, a hearse pulled up followed by the chief mourners. A lady with a black fishnet visor was handed the book, the same one I had signed, by a man resembling Eamonn Andrews.

Livre d'Or
I once signed a visitor's book;
Thought it was, but I mistook.
It really was a Livre des Morts
And not as you say a Livre d'Or.
Just imagine what was said
When what I wrote by them was read.
I simply scribed "c'est fantastique!"
How awful of the dead to speak.

I had just signed the Book of the Dead which is a custom here in France and of course thinking that it was just an ordinary visitor's book I, like an idiot, put my address. The poor distraught lady who was the man's wife must have been truly upset to think that someone thought it great that her husband had passed away. For a few days I was fully expecting a visit from either a relative or the local parish priest and to be beaten up or excommunicated.

CHAPTER 23

Back at the doctor in St Etienne the blood tests were all normal.

"Voila, comme j'ai dit, pas de problème !"

And in typical French fashion, out came the prescription book and no points for guessing what was prescribed, ye olde favourites valium and lithium. Once again I had been diagnosed with depression, the national ailment, which is almost a compliment, as in France it is associated with intellectualism, but unlike Oscar Wilde, I was not yet prepared to declare my genius and so continued to look for a cure as I was convinced I had Candida Albicans.

We were becoming rather well known in Cruis and the Mayor sent us an invitation to the annual Christmas 'Rebalun de Gros Soupa' which is a traditional meal without meat eaten on the 24th and is meant to remind us of the more meagre times encountered by our ancestors.

The French, according to George Bernard Shaw, seemed to have experienced poverty like no other nation on earth.

'In France you notice that even in the wealthiest families, food is often served most sparingly, nothing is wasted. I sometimes think this frugality may be in the blood and that the cells themselves remember the frightful poverty of the revolution.' G.B.Shaw

The meal, although meant to resemble some sort of penance, was, by contrast a grand banquet and when the Mayor discovered that we were permanent abstainers of la viande, he started to poke us with his fingers to establish how we became so tall and strong looking, on, as he put it, "que des legumes? c'est pas vrai!" It must be difficult to comprehend, such Gullivers as we were among les petits Provencaux. Being strangers to the district, we were given preferential treatment and made guests of honour at the Mayor's table, seated one on either side of him. During the course of the evening, it became obvious that our presumed good fortune at being given the two most revered places in the hall was not the envy of anyone else in attendance, as at sometime or other they had all experienced the octopus-like movements of his hands, which meant that depending which hand held the fork, either one of us was in danger of losing an eye. This was the real Provence, where semaphore gestures, like the news for the deaf, were an accompaniment to every word. Someone kindly came to our rescue and told us it was normal (and wise) when sitting next to Mayor Felix to move your chair a metre away and so we enjoyed the rest of the meal. During the recess from eating, a couple of Provencal story tellers came on to entertain us with tales from Marcel Pagnol, which was received with about as much enthusiasm as the Mistral.

Christmas Mass at the local church was a bit of a fizzer with only a handful of people and a priest who had about as much impact on the brethren as the storytellers had the night before. Christmas Day was spent trying to get a trapped sparrow out of the attic- for this task we used Mossy to help move it down towards the gable, where I had already cut a hole through the block wall, thus permitting it to leave.

CHAPTER 24

The holiday season was now over and it was time to face the realities of the New Year with our first trip back to the A.N.P.E. office in Manosque. Madame Collis had found me a job at the nudist colony in Lemans. It was basically a maintenance position which they obviously found difficult to fill, due mainly for reasons that the operative was meant to be in the nude also (not in winter of course!) I passed the interview and accepted the job of maintenance handyman which included a free caravan on site and also the possibility of a cooking job for Caron when the season started in May. Marc and Françoise were due back to take over their house, so it was a timely piece of good fortune. But then, as Irish luck would have it, an Englishwoman who was a friend of our opera-singing hosts, rang and asked if we would be interested in looking after her bastide in Auriol after we finished with Marc and Françoise. She wasn't offering any wages but the accommodation was free and we would better placed for Caron's yoga, which she did in Marseille once a week and my twice weekly AA meetings in Aix-en-Provence. Marc and Françoise had recommended us for the job but were not aware that I had already accepted the nudist number. I was in a terrible dilemma as which to take, but Bill, my sponsor and AA recovery advisor who seems never short on the right decision, said,

"If you had been offered both positions at the same time, which would you have opted for?"

"The bastide at Auriol," I replied.

"Well there's your answer."

I listened to Bill and went back to Madame Collis. When I explained the position I could tell by her face that she, no doubt like the owner of the nudist colony, was thinking that I had funked it because of the length of my penis!

CHAPTER 25

La Louviere, the house at Cruis, had served us like Romulus and Remus, but we had to move on as the adventure was not over yet. So once again we packed the two suitcases and the dog- by then the pig had regained his strength and confidence so we gave him to the old berger and asked to have him released when the shooting season was over. We continued south into Jean de Florette country. As you drive through the ravine from the motorway to Auriol, there is a strong impression of entering a lobster pot and the area where the bastide is situated is like the tacky suburbs one finds in Australia, with conflicting colours and hideous architecture, which was attributed to the Communist mayor, who had held office for the previous five terms.

The bastide was the only redeeming feature in the valley, but due to its bourgeois history, little consideration had been given to it by the planning authorities, resulting in a car wash being its closest neighbour. As we drove up the avenue past the little chapel of St. Pierre on the tree-lined avenue, Madame was waiting at the door to greet us.

Her first utterings were, "Oh I didn't know you had a dog!"

Here we go again I thought. The last time I worked for an English person in Northern France, I got a similar welcome. One morning when Moss and I drove from Boulogne sur Mer to Montreuil, about an hour away, to help an Englishman repair his roof, his wife poked her head out of the window and enquired primly:

"I hope your dog has done his toiletting in Boulogne before you left?"

"Fucking old cow ..." I whispered under my breath.

Madame Claude showed us round the bastide, after Mossy had been given approval on condition that she was house-trained. The room we were allocated on the top floor was larger than the whole house where I had been brought up in back home in Ireland, and that was for a family of six.

It was an industrial area and very tacky and we wondered about our decision.

But we thought, if Madame Claude was going away we would have the bastide to ourselves, it would be fine.

Our first evening at Auriol was certainly a change from the peace of Haute Provence, but the bustle of the surrounding busy routes leading to Aix and Marseille calmed as night approached, allowing the swollen river that ran parallel to the bastide a chance to express itself after being silent during daylight hours.

Its natural rumblings were no interruption and sent us to sleep like the soft lullaby of a caring mother. Morning came early and Mossy awoke confused and needed to get out for her morning pee. Madame was in the kitchen when we arrived down and since we were all vegetarians le petit dejeuner was a scanty affair. Madame Claude had come from great wealth, when she was a child she lived in Cannes in a house that had 26 full time gardeners. The bastide itself was home to many priceless artefacts including a table that had been custom-made for Louis XIV and was signed by the artisan. There was also a full set of tableware, hand-painted, for the Empress Josephine, Napoleon's lady, all soon to be in our care.

CHAPTER 26

Changing departments in France is a nightmare even one's car becomes victim as it is necessary to apply for new licence plates each time. We also had to re-inscribe at the nearest Assedic office, which was in Aubagne where Marcel Pagnol, the author of Jean De Florette and Manon des Sources came from.

Having seen Jean de Florette four times, I was now quite keen to see where Ugolin and Pape went to sell the carnations. Approaching the town, my fantasy was shattered by the endless condominiums, which I am sure would have made Pagnol himself turn in his grave had he witnessed the destruction of his beloved village. Aubagne had become a suburb of Marseille, with little escaping the urban sprawl except the Garlaban Mountain. At the Assedic office, the drama of changing from 04 (Haute Provence) to 13 (which is the departmental number of Bouches du Rhone), was like having a heart bypass and we were even asked why we had decided to leave our last abode. The French just cannot accept that people move without valid reasons and that we are prepared to take such a risk. They worry so much about La Retraite, (their retirement), one can even hear young people in their twenties talking about it.

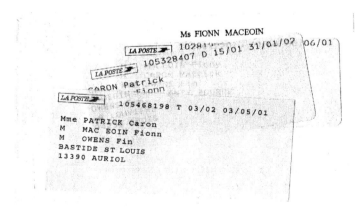

The above letter followed us from Northern France to Auriol near Marseille

We were an enigma, they may even have thought we were fugitives, judging by the line of questioning. Back at the bastide, Madame had some good news for us after our frustrating day of dealing with mini-minded functionaires (bureaucrats). A friend of hers, Michael, aka 'the Master' as his Indian house lady was obliged to title him, was acting on behalf of a business woman in Oxford and they were looking for someone to do two weeks work on a house in a village called Lourmarin. Lourmarin is situated in the Luberon area of the Vaucluse and we had an appointment to meet Michael, the Master, outside the famous Michelin Star Hotel, Le Moulin de Lourmarin.

Arriving well in advance, we got a chance to look round what could only be described as a fairytale village, which had a similar feel to Rye in East Sussex, without the sea of course. The Master arrived and introduced himself as Mr F. and Caron remarked that the handshake was of a similar temperature as that of the fish monger. If only my French teacher could have seen me, my fluency still a long way from where it might be, and here I was with a sang froid, not heeding her advice to avoid the English. The house we were going to work on was an imposing maison de village on two levels and with an entrance on two streets, built in 1667 for a Jewish merchant. The lower level on the Rue du Temple was an old shop and our mission was to totally gut it to make way for an 'English Tea Room'. French village houses are a builder's nightmare with streets sometimes no wider than a small car, making the use of skips or scaffolding a total impossibility. If there is a boulangerie anywhere close by, forget it, because the French never cease in their quest for fresh bread. This is exactly what the Rue du Temple was like, but with the additional intriguing twist, in that it had a 'No Entry' sign at both ends, though it was one way, it was the locals who decided which way that was.

The house was dark and damp as indeed are many of the houses in the village due to an underground river that capillaries through the soft sandstone which acts like a sponge. Mossy stayed at the front door and refused to go in, she must have thought she was back in Boulogne sur Mer or worse, Dunedin!

After the grand tour by the Master, we were taken to see the plans and a scale model of his conception and he told us that he was going to supervise the project. We met the Indian femme de menage and although he didn't instruct us to call him Master, we would no doubt be his lackeys, our wages were negotiated at 400 francs a day which was the minimum wage in France, known as the S.M.I.C. There were incentives of course. We were allowed to stay in the house free of charge. Also, the Master told us that we were fortunate to be working in what he described as one of France's most chic villages as he pointed out that it was the home of the English author, Peter Mayle and if we were lucky we might even see him on the street!

At 400 francs a day and no central heating I'd be expecting more than just a casual glance from the great man, but assuming it was only going to be two weeks work, there was no point in complaining and we accepted the terms, foolishly, as I look back now.

Our first task was to clear out the grenier (attic) which was full of photographic equipment and thousands of assorted postcards from the Luberon, of which the latter I put aside with the intention of selling them when the Master wasn't around. With all the rubbish on the street ready for the Master to come with his van, I was told by one of the municipal workers that the déchetterie (dump) was closed on Thursdays, but there was a secret way of opening the gate. Amazing, to be let into a village secret on our first day!

Our next project was the destruction of a perfect 400 year-old ceiling and like the German pilots who refused to bomb Paris, we expressed our discontent at the atrocity. But orders had come from Angleterre and the Master flexed his muscles and advised me that I was there to work, not to act as a Historic Places Trust advisor. What a disgrace to destroy it, not only because of the wonderful aesthetic value, not to mention the antiquity, but also because it acted as an insulator and most of all contributed to the structural well-being of the floor above. The magnificent concave curves which the ancient artisans perfected with the use of wine bottles, almost resisted demolition, a testimony to their genius. It felt criminal, compounded when the master advised us that the English lady had decided to take all the ceilings down throughout the whole house.

The open doors and the activity attracted quite a few visitors. Madame Ferlin, an elderly lady from next door told us that the Master had tried to buy the remise (stable) the other side of where we were working, in order to make the Tea Rooms larger. She refused to sell as she thought there was something shifty about the Master, despite an enormous offer. The high offer in effect, was the main cause of her suspicions and besides; she said that she did not like neither the Master nor the English woman, who had been down during the negotiations.

Mossy, also none too amused by the house nor the Master, took refuge in a doorway across the street and as a result of her sit-out protest we had a sad encounter with an elderly Swiss man who lived in the village. Some months previously, his own Foxie went missing and he got word from a villager that his dog was sitting on a step in the Rue du Temple. He came by, calling

"Ursule, Ursule, c'est toi, c'est toi!" even right up close he was still convinced, but mind you he can't have been far off ninety years old and his vision was totally impaired. Heart-broken, he related the story and warned us to take care of Mossy or the hunters might get her for chasing the cochons as Foxies are meant to be excellent for the job. We offered him Mossy to take for walks, and although he was most appreciative he said it would only restart the grieving process all over again.

CHAPTER 27

When the Master arrived I was talking to our neighbour Madame Ferlin and he asked me to try and get friendly with her to see if she would sell me the remise. Madame had already made her assessment of him by saying that he had 'un sourrire d' un commerçant, comme tous les Anglais' and I guess she should know since she had met the Queen Mother and Montgomery when they visited the Chateau Lourmarin, while she worked there after the war.

The next victim of the sledge hammer was the wooden floor which was a source for many a conversation round the village and not only because of the wonderful old wood that was being discarded, but because la Dame Anglaise was going to replace it with York stone to be shipped all the way to Provence from England. It seemed rather an odd decision, especially as the region of Provence has fine quality pavers that could match anything from England. Our neighbour's son, himself a maçon said:

"Les Anglais sont fous, fous!"

Further antics by the as-yet unseen English woman brought many enquiries as to what she was actually going to do with the building. Most of the locals seemed to think that she had another agenda as the Tea Rooms tale was not fitting with the procedure of the renovation. We of course, were kept in the dark about everything and the Master had told us on several occasions not to engage the locals as they were just inquisitive peasants with nothing else to do except nose around other people's affairs.

On the other side of the Rue du Temple there was a rather difficult to make out Englishman who invariably introduced himself as being Polish but with a west country accent. He was known as Frank the bike man. While we were in the process of lowering the floor to accommodate the York stone, or coals to Newcastle, Frank was by coincidence elevating the floor in his bike shop and he came by to ask if he could borrow our wheelbarrow and he would remove all the spoil from our excavations gratuit!

The Master, who owned a chambre d'hotes (bed & breakfast) about an hour away in Salon, arrived late one morning and found Frank wheeling away our rubble and he quickly told him not to come around again as the site was out of bounds. Right tactless and unmannerly we thought, because despite the pony tail, Frank did speak a rather nice dialect of the Queen's English. From then on every time Frank saw the Master pass in his van, he wet his middle finger and tested the wind.

"How odd" remarked the Master, when one day we passed Frank with his windometer held aloft.

CHAPTER 28

A sign on the boulangerie window read, 'Fermez pour les vacances d'hiver'. It was Valentine's Day, and although the nights were still wickedly cold, the days usually turned out sunny and often as warm as a good summer's day in Ireland. The village was experiencing an influx of well-heeled visitors, who were mainly Parisian with a variety of small dogs on tow. Our pile of sand for the plastering had become victim, despite my sign which read: 'Ce n'est pas kitty litter'. One flashy-looking doll in stilettos came by regularly with a mutt that resembled a large cotton swab with legs, connected to a fisherman's reel. While the little fluff-ball lined himself up for the morning jeter, the lady nonchalantly walked towards the fountain as she unreeled her little chou chou.

We had enough of Chou Chou and his steamy remains in the morning frost so we set a trap for him. I hid a high pressure hose just below the surface of the sand and waited. They arrived at their usual time and through the crack in the door I observed Chou Chou as he took his rectum out of gear. Then, when I opened the gate valve to the maximum, it was like an eruption, as water shot about twenty feet into the air, spraying sand everywhere with Chou Chou taking the full blast. He yelped like a cut pig as he ran in the wrong direction until he reached the end of the reel and somersaulted into silence.

"Wind him in, madame, wind him in! He put up a brave fight!"

It was the last time we saw the pair of them.

Work had commenced in tidying up the remise-stable next door and by then after almost two weeks on the job I had become friendly enough with Madame Ferlin, to pull a little stroke on the Master regarding our future employment.

I explained to her that Caron and I had only been brought in to do the basic demolition but that the Master would keep us on if he thought there was a chance of buying the stable from her.

We made an arrangement that I would visit Madame Ferlin's house while the Master was on site, making sure that he noticed me going in.

CHAPTER 29

Up until then our tool requirements were few and anything we needed could be borrowed from the locals. One such emprunte was a spirit level that had long lost its bubble, and heaven knows what I was meant to do with it. While I was in Cruis I saw a maçon fit a door lintel using a distant jet stream to sight it for level, but a floor in Lourmarin! Paul Cezanne said that there are no straight lines in nature and looking at these Provencal villages, one has to wonder if a spirit level was ever used. Lateral thinking seems to be a local invention and the Provencaux are masters at it. One such example comes to mind is when I asked a local maçon where I could find a dozen tomettes, the traditional Provencal hexagonal floor tiles, for an injured area of the floor after the demolition. It could take an age to find them because there was no standard size as each village had its own kiln and they also differed from region to region.

"Laisse-le avec moi," was the reply and he returned the following day with twelve exact replicas cut out of marine plywood and painted red.

"Voila, un peu de colle et Frenchtastique!"

Madame Ferlin was calling regularly to see if our little scam had paid off - I had not been approached by the Master, but at least we were still on the job. She usually gave us a full account of all that was going on in the village bringing us the local magazines of which there were a surprising amount despite there only being a thousand inhabitants. The regional paper for the Vaucluse had an article about Albert Camus and Henri Bosco, both writers, whom were buried in the local cemetery. Madame, now an octogenarian, had known both of them quite well and she took us to visit their graves. How similar it was to Ireland, with the Mickey Doolans (Catholics) on the one side and the Pressbuttons (Protestants) on the other. Camus' grave was a very simple affair, with just a large rock and his name engraved on it. That was apparently how he wished it.

CHAPTER 30

Every Tuesday and Thursday, Madame went to the local marché de poissons, where the marchand is attributed with inventing the wet-fish handshake, which incidentally is only a couple of degrees colder than the English one, but twice as long, thus making them about even. His business survived mainly because there are so few services left in Lourmarin as a result of the abundance of second-home owners who only come down in summer to complain about the tourists. The rest of the year, the volets (shutters) are closed and the villagers become extinct. The few that are left, feel they are becoming outsiders in their own town.

On her way back from the poissonerie, Madame, without fail, would stop to show us her purchase, with as much enthusiasm as though she had caught it herself and Caron always got a gem of a recipe because Madame had decided, as she put it:

"Vous êtes de notre famille", and fortunately it was said in hearing distance of the Master. This finally brought about an enquiry from him wishing to know how I was getting on with Madame and the remise.

"Very well," I assured him, "but it's a little way off yet!" I also told the Master how much they were going to sell it to me for which was considerably less than he had offered, but as I told Madame, I had first to earn the money and it would take Caron and I together most of a year to accumulate it. This would mean keeping us on the job until it was finished. Madame Ferlin loved the deception, especially as it was the Master and the Englishwoman who were being duped.

The Master made a phone call to the owner in England to relate the story of how I was in the process of charming Madame Ferlin into selling me the stables and on his return Caron and I were asked if we would like to stay on to the end of the project.

I met Madame Ferlin later in the day and told her the news,

"Pauvre Caron et Finn" was her endearing, and prophetic, reply.

CHAPTER 31

The tourism in Lourmarin had increased sufficiently to introduce my second postcard enterprise in France and I decided to put out a little stand on the Rue du Temple and commence selling the postcards from the attic. We put the table halfway between the Tea Rooms and Madame Ferlin's doorway, in case the Master thought it was my business. It had an unattended honesty box with Madame Ferlin giving the occasional eye to it. Most days the sales went extremely well and with Mossy sitting just by, it looked a very attractive proposition, with even the Master himself buying a few one day to impress Madame, thinking it was her shop.

I wasn't aware of it at the time, but I could have caused the other card shops to complain and we who were working on the black, could have been run off the job. The French tend not to be like that though and the greed motive doesn't prevail as much here as in other countries I have worked in. They were most likely to say nothing, but one could never be a 100% sure and when our honesty box went missing, we wondered if the locals had sent us a message! Madame Ferlin told me that she saw two shady-looking characters going up and down the Rue du Temple and they were the ones most likely to have stolen our day's take including the honesty box itself. There was not a lot I could do about it, especially when I saw what they did with the money. They were sitting happily under a tree over by the Chateau, with a couple of bottles of wine and I must say I had done far worse to get money in order to satisfy the cravings of alcohol when I was an active drinker and user.

When I was in Ireland, I resorted to taking money from the poor boxes one finds everywhere over there and things went fierce well until one day I picked on the wrong box which had a string attached to it and as I left it got wrenched out from under my jacket, resulting in my arrest. So, in a strange sort of a way I was delighted to have been robbed, a bit of restitution does one no harm.

Chapter 32

Sometimes of an evening I spent time speaking with Madame, she was a great historian and related stories about the village which the tourist would never get to hear. For example, just across from the Tea Rooms was an arched door which by ancient decree could never be locked. It was a passageway to the Laverie (wash house) situated on the river that once powered the olive mill, there was also an access to the crypt of Phillipe de Girard, a prolific inventor whose most famous creation was the linen machine which took first prize at the Paris exhibition in 1810, but was later smashed by Ned Ludd-ite in 1812. The price of a million francs was never paid to him due to an outbreak of war and he died somewhat in poverty. She told me of the secret tunnels which ran from the Castellas (now the clock tower) to the Chateau and indeed some fairy stories about the Chateau itself and the curse of the gypsies.

As part of our commitment to our guardian job in the Auriol chateau, we were obliged to go down there every weekend and like ourselves, Madame Claude of the bastide had no idea that the Lourmarin job was going to continue more than two weeks, so I rang her at her residence in Switzerland to advise her of the extension. She said:

"You had better continue as long as you can, because finding work will be difficult after Peter Mayle's comments about the Irish in his book, A Year in Provence."

I hadn't thought of that but I did recall when reading the April section of the book that he said the Irish were a liability due to their drinking, but at least now I was on the wagon and religiously attending two Alcoholics Anonymous meetings a week in Aix en Provence. The weekends were always a welcome break because of our spartan existence in Lourmarin and back at the bastide in Auriol we had all the modern conveniences including a television which neither of us had seen for over twenty years.

I watched a documentary on the life of Sam Neil, the Irish actor, who now lives in Queenstown in the South Island of New Zealand. He talked about his first experience on arriving there as a young boy. While driving from Christchurch to Akaroa, they had to stop the car because it made him vomit. Well Sam, I can sympathise with you, because I did the very same, except I got diarrhoea too, but at least I got out. Sam is still there in Queenstown next door to an artist friend of mine, Angus Watson, a man who ended up in a wheel chair after a skiing accident. Auriol gave us a welcome break from the Master, but after the Luberon, the area of Aubagne, Marseille and Auriol, had absolutely no charm and the thought of living there gave me the same feeling of emptiness as New Zealand.

I met Frank the bike man on the street, when we went back to Lourmarin after our weekend away and he told me that he had seen a rather odd-looking woman with a tea cosy on her head hovering around the Rue du Temple taking photographs. He said she looked like Cruella from 'A Hundred and One Dalmations'.

The Englishwoman had arrived and she brought two people along who she said would eventually run the business. One was a bag stitcher from Bognor, and the other an artist from the Antipodes. She told us of her plans for Lourmarin.

"It needs a shake-up you know."

The bag stitcher was known as 'Whispering Grass' and Cruella said that he was currently doing some work for Peter Mayle.

"Have you read his book, Finney?"

Here we go I thought.

"Did you read what he said about the Irish?"

Next she's going to ask me if my name is Murphy and did I come from Donegal.

"Yes miss, I did."

"Have you seen him around the village?"

"No miss and even if I did I wouldn't recognise him because we've never met."

"Well you might get a chance, if you are still here that is, because we are going to get him to open the gallery."

"What gallery is that, miss?"

"You had better keep this to yourself Finney, it's not going to be a Tea Rooms at all, but an English art gallery and we don't want the other fourteen galleries in Lourmarin to know about it."

Frank was right, it was Cruella and the tea cosy on her head was just a camouflage.

Cruella clearly had an ego problem as well as being totally paranoid because the other fourteen galleries were not in the least worried about her plans to open in opposition to them.

CHAPTER 33

Our opera-singing friends from La Louviere in Haute Provence, who had been living in sin, decided to get married and we were very privileged to be invited to the wedding.

The road up from Auriol to Cruis was like a piste noir as Saturday was the ski chalet exchange day, it was mayhem. French weddings are a different affair to other countries because they have two ceremonies, one traditional church service, and the other in the Marie, the latter being obligatory and the only one recognised. We all gathered outside the Mayor's office, where the village market consisting of one stall was busy selling regional produce to the wedding group who were making arrangements to collect their purchases after the affairs of state were given precedence. The bride arrived late, as is customary, but no notice was taken because the Mayor upstaged her by coming fifteen minutes later.

The ceremony was held in his office overlooked by an imposing photo of Monsieur Chirac and opposite a statue of Letitia Casta, the new Semeuse. She was to be the national mascot for the next ten years, though, after her selection, she vacated La France to avoid taxes and is quoted as saying that she would rather 'go bust' in England. Apparently France loses two millionaires a week due to the exorbitant taxes and charges which are designed to keep unnecessary functionaires in work.

While the minutes of the couple's last twenty years were read out by the lady who normally deals with fosses septiques (septic tanks), a photographer dressed like an F.B.I. agent set himself up in the corner to record the incident. His repetitious flashing looked as though he was arc-welding, making the event look more like a murder scene than a wedding. The Mayor (Felix, who hopefully would not be sitting beside us at the wedding feast) wore a red white and blue chevron sash and he made a short speech before handing the groom a document which resembled a prize-winner's scroll for having the best dog at Cruft's.

99

The French custom of inviting people back for drinks after the wedding is quite common, but not all stay for the actual breakfast. In Ireland there is great snobbery attached to weddings and quite often you can find young couples in debt for the rest of their lives after successfully impressing the townspeople. The French are a bit more confident and impressionism is left to the artists.

Caron and I were seated at a table of twelve, all of whom drank, with the exception of me of course and due to my vegetarianism and Candida, there wasn't a lot I could eat either. Aperitifs before the meal (unlike Ireland where it's after) seemed a very civilised affair. Then came the courses and for me an almost observer, it was like sitting at a level crossing watching a goods train go by. I took more notice of the alcohol than the food and what really amazed me was that only three bottles of wine were consumed during the entire period, they'd spill that much back in Ireland.

I was sitting beside a man from Avignon whom I prevailed upon to tell me why the famous pont d'Avignon only halfway traversed the river.

"Ah monsieur, c'est la fleuve, c'est devenu beaucoup plus grand depuis la construction!"

Mark and Françoise were now man and wife and would no doubt live happy ever after at La Louviere, while Caron and I continued our search for the ideal place in which to live.

CHAPTER 34

It certainly was not New Zealand or Australia, but the Luberon was looking like it had a chance to seduce us which was a relief to Caron because Ireland, as far as she was concerned, would drive me back to the drink within a week of being there and there was no disputing that.

While we were working in the basement back at Lourmarin, the Master was preparing to put a terrace in the roof, the latest craze in most of the Provencal villages. The permitted area was ten per cent of the total roof space which in this case was roughly three metres by two, just about enough to swing a cat. Terraces if not done properly, can cause endless problems and it is highly recommended to use a specialist maçon for the job. I had no knowledge of it but the Master said it was a piece of cake. He instructed me to cut holes in the wall for wooden beams to carry the floor and out of the four he marked, two of them ended up in chimney breasts. I told him that this was strictly illegal and when the inspector called to see the job it would be condemned for sure. Once again the Master advised me that I was there to work and not to think!

"The time has long since gone
when Irishmen and women
could be kept from thinking,
by hurling priestly thunder
at their heads."

James Connolly
1868-1916

But despite my initial reaction of telling the master to go and fuck himself I refrained and used my new-found serenity which the AA was teaching me. In the past I would have flown off the handle and stormed out to the pub, but something had changed within me and even my ego was surprised.

Down in our hole in the basement we continued to dig out the rock to accommodate the slabs which were coming any day now from Yorkshire. They were 15cm plus 6cm for under floor heating, a total of eight inches. Cruella had gone to Morocco to source art for the gallery while the Master ran riot in the attic, sometimes working until 3a.m and generally making a nuisance of himself. There was little we could do to halt the destruction. When we had the basement finished, the Master instructed us to take the plaster off the facade wall on the Rue du Temple. Caron in shorts, with the longest legs in Provence, drew a lot of attention as she hacked away the plaster from a scaffold with a jack hammer. Local builders were both amazed and somewhat challenged to see a woman doing what they presumed was a macho domain. The neighbour across the street told us that the men were talking about her in the cafes and some were not at all happy by her versatility.

'Chats castrés et protégés par la Mairie de Roquevarie.' See following page

CHAPTER 35

The days were warming up but we were surprised by the climate in the south of France, as it was not nearly as warm as people are led to believe, but then we had been spoiled by the mildness of the Antipodes. The top of the house was the only place that ever got sun, so we moved our cardboard boxes which we were sleeping on, closer to the clock tower.

Word came from Cruella ordering the removal of the ancient crepi (plaster) from the façade of the house on the Rue du Juiverie. This brought a shock response because it had been featured in all the tourist brochures, and was deemed to be the finest example of 16th century crepi in the Luberon. Sometime in the past, students from Aix-en-Provence University had come to take samples to ascertain how it had been composed all that long ago.

It was the weekend so we weren't going to worry about it until Monday. There was a new film just released called 'Chocolat', which incidentally was about a mayor in a French village and his aversion to change. It was a rather timely film as it coincided with the national Mayoral elections which were taking place the same weekend. On our way to Aix-en-Provence to see it, we went by a village called Roquevaire to give Mossy a walk and a chance to do her pee before the movie. Just outside the cemetery in Roquevaire, there is a little cabin which had been constructed by the Mairie for stray cats. On the side was a classic sign which read:

'Chats castrés et protégés par la Mairie de Roquevarie.'

Cats castrated and protected by the Mayor!

Happy must be the cats in such good hands. Reassured we went on our way to Aix and the movie.

CHAPTER 36

Our séjour at Auriol was soon to end. The bastide was going
on the market and with the atmosphere in Lourmarin changing
our future was beginning to look insecure. The Mayor of Auriol
had expressed an interest in the property and even though the
council could not be prohibited from buying it, I got the impression that Madame Claude would have much preferred to see it
go to the private sector. It was of little consequence to us and
despite being sitting tenants it was unlikely that we would be
re-housed by the Mairie. But the results of the Mayoral elections, both in Auriol and indeed in Lourmarin, were going to
affect the next stage of our adventure. In Lourmarin, there were
just two serious contenders one of them was a close friend of
President Chirac and the other a local Socialist. The nouveau
riche and the nouveau arrivé would be battling for the capitalist
candidate as the progress of the village might be hindered by
the Socialists. There were already rumours of a condominium
for the village.

We arrived back after our weekend in Auriol and discovered
a fax from Cruella who was by then back in England, advising
us of a furniture delivery. This made about as much sense as
painting a toilet seat before sitting on it. The house was a bomb
site with dust, plaster and scaffolding everywhere and Cruella
decides to furnish it! It was only days earlier that she had instructed us to demolish a classic old stone staircase, our only
access for offloading the furniture because the van wouldn't fit
down the other side of the house on the Rue Juiverie. It was
going to be, as the French say, une catastrophe. It is typical of
well-heeled people who have not an ounce of practicality and
no idea how stupid they can be. Their money buffets them from
their incredible mistakes and when they are shown up by their
idiotic decisions, they blame somebody else. The less one has
to do with them the better - I was glad we had our dog to take
walking and free us from the arrogance of these insensitive peo-

ple who my French teacher had always advised me to stay away from.

Mossy's big treat of the day was her surprise attack on the alley cats, which at 7 a.m were as plentiful around the little streets as baguettes in the boulangerie. As soon as I opened the door she was away like a bat out of hell - like Don Quixote's horse Rosinante, it was always she who decided on the direction we took.

One morning she took me past a car park where I saw a man looking at the village map and as I walked his way with a knife in my hand that I had just found, I enquired:

"Excusez-moi monsieur, je peux vous aider?"

The knife and my early morning psychopathic look hadn't occurred to me as being rather odd, but he did not seem fazed.

"Do you speak English?" came his reply, "I'm looking for the Rue du Temple?" "You wouldn't be John with furniture now by any chance?"

"I am, and you must be Finney, Cruella told me you were a bit bizarre, what's with the knife?"

John came with me to assess the delivery access, which from 7 a.m through to 9 a.m was a virtual impossibility due to the boulangerie next door, it was like Kings Road and when he discovered that Cruella had ordered the demolition of the staircase two days before the delivery, his comment was:

"Is it any wonder we lost the Empire!"

As we unloaded the baths and beds and toilet pans the neighbours looked on in amazement. Frank came by and said:

"Can you not buy toilets in France then?"

John the driver told us that the toilet pans were Victorian replicas and cost £800 each, it seemed an awful lot to pay just to show your butt to the water, was Frank's assessment of the whole affair. I recalled reading an English writer who made reference to the Dutch bringing everything except the kitchen sink when they came to Provence, well we were witnessing far more, this was including the kitchen sink. I told John that this was no time to be making deliveries but he said there were four more loads on the way !!!!

As the weather continued to improve, Mossy and I noticed a bowl of water with a cute sign outside the boulangerie for thirsty dogs 'Bar de Tou Tou' .Madame Ferlin told me that the fountain on the Rue du Temple was originally for watering the two hundred and fifty horses that congregated on the streets of the village after a hot day in the fields. They queued along the length of the Rue du Temple like taxis waiting to drink from the troughs. Her brother was the last man in Lourmarin to have a horse, which incidentally had been stabled in the little remise beside the gallery, (sorry, Tea Rooms). Today in Lourmarin, all those stables have been converted into chic galleries and shops with only this one still in existence, fortunately for us, because without it our jobs would have been terminated had Cruella not the carrot of purchasing it via me.

The tourists were beginning to flock into the village, and the Chateau, which is the area's greatest attraction, began its season of entertainment. The first event to be advertised was a lecture and film on the life and times of Henri Bosco - knowing that Madame Ferlin was a great fan of his, we bought her a front row ticket and sent it to her anonymously. I had learned much about the Chateau from her and when one thinks of how close it came to being demolished, it's a miracle that it is there at all. The current building, which is of the Renaissance period, had as many other grand buildings, suffered at the time of the revolution and eventually fallen into disrepair. By 1920 it was virtually a ruin and the then owner decided to sell it for scrap. An auction was announced known as 'une vente a la chandelle' (sale by candle) which meant that the last bid would be taken on the dying wick. A rich industrialist by the name of Laurent Vibert made the successful bid and so commenced the strange tale. For decades prior to Vibert buying it, the gypsies used it to camp there on route to the Carmargue for the annual pilgrimage at Sainte Marie de la Mer where the black Madonna was buried. But Vibert, who had different plans, decided to kick the gypsies out. Before they departed they cursed Vibert and everyone who would ever have anything to do with the chateau from then on.

Laurent Vibert
When gitanes passed this way
And rested in their lay-by haunt,
T'was fine indeed till owners changed
Then came Monsieur Laurent
Things must change in Lourmarin
This Chateau's not for you.
So take your rags, your goats and bags
By sundown out of view
The gitanes left and Vibert smiled
Victorious he knew,
But on the wall within the gate
A gypsy curse did him relate,
Your time is up.
They knew .

Vibert commenced the massive renovation with the help of some 50 local artisans giving no consideration to the gypsies or to the curse on the wall which is still visible to this day. But he never saw the fruits of his labour and died in a car accident while driving from Lourmarin to his native Lyon. It has been rumoured that Albert Camus came under the same curse though some thirty years later, because he had had an involvement with the Chateau and he too died in a crash, en route to Paris from Lourmarin.

Just a way beyond the Chateau is a monument to the family of Laurent Vibert, an erotic sculpture, which I christened the Geminis. Two sisters, one looking east and the other west. To my mind, it appears as though the artist, Louis Didier, tried to capture the reaction of each girl, one to sunrise and the other to sunset, on arriving and leaving Lourmarin. On the faces of these beautifully formed goddesses, Dawn and Dusk are so subtly defined that a photograph could not give the artist's impression due justice. It has to be visited and carefully looked at to see the difference that morning and evening has on their almost identical expressions. Lourmarin, unlike many other villages, doesn't leave the visitor feeling sad on departure, because everyone knows that they will be back a second time.

Photo of the Ferlins on Rue Basse. From right Madame Ferlin, Raymond (her Brother), Vincent (Raymond's Son) and Finn. Raymond died recently
See following page

CHAPTER 37

Photographing the locals is not a recommended pastime, but the Ferlins didn't feel as though they were being recorded as a rare species becoming extinct, so they agreed to pose gracefully with Caron and Mossy and myself. While we were all together on the street discussing the ouverture on the roof which the Master had made for the terrace, a lady who had had one done just a few doors away, gave us her thoughts. In olden days, she explained, when the animals lived on the ground floor and the residents up top, it was a logical conversion, but today all the kitchens are on the street level, making the terraces totally impractical. She said she only went up to hers twice a week to hang out the washing. In that case, Cruella's was as good as useless because of the five flights of stairs one would have to climb with trays of food. Raymond, Madame Ferlin's brother and a retired macon, was very concerned about the efficiency of a wooden structure, when everyone else in the Luberon constructed them in fer et beton (iron and concrete).

"Une terrasse en bois, c'est fou, fou." The retired maçon exclaimed.

If he saw the beams poking onto the chimney there would be a few more fou's I'd imagine but we were under strict instructions from the Master not to let anyone up the stairs to see what was going on. We knew what he was doing was a total disaster and it was not our concern, besides, it was St Patrick's weekend and we were off to Auriol.

CHAPTER 38

At my meeting of Alcoholics Anonymous in Aix-en-Provence, the group, aware of the importance of Saint Patrick's Day to an Irishman sans alcool for the first time in his life, were concerned and wondered how I would cope. If I did overcome the desire it would be the first time that I didn't become unconscious from an alcohol overdose on the 17th of March.

Madame Claude was expecting people who had expressed an interest in buying the bastide and as Caron and I were preparing lunch, the doorbell summoned us. Madame was in her bed-chamber attending to her facial camouflage so I welcomed the visitors.

"Entrez et asseyez-vous , Madame will be with you presently."

The two gentlemen commented on how nice the house was and sat patiently like two little virgins. I went back to preparing lunch as I heard Madame coming down the tomette staircase and greeted the two church mice.

"Bonjour!"

"Bonjour Madame," came the choral response.

Madame excused herself and came to the kitchen enquiring:

"Who are those two people?"

"What people?" I exclaimed, "Are they not the ones coming to look over the house?"

"They're too early! You had better go and find out, Finn, you let them in."

"Excusez-moi messieurs, êtes-vous intéressés par la bastide?"

"Oh, oui monsieur, bien sûr!"

«Bon, attendez un peu, and Madame will show you around in a couple of minutes."

I told Madame that they were interested in the bastide and that the agent must have sent them, so off they went on a tour of the out offices and stables.

From our view down the long avenue we noticed a car driving towards us, another interested group and although showing people around would have been no problem to me, Madame Claude said that she would prefer to do it herself.

"There's a sequence you know."

The second couple, Bernard and Zenia Saltiel were both dressed from head to toe in emerald green because Madame had told them that the caretakers were Irish and there I was, on our national feast day and if it wasn't for the Lacoste green alligator on my tee shirt, I could well have been a fucking Paisleyite.

Bernard, who was quite familiar with the Irish and our history, surprised me when he landed a bottle of Paddy Whiskey on the table to "wet the shamrock" as he put it. We had a lot in common - we were both fond of explosives and both of us had severe tinnitus, his from a mining accident in Africa.

Tinnitus
Some hear creaks
Or corn crakes
Cigadas even bees.
Telephones, jet plane drones
Or the jingling sound of keys
Mosquitoes got to be the worst
Bad enough to those not cursed.
But what about a dripping tap
Turns a sleep into a nap
Quasi Modo heard the bells
Others hear the sound in shells.
Samuel Morse could never sleep
He kept hearing bleep bleep bleep.
Then of course, there was poor Van Gogh
He found no cure, so cut it off.

While Bernard and I were comparing our tinnitus, Madame arrived back looking flustered. During the tour of the property, as a result of stating that there would be a clause in the sale agreement prohibiting the destruction of the little chapel at the entrance, it transpired that the two visitors had no interest in the place, they were Jehova's Witnesses who had come to convert us.

I got it in the ear as you can imagine.

Bernard and Zenia were very keen on the property and they were the couple who had rung regarding the advertisement. Caron and I left them to view the building and the bottle of whiskey remained unopened. I went to mass at Moulin Reddon near Auriol and because it was St Patrick's Day, the priest made a reference to the Fête Irlandaise and invited me to speak. It was also the day of second round voting for those Mayors who had not made it the previous week, and after the service the Priest finished by saying:

"On Calvary there was a sinner each side of Christ and today being the final round of the Mayoral elections, n'oubliez pas qu'il n'y a aucune différence entre la Droite et la Gauche! Allez et bon dimanche à tous.

Having a keen interest in politics I went along to the Mairie that evening to watch the returning officers count the votes and to see how different it was from our own system in Ireland. I was quite surprised to see how many spoiled voting slips there were and two in particular for which there was a cause for humorous giggle. In one envelope they found a photograph and details of a buxom Moroccan lady offering her services followed by another which had a condom enclosed, one has to wonder if she voted twice!

I survived St Patrick's Day without hitting the bottle and all my friends in the AA congratulated me by telephone, little did they know that the temptation had come in a bottle from Ireland which Bernard Saltiel brought with the patron Saint's name on the side, Paddy!

CHAPTER 39

The York stone for the gallery in Lourmarin was cancelled as Monsieur Gaudin, the electrician advised la Dame Anglaise that stone of that thickness would take three days to heat up and equally as long to cool down. Besides, it would be too heavy for the under-floor heating. A replacement had to be secured and the Master who knew everything about everything, found a supplier in Nod-sur-Seine, near Paris (half way to Newcastle). There was only one thing wrong, the floor was now much too deep because the new stone was only 3cm thick, so it meant going back to the dump to try and find some of the earth we had thrown away. The whole affair was becoming a bit of a comedy and the English woman was the latest subject of gossip in the village cafes. The neighbours told us that the Master had worked all of St Patrick's week-end late into the night trying to finish the terrace before Cruella came from England for a progress report. It was a disaster and I knew that even Cruella with her limited knowledge would be furious. I invited Raymond up to see it himself and his reaction left me in no doubt when he said:

"C'est fou, fou!"

«Je sais, je sais, Raymond, c'est vrai, tu as raison : ils sont tous fous!"

Having reached agreement I assured him that he had no reason to fear for his own house next door and the whole lot would be ripped out and done again. Cruella who had not yet spent a night in the house, arrived from her lodgings at the old coach station guest house, Villa St Louis, in a foul humour. Her face was like a butcher's apron having been attacked by her pet dog the previous night in England and we were all hoping that the dog was ok. But to make matters worse, her car had been broken into just outside the guest house and all the ignition wires cut. As she did not speak a word of French, I was obliged to go with her to the next village of Cadenet to file the report at the Gendarmerie. She asked me to enquire if they were going to come and inspect the car and when I told her that such an incident wouldn't warrant a waste of police time, she indignantly replied:

"It would in England!"

"In France, miss, I assure you they don't come out even for murders between midday and two o'clock unless, that is, the boulanger is the victim."

The Gendarmes requested her details and on discovering it was her birthday they wished her "bon anniversaire et bonne continuation de votre vacances en France, et au revoir!"

"Is that it? Is that all they are going to do?"

"Yes miss, I'm afraid so"

"Does he realise who I am?"

Her fury continued when she saw the mess the Master had left, and as we had anticipated, the inevitable occurred.

The Master was summoned from his abode near Salon and the last act drew to a close. He was duly relieved of his duties and I was asked to run the job from then on. The Master's departure posed a bit of a problem as he took all his tools and his van, leaving us virtually stranded. But in typical Provencal fashion, Raymond Ferlin came to the rescue and lent us all his old tools until I could afford to buy my own. No van was a problem though, but for the time being we used our own car. Word of the Master's departure soon got around the village and reluctant artisans who had refused to work under him came forth like the timid blossoms of early spring. The door bell rang and Monsieur Matteau the plombier was the first to announce his delight at working under the new management. Soon after came the electricians, who had abandoned the job over a dispute with the Master and they gave us a new start date. It was a renaissance and our isolation ended. Cruella, now happy that the project was in safe hands returned to England, but before she went she had a meeting with Monsieur Gaudin at his house in Puyvert. Afterwards she said to us:

"How can an electrician live in a grand house like that?"

Cruella was of the old school and the thought of peasants in bourgeois mansions left her questioning her decision to buy in France.

The English passion with France is not the food, nor indeed the weather, it is purely their fascination with the 'peasantry' in a derogatory sense.

With Cruella out of the way, we were all relieved and the work progressed much better without her interference.

Madame Ferlin visited and brought us all the literature from the film and lecture at the Chateau on Henri Bosco.

She told us that she had the best seat in the house and that someone had sent the ticket to her anonymously. It was a wonderful start to spring, positive and cheerful like no other we had experienced.

CHAPTER 40

The villagers had taken to the hills in search of wild asparagus and of course Madame Ferlin with her four score years didn't forget to pick a bunch for Caron which, as usual, was presented with yet another Provencal recipe that even the Michelin Star *Moulin de Lourmarin* chef hadn't heard of.

During our lunch break, which we had now extended by an hour because Cruella had not increased our minimum wage despite making me foreman, we went north of the village into the Luberon hills in search of the prized delicacy and there among the wild thyme and rosemary we found it in great profusion. To our surprise we also saw Edouard Loubet, the afore mentioned famously eccentric Michelin Star chef of the *Moulin*. There he was in full uniform, collecting wild thyme and rosemary for his restaurant. One had to wonder, is it such attention to detail and the eternal quest to find the highest quality ingredients that makes a chef of this standard. Loubet was the youngest chef in France to receive this honour, one which the French hold in higher esteem than the British do their Knighthoods.

A phone call from Bath in England, it was Cruella, in a demolition yard where she had just bought a cast-iron staircase to replace the conventional one we had broken out. As usual there had been no prior consultation with us regarding the size, height, width or indeed if it was left or right hand twist, all of which have to be considered before purchasing a spiral staircase.

"It's too late Finney, it's already paid for!"

She was in her car and on the way home. The hole in the floor through which the stairs would have to pass was walled on two sides and there was an old wooden beam which could not be touched on the other. Having fitted a spiral staircase once before, I knew that it could be a right pain in the neck. But as in most cases, the tradesmen of this world are expected to work miracles for non-thinking whimsical prima donnas, who occasionally flutter our way. I rang the yard in Bath myself and spoke to the foreman who was as helpful as Cruella and told me that the stairs had been dismantled and other than the colour, which was black, he had no other information about it.

"Could I have the measurement of one tread and the diameter of the pole?" And back came the measurement in feet and inches and I here in France with a metric tape, long live the empire!

Working for English people who are renovating in France is the biggest headache one could ever encounter, because they insist that every single item has to come from Blighty and they even change the French power points for English ones. This is a nightmare for tradesmen because adaptors must be used for every power tool. According to one Englishman I met:

"The only thing the French do well is perfume and they only got that right because they never wash!"

CHAPTER 41

Whilst I was in New Zealand in an effort to improve my health I had had all my amalgam fillings removed and replaced with white composite of which one had been set too deep resulting years later in a toothache that would fall a horse. Too late to go to a dentist, so I went along to the local chemist in Lourmarin who obliged me with a few pain killers to keep me going until the morning. I took my first pill in the shop and I was offered a choice of *eau, plate ou gazeuse* to get it down, which again, could only happen in France. Nightfall brought more than the toothache to contend with, the *Mistral* had returned and all those loose shutters I meant to repair since the last storm came back to haunt me. My sleepless night provoked an early morning rise which Mossy and I availed of by taking the opportunity to see the village in darkness and just like the tumble weed in those dreary American films, the badly-glued posters were having a rendezvous at the corner of the Rue du Temple and the Place d'Ormeau, just by the *tabac*. The most visible contributors in attendance were those of John Fratellini, the circus people who go around Provence like the painters on the Golden Gate Bridge; as soon as the circuit is complete they're back again. Their Metro Goldwyn Mayer Lion seems to be eternally looking at us from different walls and trees around the Luberon.

Having no comfort in Cruella's house, there was little one could do to make life more pleasant and walking around Lourmarin until the dentist opened was as bearable as lying on the cardboard boxes with my eyes open.

My visit to the dentist was a rather novel experience. Although the French are not noted for having the best of teeth, I could envisage a change in Lourmarin, because this was a surgery with a difference. Doctor Ronan, a young vibrant surgeon originally from Brittany with an amazing Celtic personality, gave me the traditionally Gaelic welcome of *Cead Mile Failte*. His female assistant or human anaesthetic in her white see-thru nurse's outfit with virtual reality black underwear, was enough to encourage anyone to come in and have their teeth straightened out.

"Do you mind the sound of the drill?" Dr Ronan enquired and me with my mouth opened to the maximum,

I responded with the only oral sound one can make in that position and said:

"*Aaaaarrrggghhh!*"

Satisfied that I was not going to be disturbed by it, he proceeded to dismantle my tooth, but at least he asked. The pain would soon be gone, but there was little that could be done for the headache which I was about to experience at the hands of Cruella.

She faxed us from Burford and said I had to go to Oxford to pick up a van to replace the Master's one and drive it back to Lourmarin. The idea of going all the way to England for a fifteen year-old Volkswagen seemed ludicrous, but I suppose if she was sending everything else down, why not a van. I flew Ryan Air from Marseille to Stanstead and took a train to gloomy Oxford. The van had a six cylinder petrol engine and I was assured that it had been totally serviced for the grand trip south. After arriving at Burford, where Cruella had another gallery, I was handed the keys and in typical English fashion I wasn't even asked if I was by chance hungry and was ushered off back to France like a stray dog. Five miles from Burford I noticed the petrol gauge was reading empty and one of the six cylinders was misfiring. I attended to the petrol, but if Cruella was insensitive enough to expect me to drive off to France with a vehicle in that state, I was not going to be wasting my time trying to fix the problem with the cylinder and the extra fuel it was going to consume on the journey south was her problem. It rained all the way to Dover, where I caught the night ferry to Calais. It was my intention to drive to the first motorway stop and sleep for the night, but coming out of Calais the oil light began to flash. Although angry by the whole affair, especially Cruella's lies about it having been serviced, the thought of continuing and letting the engine seize was no longer my *modus operandus* since joining the AA, so I stopped and decided to wait until morning. Around 4 a.m I was abruptly awoken by the back draft from the juggernauts which had just disembarked and the cold damp atmosphere of Nord Pas de Calais which was by then an alien climate to me, caught me by surprise. I had no blankets or sleeping bag and the cold had gone into my bones. At first light I drove to Boulogne-sur-Mer to see Emmanuelle before heading off for Lourmarin. The drive down wasn't without incident as all the electrics packed up outside Amiens and after spending hours trying to trace the fault, I was forced to call the local *dépannage* (breakdown) service. At every second service station I had to put 200 francs worth of petrol in the tank due to the faulty cylinder. It was a nightmare and the total cost of the exercise between flight, food, ferry, fuel, *péage*, repairs, wages, came to far more than the van was worth. But it had ye olde G.B. sticker with the steering wheel on the wrong side and that's all that mattered to Cruella; letting the Frogs know where she came from seemed frightfully important to her. I arrived home at an ungodly hour and left the van outside the house for the convenience of unloading the famous spiral staircase which I had carted from Burford.

CHAPTER 42

The following day while I was parked opposite the work site on the Rue du Temple, I had my first-ever experience of what it was like to be English in France. The local policeman, on seeing the Union Jack parked outside the house, came by and gave me a right telling off and no amount of Irish brogue could redeem me. It was then that I decided it was necessary to disassociate myself from the common misconception the French are under, that if one speaks English, one is English. So I quickly made it known around Lourmarin that I was an Irishman. However as Frank informed me, I might have been better off letting people think I was English, because of Murphy, the character in Peter Mayle's book who was also a builder with a bad reputation and supposedly the spitting image of me.

The first day of real tourism arrived, and although Madame Ferlin said that we were only experiencing fifty per cent of the normal quota, it was hectic and parking became a virtual impossibility.

Mossy had to be put on a lead due to the influx of macho dogs and our usual haunt behind the Chateau was no longer possible because of the picnickers. Extrovert Frenchmen urinated against the trees with no consideration for passers-by. 'Le droit de pipi' illustrates the French penis is by no way as bashful as the Anglo Saxon's and not nearly as selective either, it will hang out anywhere!

Now that we had a van I could begin to haul back the soil that was necessary to elevate the floor again.

The man at the *déchetterie* (dump) said that he had never before seen anyone come to take stuff away from there and when I was offloading the soil on Rue du Temple, Frank came by and asked us:

"Would that be English top soil by any chance, that Cruella has had shipped down from Oxford?!"

Everyone knew what the Brits were like and even though I had heard about their distrust of things French from those who initially refused to travel through the Channel Tunnel, I had never seen anything like what Cruella was doing. She was making a total mockery of everything and everyone in Lourmarin and despite Mayle's Mr Murphy being a bastard, I was glad to be Irish and relating Cruella's antics to the locals became a daily pastime. I was also keeping a diary and a scrapbook of all her faxes and notes that she was sending to us from Oxford.

A second load of furniture arrived from England and the driver told us that it was official, Peter Mayle was definitely going to open the gallery.

Cruella asked me to write a poem reflecting the mood of the event. It was my big opportunity and who knows, she added, maybe Mayle himself might even get to read it.

Signs around the village for a forthcoming *vide grenier* (literally 'Empty attic', the French equivalent of a car boot sale), attracted my attention and residents of Lourmarin were given first option on the spaces available to sell their goods. For some weeks previously I had been picking up interesting items from the local dump which had been thrown out by the *nouveau riche* who frequently week-ended in Lourmarin. One could find anything and in most cases in reasonable working order. Fridges, washing machines, microwave ovens, lawn mowers, virtually anything, and as I was a great seller with a neck like a jockey's bollocks, I amassed as much as I could in preparation for the big day some weeks hence.

The *vide grenier* always coincided with the tourist season and the foreigners loved the atmosphere and bought just for the pleasure of being involved. All the houses and apartments were occupied by people from every corner of the globe and some who came back year after year felt as though it was their village.

An elderly American couple who were on holiday from California became regular visitors to our worksite on Rue du Temple and were fascinated by my postcard stand and what an odd bi-product it was for an Irish builder in France! "You'd do very well in the U.S. you know, because every time we come down this "roo" there's a crowd around you."

They were off to 'Aches' (Aix-en-Provence) for the day and the permitted time allocated by their tour handlers back in the States was only six hours for the round trip.

"We can't stand around talking for too long!"

How sad, we thought, here they were on holiday and still governed by some silly schedule that almost told them when to piss! But despite their somewhat regulated lives, it is difficult not be fond of Americans. Their generous nature, constant good humour and positive character is a great advertisement and Europeans would do well to take a leaf out of their book. When they came back from 'Aches' they presented us with a punnet of strawberries and a bottle of olive oil!

Madame Deliso, the wife of a wealthy American who resided in Lourmarin became interested in our project due to the talk around the village about the strange methods being employed by a mysterious English woman who wore a tea cosy on her head. Questions about the 'Tea Rooms' were constant, and although what we were doing did not correspond with the work needed for such premises we were under strict instructions to continue with the charade.

Madame Deliso, unlike most other people, seemed to understand builders and rarely interrupted us as she passed for her morning coffee with her dog Tattoo, a little West Highland terrier that was well known for his amorous encounters and, if his tail was any barometer for his thoughts, the rumours were to be believed!

CHAPTER 43

It was May day weekend, which is a big occasion in the French calendar especially for the construction industry. *Bétonnières* (cement mixers) and ratchet pulleys that survive the Provencal sun without oil or grease, go silent as the *maçons* tidy up for the *Grande Fête de Travailleurs*. We availed of the weekend and left Lourmarin to the tourists. Auriol was suddenly becoming more pleasant and our usual trip to the bio market provided a tale that I am sure will become a legend with the locals. Just opposite our organic vegetable stall holder was the butcher, who every Saturday tried to tempt people to buy his meat by holding up a prime cut of steak to passers-by and this day was no exception. We had just commented on how revolting the smell of the meat had become since we gave it up some fourteen years previously. We told him that we were vegetarians which went down like a load of bricks, but he didn't give in and tried it on with Mossy. Again we let him know that Mossy did not like raw meat and this he just would not accept. It was certainly bad enough to encounter two six-foot, extremely healthy looking vegetarians, but a non meat-eating dog! He vibrated with disbelief and decided to pursue the matter himself by offering Mossy a piece of his finest prime beef saying:
"C'est pas vrai, c'est pas vrai."
We were in no doubt whatsoever as to how Mossy would react. She was always an almost reluctant eater. When the butcher shook the piece of dangling flesh in front of her nose, the scent became irrelevant and in typical fox terrier fashion hand and meat became one and like Marconi's first signal on his land line, I felt the vibration of her larynx all the way up her lead. The butcher, with his profession in question, persisted to taunt her, with the occasional glimpse at us and Jerome the vegetable man. Mossy, feeling that she was a victim of ridicule exposed her stalactites and I knew it was only a matter of seconds. Then *"Graaaaaawl!"* and the lead was wrenched out of my hand as the butcher took to his heels and Mossy was in hot pursuit. The

piece of lean meat was early abandoned by both parties and the chase was a spectacle for all in the market place, but as the overweight butcher climbed the stairs to his caravan, he was no match for Mossy's agility. With a firm grip on his trouser leg Moss continued to express her discontent at being ridiculed to the delight of a now assembled arena. Safe in his carnivorous cockpit the butcher kept repeating:

"*C'est pas vrai, c'est pas vrai!*"

We bid farewell to Jerome and as we walked off we heard the butcher say to his next customers:

"Etrangers, vous savez, leur chien est fou!"

Afterwards, we went to the *Fête d'Anes* in Roquevaire, where the Mayor castrates the cats. It was a bit like the fairs in Ireland frequented by tinkers, with lots of gypsies from the Carmargue and all sorts of gimmicks to make money. One had a stuffed donkey which was marketed as the oldest ass in France with a plaque stating that it had come under the hands of the taxidermist since *1890* and it was mounted on wheels. Dead donkey rides were popular at twenty francs a go!

A.D.A.D.A., the *Association des Amis des Anes* had their representatives handing out leaflets on the renaissance of this once threatened beast of burden, while opposite, ironically, a charcuterie was doing a fine trade in *saucisson d'âne*, donkey sausages.

Further off in a corner, five men dressed in blue t-shirts and Sandeman port hats with Roy Rogers handkerchiefs round their necks were struggling to push *Têtu* (this stubborn ass) into a box out of harm's way from a frisky jackass who looked like pole-vaulting in after her.

There was a dog show and any dog was allowed to participate, so we entered Mossy in the *Milou* category but we were told that her *barbe* (meggle or beard) was illegal because she was female, apparently in France only males are allowed the tuft under the chin. We explained that in the world famous 'Cruft's Dog Show' in England, they permitted both the male and female to wear the beards. This brought the what had now become common reaction:

"Les chiens anglais sont bizarres!"

Chapter 44

Our weekends away from Lourmarin provided Cruella ample time to create enough obstacles to hinder our progress and thus slow the job down totally. Both she and Whispering Grass (the bag-stitcher from Bognor) had started to furnish the house even though none of the rooms had been wired or painted. There was currently enough furniture for two houses and I was informed that there were another two loads to come. Perhaps she thought I had managed to charm Madame Ferlin for the stables next door! Cruella fancied herself as some sort of interior designer and told us that the practicality of a kitchen was of no consequence but aesthetics were. She maintained that worktops were not necessary because her mother never used them and in typical English fashion the washing machine was located in the kitchen beside the fridge. Cruella said that bathrooms were places of beauty and not places for washing-machines.

The beds, of which there were eight (and we still sleeping on cardboard boxes), were all antiques and one had rather a unique story attached to it. It was a two hundred year old Italian iron frame bed with a hand-painted Virgin on the headboard and according to Cruella, she had bought it on the King's Road from a dealer who refused to sell it to one of the Rolling Stones after he requested that the painting be erased. He seemingly didn't want to be watched over by a virgin while he made love!

I remember when I was growing up in Ireland where our houses were full of icons and paintings of the Virgin Mary which we would solicitously cover before we masturbated. I'd have expected the Rolling Stones would have been past that kind of stuff by then.

The aroma of fresh baguettes from our neighbouring *boulangerie* often woke me prematurely. On my anti candidia diet I had been six months now without bread and it was becoming more of a temptation than alcohol. With alcohol at least one doesn't smell it that often, but here in Provence you can't turn a corner without being poked in the eye with a French stick. An early rise meant an early walk with Moss and on this particular occasion we had a rather humorous encounter with the only other early riser in the village, Super Taff, one of the village bakers. Mossy, as usual, was out front and as we passed by the *Tabac* I noticed her sniffing something that from the distance resembled a dog turd, still steaming in the morning air. On closer inspection, as I had shooed Mossy away, it transpired to be a freshly made croissant which I assumed someone had dropped right in the middle of the cobbled street. The magpies on the rooftops were eyeing it as were the sparrows and the occasional builder's truck passed over it without injury. Super Taff who had a charcuterie/épicerie fifty paces away, was making his way towards me with his usual Long John Silver impersonations on his aluminium crutch, which had lost its rubber and thus made an awful din in the quietness of the morning. Arriving at the croissant, he leaned over like a competent horseman and picked it from the ground as though it was a damsel in distress. After retrieving it from a fate of numerous possibilities, he gave the street a quick scan before hastily wiping it on his already over-wiped butcher's apron. Then with a firm grip, he click-clacked back to his display stand and carefully placed the croissant in the front row with a delicate re-arranging of the others and got on with his business. I related the story to Frank, who, in turn told me an even better tale about Super Taff.

Some years previously, a Health Inspector paid him a visit unannounced but Taff was in no mood to show him around the premises to see if he had cockroaches or not and with his Provencal temper, he locked the Inspector in the fridge. It was apparently a customer who reported the incident to the local gendarme and when the gendarme finally made it round to check on this most likely fictitious complaint, the Inspector was by then looking like he had been standing in the snow. But because Taff was such a famous French cyclist of times past, he was by an unwritten French law, exempt from prosecution and it was the Inspector who was at fault for going into the fridge and closing the door behind him! Taff said he never heard the screaming because he had suffered a serious accident during the tour of Italy and his hearing was impaired. He said that he assisted the Inspector in every way to carry out his assessment of the premises and that the fridge incident was an accident. The gendarme was satisfied and the Inspector was sent back to Avignon to thaw out. The name 'Super Taff' is in itself worthy of explanation. It came about after a supermarket opened not far from the village called 'Super U'. So 'Taff', which had been all that was written over his door previously, changed to 'Super Taff'.

CHAPTER 45

Cruella and Whispering Grass decided they would like to give a pre-Vernissage dinner party for the exhibiting artists at the Gallery, which was still officially an English Tea Rooms to those enquiring peasants on the street.

It was only months earlier that we had read 'Michelin Guide now under Anglo-Saxon Management'. Could it be possible the English had learned to cook while I was in New Zealand? We were about to see.

It was Friday and anyone who has visited the South of France, will be aware that one will not find a better market than the one in Lourmarin, but guess where Cruella went to buy the materials for this grand Impressionist meal! To Super U. Caron and I, who had run a successful café in Auckland, were not allowed near the kitchen, while these culinary laureates spent the day in preparation. An occasional glimpse through the window gave us an insight as to how it was going to pan out. I recalled a quote from the Pall Mall Gazette in 1885 by a fellow countryman.

'A British cook is a foolish woman who should be turned into a pillar of salt'.

Oscar Wilde.

The artists, who incidentally were all French, arrived for what some writers would have us believe is the only occasion the Provencaux keep an appointment, *pour un repas*. Caron and I were also given an invitation and without doubt, it was the most disastrous meal ever prepared and the French, who have an ability to say that almost everything is *trop bon*, were silenced by the execution of the dinner.

Menu

Over-cooked rotisserie chicken

With under-cooked broccoli;

Served with tepid hard potatoes

And tomatoes filled with

Raw garlic cloves

Over decorated with herbs

De Provence.

Supermarket bread,

Supermarket cous cous and

Supermarket salad.

Supermarket apple tart

And aerosol cream

Cheese and after eights

Maxwell House instant coffee

Just as we sat down to dinner, a lightning storm erupted causing the electricity to fail and I'm sure the guests saw it as divine intervention as we were forced to eat by artificial light. It felt more like the opening scene of Macbeth than a joyful occasion with the French.

Candles flickered
And lied about their height,
Ventriloquistic munching sounds
Denied the cooks
Those second round
Diplomas or delight.

There is no doubting but it was the worst meal I had ever participated in and we were so fortunate to have had the lighting failure. Cruella and Whispering Grass were unaware, but people were wrapping food in napkins and stuffing their pockets rather than try to masticate the raw and undercooked food. We were delighted, because it was all we expected and the occasional expression of dismay on the faces of the French visitors was better than applause for a trick that had gone wrong.

Oscar Wilde was right and all of the guests that night would have agreed, but Cruella was never to know- her attempt to show the frogs (as she put it) how to entertain, was a bigger disaster than the Battle of Fontenoy.

CHAPTER 46

My application for a stall at the *vide grenier* had been accepted and we were requested to be at the Place Rayon by 7.30 a.m on Sunday morning.

Madame Claude, our host at Auriol availed of the opportunity to get rid of some rubbish so I took a boot load from the bastide to Lourmarin.

All of the merchandise that I had amassed over the previous months had to be delivered by wheelbarrow and Caron, once again just like when I went busking in Boulogne-sur-Mer, didn't want anything to do with my little venture. The spaces had been marked on the road the previous night and although each had an allocated number, the French resistance to being told what to do or where to go, put the whole street in chaos. Even the stewards knew best and went for a coffee. For me it was a familiar sight as the Irish have the same character traits, but what caused the most problems were the early morning bargain hunters, milling around in what must have looked like an aerial view of an ant's nest. Then, as the first rays of sun penetrated the leaves of the majestic plane trees, a sense of order which defied all possibility a half-hour previously, prevailed and so commenced the sales. Most of the stallholders were inexperienced sales people and they sat in little groups resembling the spectators at Wimbledon, just looking at people going each way along the street and making no effort to promote their wares. Mossy and I had a different approach - we attracted the crowds by my harmonica playing and Mossy's canine chorus.

The Gendarmes paid us a visit to see if we had any contraband or firearms on display and an extremely old 'Men at Work' road sign, which I had found at the dump, was a cause for concern, but like most things here, it ended in a jovial comment followed by a *"bonne continuation!"* Virtually all the visitors to our stand recognised some item which they had thrown out earlier in the year and here I was trying to sell it back to them!

I had a Slazenger tennis racket, in its sleeve, which when asked by an interested visitor:

"Combien pour la racquette monsieur?"

"*Trente francs,*" I replied.

"Acceptez-vous cinquante?"

"*Bien sûr!*" I told him and it was sold to the man with the bad hearing. He must have thought I said '*cent*' at the onset thus proving that my '*coccinelle*' French was finally beginning to make good business sense!

An old typewriter, which again I had found in the dump, only required a little marketing and I was sure I'd be able to sell it. All the keys had been fused together from age and when one hit any key, they all popped up. I had also found a copy of Albert Camus' 'The Plague', so I placed them side by side with a little sign which read, 'From the typewriter of Albert Camus', referring to the book of course, but misleading the customers into the illusion that I had Camus' typewriter. Being in Lourmarin it was not questioned and it sold for 100 francs in the first five minutes of the day. The delighted buyer walked off and said to his friend:

"The French are so fucking stupid - imagine selling Camus' typewriter for a paltry sum like that!"

If only I had another, I thought. It reminded me of a story about an American, who visited Ireland some years back, and on arrival at Shannon Airport he encountered a man with a stall full of ancient artefacts, one of which was the skull of Saint Patrick. He bought it and went back to New York where he opened a pub displaying the skull. It was a phenomenal success, so he decided to go back to Ireland to see if he could find more artefacts for another pub. Again he chose Shannon as his destination and of course the same stallholder was there with another smaller skull which also had a sign 'Skull of Saint Patrick'. The American immediately expressed his anger and said:

"But I bought the skull of Saint Patrick from you last year!"

The stall holder replied:

"But sir, this one was when he was a wee lad!"

By ten o'clock I had sold everything and made 800 Francs all from their own rubbish, but it wasn't about money, it was just another social occasion where the French get together to enjoy their own company and most of them came every year with the same old junk. But one never knows what can be found there. An exhibition of sketches by Paul Cezanne in the Cours Mirabeau some years back, was as a result of someone buying an old suitcase full to the brim with art paper that Cezanne had used in his Chateau Noir gallery in Le Tholonet just outside Aix en Provence.

When Madame Claude, the English woman, heard that I made 800 francs at the *vide grenier*, she asked me for half of it. She was selling the bastide plus she had two houses in the Alps, a house in Tuscany and she had just bought an apartment in Aix en Provence but felt the need to ask me for 400 francs.

CHAPTER 47

The atmosphere on the job was changing as Cruella's relationship with Whispering Grass had become similar to the one she had had initially with the Master. Whispering Grass had gone from bag-stitcher to assuming the title of site manager, despite knowing absolutely nothing about the building industry and all the tradesmen were complaining to me about him. They referred to him as the Mistress. We had had the Master and now, Whispering Grass had become Cruella's lap dog/lackey. He agreed with everything she said by adding "Yes Yes *Yes!*" after every command. Caron and I had to be extremely careful from then on, because we knew that as the difficult aspects of the job were under control, Whispering Grass was trying to get rid of us and as everyone knows, there is no better person to put the knife in one's back than an Englishman. Cruella had gained a reputation in Lourmarin as a subject of ridicule; hiding behind a pair of dark glasses which were as big as ping-pong bats. She looked like a bumble bee, especially when she had the tea-cosy on her head and Frank's initial observations of her when she first arrived in the village were only too accurate.

Our weekends became more treasured as we escaped the Angry-Saxon syndrome that was raising its ugly head.

In Aix-en-Provence the Cours Mirabeau was windy and the air was full of spring eroticism, mini-skirts and tight shirts with short messages in Braille which created traffic jams as imaginations savoured the possibilities of the Provencal's favourite pastime *'le rêve'*. Our little Utopia in Lourmarin had been shattered and so were our weekends, affected by the thoughts of having to go back on Monday wondering if we were still going to have a job. Cruella had given up her designs on the stables next door and it was becoming evident that she had no affinity for the house we were renovating, even the locals had been saying that she was just a speculator and did little to assimilate into French culture. Like many of her fellow countrymen, she had absolutely no French and had no intention of ever learning either.

"It is only a matter of time," she said to me one day, "before everyone will be speaking English."

The electronics for the house and gallery (Tea Rooms) had to be recessed into a box of a metre square and 400cms deep on the party wall between us and the stables next door. Although the wall was a meter thick, it was a tricky exercise to open it up without bringing the whole thing down, especially as Raymond was keeping a close eye on us since the Master's episode on the roof, also due to a major catastrophe some years previously, when an inexperienced *maçon* caused a virtual total collapse at the present *Moulin de Lourmarin* Hotel, when he undermined too much of the foundation during renovations- it resembled an earthquake. The dust could be seen as far as Aix en Provence and the dogs are still barking in Lourmarin.

Most of our x-rated work had to be done during lunch when no Frenchman would bother himself with such trivia as a house falling down. We did manage to do it without any incident and when it was all finished, I invited Raymond to see what he described as *"une niche extraordinaire"*.

CHAPTER 48

The smell of freshly cut hay around the Temple, ripe cherries for sale and evening sunsets, started the Mediterranean tradition of sitting round in the evenings while the locals played *boules*. I spent many an evening with Madame Ferlin, who related more wonderful stories about the village when she was a girl. She had ventured once to Marseille in her youth but the journey made her sick and thereafter she contented herself with forays to Cadenet some 5 kms away but no further.

Une Dame
And as we sat
A jet stream like
An infant's chalk
The sky had marked.
Her eyes attracted
By a setting sun
Spoke in silence
Of a passing time,
Lamented by a Skylark
And bees content in
Lime abundant blossom.
Then curfew called
and on our separate
Ways we went
Both wondering of
Each others thoughts
And of the time
Together spent.

Another truck of second hand furniture arrived from England, bringing the loads to three and turning the house into a permanent obstacle course for all within. The plumbers had already encountered enough trouble with the imperial fittings of

Cruella's Victorian sanitary ware and the electrical equipment posed a similar problem with no French explanations.

"*C'est une catastrophe!*" exclaimed Monsieur Mathieu *le plombier.*

In the midst of all this chaos, the phone rang. It was Cruella calling from England.

"Finney, we've got to get a move on now, because there was an article today in the Country Life about the Gallery (no longer Tea Rooms) and it's being opened officially on the 29th June by Peter Mayle, I'll fax you the page!"

"Peter Mayle to Open Gallery in Lourmarin" was what it said.

Cruella meant business and as Whispering Grass had been given *carte blanche,* we had become virtually superfluous with regard to the management of the project.

CHAPTER 49

The Friday market in Lourmarin was now becoming a spectacular sight, not only with the regional produce but also with the numerous artists and artisans who had come to sell their wares. A poet called Patrice Aubert had a stall and was selling his most recent book 'Maison des Yeux'. Browsing through it, I fell on a poem which was titled 'Ventry Irlande', and although I can't say I understood it in its entirety, I bought it. Our ensuing conversation aroused his curiosity as to why I purchased the book. When I explained that I too was passionate about poetry, he asked to see some of my work, and I showed him L'Heure Matin, which he offered to translate into French, and it later appeared in the local paper, titled Levant and underneath, 'pour un poet de Lourmarin par Patrice Aubert'. It was official, I was now the 'Laureate de Lourmarin!'

Levant - Pour un poet de Lourmarin
Matin de marche.
Petit temple en retrait du château.
Aube triomphante d'une douce simplicité.
A la lumiere naissante.
Des ombres fugitives se livrent un duel inégal.
Au loin s'enfuit la rosée
La danse de montage éclairé un jour nouveau.
Les nuages s'éloignent.
Le village en sommeil aux maigres volets clos
Résonne d'une eclatante lueur.
La route aux yeux couleur de marbre
Releva fécondité
Deux statues en offrande
Eveillent les premiers instants.
Deja, un carillon te salue, Lourmarin.
Traduction par Patrice Aubert

Levant was a superb translation and like the Rubaiyat of Omar Khayam, which was translated by Edward Fitzgerald, most people agreed that Aubert's translation was better than my original. I have yet to understand french well enough to agree!

But here is my original version in English which I entitled *L'heure Matin.*

The poem is about a walk through the village with Mossy at sunrise,.

L'Heure Matin
The early morning walk brought us past
A temple, though smaller than the chateau,
was, in its simplicity as grand.
Shadows resisted the rising sun's
attempt to measure their importance, but
the dew drops would soon decide.
In the distance, watched over by the mountains,
more serious with age, such trivia was not pursued.
Unwelcome clouds were wished away and
Preparation for the perfect day was in progress.
Volet's cheated an unerring light while the village slept.
Then passing by the marble carousel with a bouquet
of the regions bounty held high by the fairer gemini's ,
my heart felt like announcing the sextons chime,
because we were first to see, Lourmarin.

On Rue Juiverie, a French *maçon* and his crew arrived to do some plastering for one of our neighbours. They had an electric mixer with a loose belt and rather than spend five minutes to tighten it, one of them had to assist the drum by hand when it was fully loaded; he looked like the captain of the Titanic trying to avoid an iceberg. This went on for weeks. They tipped a load of sand against our wall, paying no attention to the air vent that served the basement and the new shower, just fitted by the plumbers had a half metre of sand trickle down during the night thus blocking the sump of the wizzer system we had been obliged to fit because we were below the sewer level. When we challenged the workers about the sand, they simply replied:

"C'est pas grave!"

This was a typical reaction and *pas grave* is a Provencal band aid, the cure all. After work every evening, they would wash out all their tools and the mixer, letting the spillage run down the street, causing a permanent cement stain, which one sees everywhere in France. Someone complained and we were visited by the local gendarme, the one who got the Health Inspector out of Super Taff's fridge.

"*Où sont les maçons?* " he demanded of the plumber, thinking of course that it was us, *les anglais'* with whom he had no doubt an axe to grind. The *plombier* was quick to put him right by showing him the sand in the basement after the *maçon's* carelessness the night before. But in true Provencal fashion, the incident no longer interested him, because the Angelus was ringing which meant only ten minutes to midday and being Friday as well, it had already gone into last week's basket, meaning that there would be no more heard about it.

With just two weeks to go to the grand *ouverture*, which we were assured would go down in Lourmarin history because of the Mayle connection, the stress levels were again artificially induced. Cruella was back and the classic remark of the job was coined by her on this occasion.

She was aggravated at the French tradesmen because they went home to their families for lunch and more so because they took two hours to have it.

"Haven't they heard of the sandwich?"

Naff
Deux Chevaux's and tapes
Of Edith Piaf,
Typical of Poms away
At least the locals laugh.
Acceptance is the word,
Must pretend we like the French,
But living here is such a wrench.

Don't they know
We've got a Queen
Where bread is buttered in between
The Earl of Sandwich set the tune,
No need to close our shops at noon!

Cruella expected the French tradesmen to eat crisps and Mars bars like they do at home in Blighty and thought it an affront that they deserted their posts for two hours every day and refused to work Saturdays and Sundays.

She was going to change the art scene in Lourmarin and no doubt the French work ethic. Cruella reminded me of a character in the autobiography of Sir John Lavery, The Life of a Painter, Cassell 1940. Lavery was in Tangiers with a Brit called Cunningham Graham and in the market place Mr Graham, who spoke a little Arabic, decided that he would like to take the platform and address the Moors.

The House of Commons at the time were discussing the eight-hour day and Graham felt as though the Arabs should be informed of its benefits also.

Up on the podium he went and commenced his impassioned address to the nodding heads of the Moors. He didn't get very far and soon realised that his audience was not very sympathetic to the address. In fact, they were examining their flintlocks and feeling for their daggers in a very unfriendly fashion when a kindly Moor, summing up the situation, whispered in Graham's ear:

"These men have never worked one hour a day in their lives and are prepared to wade through blood before they would even consider doing it for eight!"

Cruella had simply no idea about anything French and her adviser and lackey, Whispering Grass was no better and hence the continuous problems they encountered from the workers. We could have put them right, but as it was so comical and entertaining just watching their total disregard for everything French, we permitted it to continue.

By then, everyone in the village knew that Cruella was bad news and being involved with her was no doubt going to tarnish all of us. But for Caron and I who were still only learning French, our chances of getting work elsewhere with accommodation was unlikely and besides, the notion of writing a book encouraged us to stay. Cruella was a great source of inspiration for my pen, as indeed was her new lackey.

Yet another load arrived from England which got the electricians and plumbers asking:

"Is there going to be anything French in this house?"

"Electricity and water', was Frank's answer to that. Frank was never stuck for a quick retort and he too was enjoying the gossip around the village about Cruella and her puppet.

The first literature advertising the opening arrived with as much excitement as the *Beaujolais Nouveau*. Beautiful posters and colourful cards announced Peter Mayle as the star attraction and we were sent around the local villages like town criers bringing forth the news of a truly great happening. It was to be a memorable occasion, a sort of English Crusade into the heartlands of French culture. Cruella was using the Gallery as a means to access the status in life which she was not born into.

"I was thinking in my bed this morning that the great superiority of France over England, is that in France, every bourgeois wants to be an artist, whereas in England, every artist wants to be bourgeois." Oscar Wilde.

Peter Mayle was expected to come to the opening via the Rue du Temple and it was from here that he would access the upper house to formally cut the blue ribbon and declare the gallery open. The *ferronier* arrived with a large black metal sign which he hung from a pole on the street and that in itself was to be envied by all the other galleries.

The time at last came to fit the famous spiral staircase from Bath and what a drama, it was too short and too wide and we wrestled with its weight as we hacked away at the wall to try and allow it to pass through the hole above. The only solution to its lack of height was to fabricate an artificial step on top or mount it on a platform at the base, either way it was going to take time, a commodity of which we now had little due to the deadline. We had to forfeit our weekend at Auriol because it had to be ready for Monday morning to allow the tradesmen to pass by the only access from the gallery to the main house.

Mossy was being somewhat neglected while all of this was going on and she couldn't take herself for a walk because the roads were too hot for her paws. We would take her by wheel-barrow to the park just opposite the Temple which of course the tourists loved every minute of it and we were both pho-tographed on numerous occasions, especially by the Japanese visitors who seem to have a thing about dogs and cats though it doesn't extend to actually touching them. Lourmarin was a booming destination with everything one would find in a chic Parisian suburb, it was no doubt the most sought-after village in Provence, if not France. With the gallery opening only round the corner, we were fully engaged in the last minute make-over of the reception area where Peter and Jenny Mayle would be cut-ting the tape. The *tomettes* (Provencal tiles) on the terrace were all cracked and though looked wonderful, were condemned by Cruella and replacements had to be acquired. Quickly.

At the *déchetterie*, I had found a hundred or so really old Provencal floor tiles and as I had no use for them I offered them to Cruella to repair a broken area on the floor over the gallery where the guest of honour would be entertained in a few days.

Hoisted by our own petard, Cruella asked Caron and I at ten thirty in the evening, to go and do this repair. I declined as we had done our day's work and were already showered, but Whispering Grass, who had now become her bell-hop, defended Cruella's honour and protested at our refusal, citing it, as he put it, as 'A declaration of war!'

They commenced to do the job themselves and were banging and smashing until one in the morning with no consideration for us nor the neighbours.

When we arose, we found a note from Cruella asking if we would go and fix their mess. Whispering Grass had thought to impress Cruella and show us up by setting the tiles, but he used cement instead of plaster and everything had to be pulled up again. From that point onward there was no more verbal communication from either of them, everything was by note or fax, Cruella and Whispering Grass were giving us the silent treatment. Caron said that she was fed up with being treated like dirt and she wanted to leave, but once again I managed to calm her anger and assured her that I would not let them get away with it.

With the opening only a few days away we had finished all we had to do and were put on another contract to remove the *crepi* (plaster) from the façade of the house on the Rue de Juiverie, while Cruella and some other people began to hang the Gallery. A permit for scaffolding had been approved, but due to it now being peak tourist season, only a months use had been allocated. While we were erecting it, I made the acquaintance of a man who was living across the road which at that particular spot was only about 3 metres wide. Until then I had assumed that he was a recluse, but he was a writer. I related some of the goings-on with Cruella and her bizarre Anglo-Saxon antics and I said there were enough incidents to fill a book.

"Then why don't you write it?" came his reply, and that reinforced my determination to expose Cruella and Whispering Grass for their xenophobic attitudes as guests in another country and generally of the Brits abroad.

Nothing was going to silence me though we knew that our time was limited as Whispering Grass was hell bent on getting rid of us at all costs. The tradesmen were only too aware of what was going on and they supported us, but little could be done while this lackey was in Cruella's good books.

CHAPTER 50

The swallows were still nesting in the *génoise* (Provencal eaves, a term deriving from Genoa) so we deferred the last section of scaffolding until the young had flown. Fortunately Cruella wasn't aware of this, for had she known that progress was stopped because the birds were holding up her venture, I'm sure it would have caused a cessation of our employment as we would have refused orders to proceed rather than disturb the swallows. Whispering Grass would have seen it as a mutiny and as neither of them had any nature, there was no doubting their reaction. I remember once back in my hometown of Mallow, the station master refused to move a train because there was a crow nesting in it. All of the carriages were unhooked and the engine was moved at a snails pace into the siding, where it remained until the young flew the nest.

The destruction of the ancient *crepi* was a painful exercise that had us both apologising to the building before we commenced.

The Provence heat that Pagnol spoke of was now on us and the lady across the way was concerned that we were actually working in it, especially as we were vegetarians.

"C'est incroyable!"

She had never met vegetarians before and thought we should have no energy. Cruella had only one passion and that was money and her lackey Whispering Grass who was of Scottish origin, was not too far behind her on that issue, it was said that he wouldn't give you the steam of his piss, he was so mean.

In the park where we walked Mossy we noticed a group of municipal workers in heated debate with a Gendarme, and although my French had improved immensely, I was in no way prepared for the auctioneering diatribe of the *Provencaux* in argument. But we did manage to discover the source of the disharmony. It was the old mill stream that runs through the village. It had become totally polluted overnight, *une catastophe!*

Especially in the tourist season and furthermore on the week of the gallery opening by Peter Mayle, when the village would be swamped with people and journalists coming from all over the world country to see him !

Pollution
Exhausted by emission
Taste buds tarnished
By some sullied fad,
Optical illusion mist or smog
Spring water or some holey grog.
Enemies of earth
God given rights abused since birth.
Just saw an abortion floating boy,
All condom wrapped in pink, but why?
Such a stench,
Each passing wench can live the lie.
Maggots thriving
Called surviving,
Symbiotic!
Makes one want to cry.

The stream was in a terrible state and full of all sorts of rubbish without explanation or solution. Mayor Blaise was brought in to look at it and other than diverting it or putting a green vegetable dye in it, there was apparently nothing to be done, not even a *"pas grave"*!

Cruella had her own problems and we were called down from the scaffolding, and told to go out to the neighbouring villages and quickly pull down all the posters announcing the *'Ouverture par Peter Mayle'*. Something had gone wrong and it must be serious by the urgency of her latest despatch. We initially thought it was something to do with the polluted stream, but no. The printing press had been instructed to re-write the text on the advertising posters and to delete *'Ouverture par Peter Mayle'* and instead, stating in the 'presence of Peter Mayle.' The writer's contract to cut the tape had been withdrawn and we were not informed as to the reasons why. But rumour had it that he was temperamental and could not be depended on as he had a reputation for changing his mind and landing people in the merde. It was also rumoured that he thought Cruella was a proper vache and on that score, there were few if any, with the exception of her new lackey Whispering Grass, that disgreed. We wondered if Mayle was going to be there at all and would all the journalists who were expected to arrive be disappointed. Cruella requested a poem and in it I was to highlight 'In the Presence of Peter Mayle'. It was a bit of a come-down for Cruella but as far as I could see, his presence must surely be as good as him opening the gallery. The journalists would still flock there no matter. With only two days in which to write the poem my ability as the Laureate of Lourmarin was truly being tested!

Infallible (for Cruella)
Perhaps a little
To the right
Or dare I say
There's too much light
Caché hidden
Out of sight
Just two more days
To opening night
Exotic Floras,
No simple lace
A piano tuner
Sets the pace
Red wine from Papal bottles
Intelligent talk from Aristotle's
The English Swan
Is set to sail
And "In the Presence"
Of Peter Mayle

Why Mayle had pulled out of his commitment would be for another day.

Lots of people were asking a lot of different questions, but perhaps even Cruella did not know the answer. Perhaps he was ill or as Frank put it, he most likely did not want to be associated with Cruella because everyone thought she was just another *sans noblesse* (SNOB) , giving the Brits a worse reputation than they already had. Frank said that Cruella should do something really arty and instead of cutting the tape, she should burn it and while she was at it, the gallery also.

Country Life stated emphatically that Peter Mayle was opening the Gallery. It was yet another Cruella fuck-up and no matter what the reason was, once more the villagers were having a field day at her expense. Frank said that she would soon have to wear a Ned Kelly style hat to hide from the ridicule, or simply sell up and leave.

CHAPTER 51

We were given ten easels to paint in advance of the gallery opening and since there was no room inside, due to the insane activity, we set up on Rue du Juiverie. After giving them all a first coat, the Mistral gusted like the backdraught of the London underground, bringing all the flies and dust of Lourmarin funnelling down the tubular little street and leaving the easels looking like fisherman's hats.

Removing the flies proved impossible so we were forced paint over them -they produced more inquiry than the art itself.

Opening day, and Cruella had an English bar attendant flown down especially to open the wine bottles and to pour Perrier into *Accroc* glasses, which I must add that he did it extremely well, especially the latter. It was quite obvious from all we were seeing, that this whole charade had absolutely nothing to do with art which we had already deduced from another classic Cruella remark that she had coined some months earlier:

"If you want to integrate into French society, the best way is to open an Art Gallery."

I recall a wonderful story about an Italian customs officer on the French border at the beginning of the 1900s. It was his first day on the job and he was confronted with a shipment of art which he was obliged to tariff. Unable to arrive at a pricing he decided to weigh the art and charge accordingly!

At 5 p.m the guests began to arrive and I had great reservations about the terrace where most of the entertaining was to be held. At the beginning of the job, we were instructed to remove the reinforcing plaster from underneath against all good counsel. I told all our friends not to stand there as a collapse was quite possible.

As I saw Peter Mayle with his lady arrive and stand beneath the large Blackpool awning, which protruded into the Rue du Temple prohibiting any further commercial activities taking place on the street while Cruella entertained, a horrible thought came to mind. Just imagine, I said to Caron, if the floor did actually cave in and Mr Mayle was fatally injured!

Headlines in the English tabloids announcing his death would certainly provoke enquiry. Scotland Yard detectives would be swarming around the place and Cruella would be the centre of attention and she couldn't have asked for better publicity, despite the writer's refusal to cut the tape.

The catastrophe would most definitely have been associated with criminal negligence, and despite my advice at the beginning of the job to leave the plaster on for structural reasons, Cruella and Whispering Grass would never admit to it. I'd be portrayed as the Irishman masquerading as a builder arriving out of nowhere without references, C.V. or indeed any tools, come to think of it. It would also be discovered that I had written to Mr Mayle about his reference in 'A Year in Provence', where he depicted Irish workmen as being a liability due to their drinking and that one would be advised not to employ us. Being an alcoholic, even though dry for two years at the time, it would be seen by the detectives as a revenge for the character assassination of my nation and our national pastime. The Gallery owner would add that Finney was a bit of a dreamer with delusions of being a latter day Don Quixote, who came to the Luberon to right the wrongs and to redeem his nation from the Mayle insult.

We didn't wait around and probably missed my only chance to meet the author, but it was Friday night and I had an A.A. meeting in Aix-en-Provence.

CHAPTER 52

On returning from our weekend we heard all the news and to my relief the floor hadn't collapsed but the newly elected Mayor, whom Cruella had neglected to invite, paid her a visit after receiving complaints from the locals about being unable to pass by the Blackpool canopy, which incidentally had been erected without permission. The Mayor, a reasonable sort of a chap, didn't exercise his power by demanding its removal, but later in the night it was slashed with a knife and a message pour *la dame anglaise*:

"*Vous êtes en Provence Madame, et pas en Angleterre*". The Provencaux had sent their first message and it was becoming obvious that the English woman was not wanted in the village.

It was all beginning to make sense. Even Frank had told us that he overheard a conversation where Cruella was mentioned and they said that there was more to come and they called her "*une sale vache*" (dirty cow).

We continued with the ancient *crepi (plaster)* removal and Raymond as always was there to explain the best procedure and the correct tools to do the job. He took us to the local hardware store and introduced us to what all the *maçons* use down here for the *crepi*, '*Picolas*', a sort of a geologist's hammer. Both he and the hardware assistant explained how to re-point the joints and the right type of sand to use. Without them we would have been lost, but I have to say that the Provencaux are the most helpful people under the sun and all one has to do is simply ask. It was so hot now that we could only do the pointing between 7 and 10 a.m and again in the evening between 5 and 8, otherwise it would crack. So instead we spent lots of time behind the Chateau with Moss while Caron read and I wrote poetry. Because we knew that it was only a matter of time before Whispering Grass would have Cruella fully primed into making us out to be a liability by some fabrication or other, we had put some feelers out to see if we could find a cheap place to renovate for ourselves.

Frank came by and said he had found an old mill with five thousand square meters of land near Cucuron for sale and if we were interested he would take us to see it one day. Having come to know Frank it was unwise to push oneself on him or he was likely to go dark on you, so like everything else in Provence, or indeed in France, we would have to wait until he was ready.

Due to the rush to finish the gallery, we lost two weeks of scaffolding time and our permit had expired prematurely, therefore it was necessary to call at the Mayor's office for a renewal. I met Mayor Blaise, whom we christened 'Modesty Blaise', which he truly was.

"Pourquoi demandez-vous une extension, un mois c'est assez pour peindre des fenêtres, n'est-ce pas?"

When I told him that we weren't painting the windows but removing the ancient *crepi*, he nearly blew a head gasket. He was furious.

"Arrêtez tous les travaux immédiatement!" was his reaction.

"Mais Monsieur le Maire, c'est trop tard, on a déjà enleve le crépi."

Cruella had flaunted the rules yet again and I got the impression that the Mayor had had just about enough of her English arrogance.

A site meeting was arranged with the regional architects for the *Sites Historiques*. Cruella was in the *merde* and we were delighted. As she was in Angleterre, she appointed Whispering Grass to meet with the representatives, indicating to us that our roles as site managers had been undermined and a replacement for the Master was in our midst.

On the morning of the rendezvous everyone arrived on time except Whispering Grass. This gave me enough time to express my total opposition to the removal of the *crepi*, especially as we knew it was classified and I told them that Cruella and Whispering Grass had no respect for the French or their traditions. I also let them know that they paid no heed to my earlier requests to save other aspects of this once wonderful building, but like the *crepi*, they had fallen on deaf ears. Caron and I had renovated and preserved two historic buildings in New Zealand - St Patrick's stone chapel in Wanaka and an old gas valve house in Auckland, so we knew what we were talking about.

Whispering Grass, with his late arrival did little to change the decision which had already been made. The Architects and the Mayor were comfortable with my explanation. The Regional Architect insisted on the total restoration of the *crepi*, stating that *pierre apparente* was *interdite*. The Mayor said that the scaffolding would have to come down because of the imminant influx of tourists and Cruella would be obliged to finish the job another time.

Cruella was like a viper and proclaimed that she didn't know anything about the *crepi*'s ancient status.

It was like the story about Livingstone who spent years searching for the source of the Nile, it has been said, had he not been so arrogant and had asked the locals, he could have found it in a day! This was Cruella's problem, the locals in Lourmarin were just like the blacks in Livingstone's eyes and the less she had to do with them the better.

The man living opposite, whom I had earlier assumed was a recluse, took time out from writing his book to speak to us, saying that he had overheard virtually all of what went on regarding the *crepi* and said it had the makings of *une bonne histoire*.

He advised me to commence immediately *'à écrire votre livre'*

"J'ai déjà commencé." I replied.

"Bonne chance, alors!" was his response.

Caron and I were transferred inside to start the renovations and decorations of the house proper while the gallery was preparing for its second *vernissage*. It had only been a month since the *Grand Ouverture* and Frank, who had the wit of Wilde, had already christened the gallery 'The Dead Duck'. And so I wrote another little ditty

The Dead Duck
Swan song, dead duck, wild goose
English art in Lourmarin is loose,
In café and in bar there is debate
If and when the blackbird will migrate

There was a curse on Cruella and her paranoia was beginning to show, despite her buying bigger sunglasses and completely covering her head with the tea cosy.

We were given the colour chart for the entire house and the paint, which came from England, naturally, was supposedly approved by the royal household at Windsor Castle. The first room we engaged upon was on the ground floor on the Rue de Juiverie, which had a beautiful traditional Provencal ochre and our instruction was to get rid of it. The weather being so hot, we had all the windows open and a group of French tourists looked through and enquired what colour we were repainting the room. I came down the ladder tin in hand exposing the Farrow and Ball can of green camouflage paint which excited them as much as finding a knotted condom in a pillow case.

"*Oh non, monsieur, pas cela!*"

"*Quel dommage!*» they remarked as they took scrapings and a photo of the original ochre. I had but to agree with them, that the Farrow and Ball looked like some army surplus leftovers from the Second World War, but one must admit, the English have a knack of making dark, darker!

Francophobic (for Cruella)
Bedroom suites with iron frames
By Ashley, or some other names,
Coloured sheets and floral quilts
Fancy paper, expensive prints,
Chandeliers and Royal paints
Queens awards, so no complaints,
Imperial baths and matching sinks
Ceramic tiles in panther pinks,
Union locks but metric spindles
Leaves us doors without handles,
Forgetting not those English taps
Gets local plumbers lifting caps
Best of all, those three pin plugs
On toasters, fridges, water jugs,
The biggest laugh of course, the van
Brings ridicule from the peage man,
What about the English News
Ex-pats express their points of views,
Must be time to rearrange
Oh, those French will never change.

CHAPTER 53

At Auriol, we picked the last of the cocktail tomatoes, figs and apples. They were now at the end of their tree life resulting in all becoming victims of the ants. Hazel nuts were falling and had we known the bastide would still be on the market, there was lots more that could have been done in the garden. It was such a shame the way *la dame de la bastide* left everything uncared for, nature's generosity refused.

She had become rather restless and couldn't be bothered to wait for the sale of the house, so she went off and bought a luxury apartment in the most fashionable district of Aix-en-Provence, on Rue Fredric Mistral. She also bought a house in Italy. We were invited to do some work on her Tuscany retreat not far from Sarteano, on the old Tuscan road. It was about an eight hour drive from Lourmarin. Our 4 a.m departure was a wise decision due to the intense heat in the afternoon. After crossing the border there seemed to be about 250 tunnels in succession, which act as sort of air conditioning, for those of us not fortunate enough to have the real thing. Having never driven in Italy, I was pleasantly surprised to find how courteous the Italians were in comparison to their French counterparts.

Arriving at her Ladyship's country retreat, which was situated on a hillside overlooking all of Tuscany, we found clusters of cypresses resembling the pegs on a General's war plan wth the expanse below seeming like a fertile oasis with recurring hills diminishing into infinity. The house itself had a certain resemblance to the one we had looked after in Cruis, probably as the previous owner was also from Switzerland. The windows were barred like Fort Knox and the whole interior painted in brown. Madame didn't seem to mind. As well as an olive grove, she had inherited an old Italian gardener who operated a time-share gardening service and, as in many such cases, these people cannot be got rid of or mysterious things start to happen on the property in one's absence.

The house would have originally been a farm worker's cottage and although charming, had little more room than the council house I had been born in. Madame, only a week after buying it, said she regretted the purchase.

As much as I believe that money does not make one unhappy, I am sure that it is the fear of losing it which causes the discontent. Madame du Chateau was without a doubt the most unhappy person we ever met despite her vast wealth. She probably still had her Holy Communion money, thus we deduced that meanness is a prime cause of melancholy. One has to be cautious of people who live alone and so far we were surrounded by them. Whispering Grass, Cruella and Madame du Chateau were all of the excommunicated solitary people who either had been abandoned by their partners or were too mean to make a commitment to a relationship in case it cost them.

After I had cut off all the iron bars in the windows of the Tuscan retreat I had had enough and decided to return to France.

CHAPTER 54

My American Alcoholics Anonymous sponsor was in Paris and quite ill with cancer of the throat, but despite that, he wasn't going to neglect my progression from step four to step five of the A.A. twelve step programme. When he rang, he croaked like Tom Waits and asked me if I would like to come to Paris to do the step. Just back from Tuscany and now off to Paris. Here was a man who could well be at death's door if the treatment failed yet he was worried about my fifth step, it was incredible. He would take time out from his treatment while I took this very important A.A. step and asked me to pick 5 places of interest to visit in Paris.

My first time on a TGV (Train de Grande Vitesse), I bought a ticket from Marseille and arrived at Gare de Lyon where Bill was waiting on the platform, with his neck looking like a butcher's apron from repeated radiation treatment. He had arranged accommodation in a vacant apartment of a friend close to Notre Dame Cathedral, which was one of my five choices. The following day we met there for eight o'clock mass after which we proceeded to do the fifth step en route to the other four sites, which were the Musee D'Orsay, where I dearly wanted to see the Daumier Painting of Don Quixote, finding the dead donkey, the Eiffel Tower, not because it was the most prominent structure in the world but because I had developed a respect for steel due to my welding career and more so, because it was a completely riveted structure, Napoleon's Tomb at Les Invalides, and finally to 7 Rue Peronnet, Neuilly, to see if Sylvie Bodennen, a girl I met in Ireland when I was a teenager and fell in love with, was still there.

We walked and talked, stopping here and there for coffees and by afternoon we had completed the fifth step. As Bill was quite tired from such an intense day, he went to his apartment to rest while I followed up on a lead on the whereabouts of Sylvie, but to no avail. It was the most memorable weekend of my life and as I left Paris I thought what a wonderful diplomat Bill was for his country and indeed for the A.A. and I asked the same God that blessed America, to spare a little for one of its countrymen struggling in Paris.

In Samuel Beckett's house in Rousillon. Beckett spent 5 years here during the war. It was here he wrote *Waiting for Godot.*

CHAPTER 55

When I arrived back in Lourmarin, I found a note on the door, "Had to rush to the veterinary surgeon with Mossy, she's bleeding from her vagina." Negative anticipation had me thinking all sorts of scenarios and in the past I would have been right into the bottle, but it transpired that she only had a rye grass arrow head in her uterus, a common enough problem here in Provence for dogs in summer.

September sees an end to the national school holidays and Lourmarin is graced with a more well-heeled type of tourist, the ones who buy art, or as Frank put it when he came to take us to see the *cabanon* for sale, the ones who buy art galleries. The rumour was going round that Cruella had the Dead Duck on the market as it was doing no business and her reasons for opening it had not come to pass either. She was expecting to be catapulted into high society because she had a gallery. Perhaps in England one would, but the French are not impressed by such silliness and so "The Dead Duck" was stuffed.

Frank finally took us to see the old mill *cabanon* which was situated within the sound of the village bells of Cucuron and only seven kilometres from Lourmarin. It dated from 1365 and was still in good condition despite having been neglected for many years. It had a wedge-shaped roof which had been recently renewed and the total area was of 75 square metres with enough height to put in a mezzanine. In front there was a neighbours vineyard of about two acres and at the side, a little stream with a pond which was used for irrigation. The land to the rear comprised of two small fields with the most amazing top soil which went to a depth of about half a metre, ideal for growing our own vegetables. At 200,000 francs (about £20,000) it was an incredible bargain, but as always, there was a catch. There were three owners and due to psychiatric problems, all of them were under the care of tuteurs (judges), which meant they were not in a position to make decisions for themselves. Another problem was that in France if land is classed as agricultural, the local farmers have the first right to buy and finally, the Mairie also has an option. It was extremely complicated, but Frank with his unusual optimism put us on a positive note by saying that in France, unlike the UK, anyone can become President!

September 11th in some way or other affected all of us, and for me, who had made a lot of American acquaintances since coming to Provence, I shared their grief. But much as I like Americans, I can't say that I agree with their Government's foreign policies, especially in the Middle East, and as is often the case with empire nations, the populous have no idea what has been done to provoke such a response. How often while I lived I London did I hear English people say:
"Why are the I.R.A. bombing us?"
I was requested to write a poem to mark this incident.

Scars and Gripes
Imperialism being the fate
The target be the empire state.
Democracy said Tony Blair, a
Stupid statement, as if they'd care.
Besides, they'd hit old mother Liberty
With torch the symbol of eternity.
No, they hit the world of trade, where
Men of greed and anger made, a great
Divide between east and west.
Bin Laden chose what he thought best.
Now Uncle Sam's one eye for tooth
Creates the smoke to hide the truth
Occidental catechism promoting evil
Capitalism. Allah has no taste or need
The infidels' Bubonic seed.

CHAPTER 56

After a long absence I was invited to a family wedding back in Ireland though had I not been in the A.A. an invitation would never have been considered owing to my past performances when I got drunk. Bill said that if I survived an Irish wedding without drinking, it would indeed be a great test of my sobriety and the A.A. would certainly have proved its purpose.

The security at Charles de Gaulle was like Heathrow after an I.R.A. blast and the fragile present I was carrying was prohibited from going as hand luggage. It was a hand-made clay Provencal bowl filled with produce from the region which the Aer Lingus ground staff assured me would not be put on the carousel when it arrived in Ireland. On arrival to Cork, I went to the office as requested by the Paris people but they had no notification regarding the safe handling of my bowl. I went back to the turn table and there it was jingling along in harmony with the conveyor belt. Attempts at compensation fell on deaf ears so I sent the manager this short poem and prayed for the day that Michael O' Leary (of Ryan Air) would banish them from the skies of Ireland just as Saint Patrick had done to the snakes in 432 AD.

Bumble bees, Boeing, Buzz.
Aeroflot and Qantas does.
But there's one which all the other
Licks, Cunni Lingus run by pricks.

A group photograph at the wedding of all my family including the prodigal son just back from France provided a humorous interlude when the photographer in an effort to impress the French contingent and show off his school French asked the group to say *"Fromage!"*

At the wedding itself, I met all the people I had crossed swords with during my drinking days, including the doctor who committed me to the psychiatric hospital, and although I felt like giving him a piece of my mind, or a kick in the bollocks, I refrained and tried to practice some self control. To everyone's surprise I managed to go the whole day without touching a drop and for a country whose alcohol consumption has increased by 40% in ten years, I felt like a complete foreigner with a glass of Ballygowen spring water in my hand! At the actual wedding breakfast at the Dunloe Hotel in the presence of 250 well-heeled guests, I took the opportunity to make a class action amend by declaring over the intercom that my 'boyhood's fire' had been fuelled by alcoholism. My brother took the microphone and added:

"Sure even the dogs in the road knew that!"

CHAPTER 57

Going back to France was a relief from the continuous peer pressure to drink, but Lourmarin had its own obstacles to overcome.

Cruella was back when we arrived, and we found a note saying the house was depressing her, which came as no surprise now that all the original charm had been covered over. Frank as always, never short of a nickname, said the house looked like Bin Laden's cave in the Afghan hills and he newly christened it 'Tora Bora'.

Tora Bora
Camouflaged in Laden Green
Halls and doors not European.
Nocturnal shades, all the rave
Prehistoric like a cave.
Silkworms, mushrooms and endives
Growing happily in the eaves.
Dampness rot and mould was rife
But not a word in Country Life.
Moonlight mistral not Aurora
Locals call it Tora Bora.

There was a new *maçon* on site to finish up the Master's mess, his name was *Pere Noel*, though nobody knew the relevance of his nickname other than perhaps that he worked alone. The first thing he did was to condemn everything that the Master had done by pulling it all to pieces and told Cruella to get it out of his sight. There was over 10,000 francs worth of wood ruined but it didn't seem to faze Cruella, we were told that money was no object to her, an only child of wealthy parents. We were given the task of clearing it away, and where better to take it than our *cabanon*, to which we already had the keys, even though it was not yet ours.

Cruella and Whispering Grass were going away for a few days so I took the liberty of using the van to move the load of wood and what a disaster that turned out to be.

It was an unusually wet day and autumn was closing in. With the evenings being shorter and on strange terrain around the *cabanon*, I miscalculated the turn and the van slipped off the road, burying two of the wheels in the muck. An absolute catastrophe, how was I ever going to explain the incident to Cruella?

We started to walk home to Lourmarin and with the French already at their evening tables there was no hope of hitching a ride, let alone assistance, even though it was only 9 p.m.

"What the hell," I said to Caron, "Let's knock on someone's door!" And to our surprise, a man and his son came with their 4 x 4 and pulled us out without further ceremony.

Gallic Knight
Revving, skidding, clutches smelling,
Cursing, swearing and despairing.
Raining, pouring, darkness falling
Mossy lost and Caron calling
What a night it was, in Cucuron.
No lights, nor coats and no cell phone.
Our camping car was truly stuck
Falling over in the muck.
On foot to Lourmarin our fate
A stranger's door now far too late.
But through a window in peopled light
Provence and Irish luck I might.
And what response did we get
One we'll surely not forget.
Four wheel drives with lamps and chains
Mini-jacks and hoisting cranes.
All hooked up then heave and ho
Didn't look like it would go,
The old man told me change my lock
And then with one almighty shock
Our Gallic Knight had saved the day
Bid au revoir and went his way.

CHAPTER 58

Every four weeks we collected our wages from Cruella's account at the bank in Cadenet, a village just over the hill, and there by chance we met Cruella and Whispering Grass, who had just come back from a weekend at St. Tropez. Cruella informed us that she had bought an apartment overlooking the sea, for 2.5 million francs and that we could not collect our wages that week as she was a bit short. We were advised to wait until the next month.

Caron was furious and said again for the third time:

"Let's get away from these two, they are evil,"

"But what about my book, I need more time and more material!"

I promised her that if she hung in there that I would finish the book and expose Cruella and Whispering Grass for their evil ways. Little did Caron know that I wanted to leave far sooner than she did. But it was time that somebody let the world know what the English in France are all about. People had about enough of the Lady Fortescue (Perfume from Provence) type books which set out to patronise the French peasants just as Mayle succeeded in doing 40 years later with a somewhat similar version of the afore-mentioned. Obviously my history gave me ample reason to be cautious of the English and the old saying, "The Irish never forgive and the English never forget" could be part of our mutual misgivings for each other, but the way we were being treated by these two here in Provence had no justification whatsoever. Even the tradesmen recognised it and they not having a word of English. My wife is a yoga professor and her philosophy would not permit her to falsify anything that had gone on and what I was documenting was an accurate and honest observation. She just wanted me to leave the job and to get away from the tormenting which she feared was going to drive me back to the drink. I had a mission and I was going to complete it and the day my book was ready for publication

I was going to be able to present the photographic and written proof of everything stated therein. I was collecting Cruella's letters to me and documenting by photograph the abuses plus I had the support of the tradesmen who were appalled by the behaviour of Cruella and Whispering Grass.

I knew I needed to stay a little longer because I just felt that something incredibly sinister would occur if only we waited and whatever it was going to be would give the story an ending which would be worthy of going to press.

It would be my trump card and I was prepared to play the ball back into their court with more force than it had come out. They had taken on the wrong Irishman and it was not I, but Whispering Grass who had used the term "This is a declaration of war", when we refused to go back to work at ten o clock at night of the tiles incident before the Mayle visit.

It had become a battle of wills and even though I was in a much weaker position than they were, I was Irish and endurance is in our genes. There was no way that these upstarts were going to get off lightly either then or when I published my book.

Finally we got word from Madame Manet the *Notaire* in Cucuron regarding the Moulin or *cabanon* we wanted to buy. We had a rendezvous to go and sign the *compromise de vente* and put down our ten per cent deposit.

Only one of the three owners turned up to sign, the others were under psychiatric care and would have to do it under guidance. The *Notaire* went through a whole litany of laws and regulations with the water rights being the most talked-about issue. We felt like characters in one of Pagnol's books and the future cohabitation with a xenophobic *paysan (farmer)* did not bode well. We would have to share the water rights and would only be allowed to irrigate twice weekly and only twelve hours at a time. There and then it didn't matter to us what the deal was, as long as we had somewhere to go when Cruella and Whispering Grass committed their final act against us.

CHAPTER 59

When Cruella's kitchen was finally completed and totally fitted out with cooker, fridge, and of course laundry, we thought that we would at last have somewhere decent to prepare our meals, but not so, and just as Luther nailed his thesis on the door of the church in Wittenburg, Cruella did likewise.

The note, which was mainly targeted at Caron and I, read as follows:

"From now on I don't want any of the work-force entering the kitchen and I have advised Whispering Grass to keep it locked permanently."

Permanently!!!!!!!!

The workforce, as she put it, thought it rather odd, and although they all went home to their families for lunch everyday, they were concerned about us. They all had, at sometime or other worked for other English people and agreed that:

"Les Anglais sont tous comme ça!"

Things were really changing and we had no idea why, until Frank told us that there was a law in France which stated that a tenant cannot be put out of a house between the months of December and March. These months were deemed to be too inclement and even though Cruella had stated in writing that we could stay until March if we wished, she now had second thoughts as the work was coming to completion.

The eviction had commenced and from then on every room we finished was locked immediately. We were sleeping, cooking, showering and toileting in the bathroom, which incidentally was the only room in the house that had purposely been left without heating and the electrician was furious about that too. Cruella had purposely omitted the heating in an effort to get us out without having to face telling us we had to leave. She was no doubt afraid that I would have the 'Inclement Weather Laws' enforced and thus stay until March at our leisure.

The bathroom on the top floor, which up until then had been used by the artisans, became out of bounds also with another note appearing.

"The upstairs toilet is out of bounds to the workers and should the electricians or plumbers require access for anything work related, I wish to be contacted in England first."

This tactic was designed to make our living area even less private, because the artisans would have no choice but to use the bathroom which was our bedroom and kitchen. Direct dialogue being severed, the fax machine was pumping out edicts on a daily basis from Cruella, who was back in Burford. Caron said that Michael Collins would turn in his grave if he knew I allowed myself to be treated by an Anglo Saxon in this way. I did feel as low as a snakes belly, but everything was coming to pass and the last chapter was showing all the signs of being just what I needed to complete the story.

Pere Noël, the builder who was brought in to replace and repair the incredible mess that the the Master had left behind, had turned a four week job into a four month one and we eventually discovered why he was called Pere Noël - he only turned up with the frequency of Santa Claus. We were getting the impression that he was only slightly more capable than the Master. One day he ran into a problem with a wooden roof beam that needed to be cut, but no visible means of support was apparent for upholding the roof. It was a disaster and Cruella called a site meeting with Pere Noël, Whispering Grass and another English friend of theirs, who had a degree in English literature from Oxford . The site meeting lasted two hours with no conclusion and Pere Noël was first to leave amidst accusations of ineptitude. The other three, none of whom would know the right end of a hammer, followed in hot pursuit. Caron and I went to the *grenier* (attic) to see if a solution could be found. I was quite surprised that Pere Noël had failed to see the extremely evident alternative to his stalemate, but then he was a Parisian and not a lateral-thinking Provencal. We phoned him and explained how it could be achieved without any fuss which resulted in another site meeting, from which we were again excluded and therefore recieved no acknowledgement for our genius, as Oscar Wild- would have put it!

CHAPTER 60

Caron had started an Al-Anon Meeting (for wives, children, friends etc of alcoholics) in Lourmarin, it was held in the Catholic Church hall and slowly became well attended. However, the curator changed and the woman who took his place decided that Alcoholics Anonymous was a sect and should be banned from Lourmarin. The meeting was then moved to Cruella's house, but Cruella took a hard attitude on it and banned the meeting from the premises. So ended the fledgling group.

Lourmarin in winter is a sombre place, deserted not only by admirers but also by its inhabitants. Cruella herself said it was too depressing before she departed for Oxford. We were left to finish off the remaining details and were told in her departing note that we only had until the 21st December, there were to be no wages after that date. We were a month in arrears over her purchasing the house in St Tropez at that stage anyway.

Winter was really on us and our only source of heating in the self contained bathroom was a halogen light that Mossy sat in front of and thought it was the sun. Her teeth chattered like castanets at night and Denny the electrician, said that it was attitudes like Cruella's that caused the French Revolution, but as we hadn't much time to go before we left, we decided to grin and bear it.

Monsieur Gaudin, the *patron* of the electricians, came to see how the job was progressing and when he discovered that the only room in the house left without heating was ours, he expressed his anger at Cruella's disrespect for us and immediately asked his employees to rig up something temporary until Cruella gave him the go ahead to do the definitive wiring. Pere Noël in the meantime, had got himself into trouble on another job so he asked Caron and I to go and help him out at the weekend. Cruella heard about it and yet another fax arrived from Angleterre stating the following:

"It is prohibited to work for someone else on weekends whilst you are in my employment. Doing so would be conducive to fatigue and therefore affect my interests. Should you persist in these activities I will have no option but to sever your employment. Furthermore, *Pere Noël* is months behind and he doesn't need encouragement from you to detain him longer by working elsewhere."

This last fax got my temper up but we had nowhere to go since the Chateau had been sold to the Mairie in Auriol and Whispering Grass was likely to dump our possessions on the street if I told Cruella to fuck off.

The writing was on the wall and returning to Ireland was becoming a reality despite our wish to remain in the Luberon.

CHAPTER 61

The olive-picking season was in full swing, shakers and rakers could be seen all round the village on triangular ladders like umpires at Wimbledon. There was an air of Christmas about the place and a young trainee chef from the Moulin Hotel called to the house to see if *la dame anglaise* would like him to prepare her Christmas dinner. I don't know if he had heard about her attempt at cooking the first vernissage meal or whether it was a French tradition that brought him round.

November 2001. This is how Cruella treated us. We lived in the bthroom/ toilet. The bath was our sink and the only heat was a halogen lamp. All the other rooms were out of bounds and they all had heating except ours.
This is why I wrote this book, 'Lest we forget'

We invited him in and explained that we had been locked out of all the rooms, with the exception of the attic where the work was still going on and our living area, which he came to see. Our fridge was the window sill, the bath was our sink, and we peeled the potatoes down the toilet and all without getting out the bed. We could see by his expression that he had never encountered anything like it before in liberated France. We were still sleeping on cardboard boxes after almost seven months in a house that by then boasted four bedrooms, all fully furnished.

The young man left, and so began the rumours about Cruella in the restaurants and cafes which had been partly our reason for bringing him in. Up until then people were assuming that a lot of the stories which abounded regarding her snobbery may have been exaggerated, but this was now witnessed by someone who, we knew, would pass it on in the right circles.

Rumours
Imagined fabrications.
Three blind mice
With monkeys tales
Confessed their secrets
To the northern wind.
Migrating swallows
Going south
Conveyed the news.
Humpty Dumpty
First to hear,
Aback did fall.
Chinese whispers
Told the grass!
«The trees,
they need
to know»
Then falling leaves
Obliged they felt
To spread their views.
Petite Bo Peep
Even went and told
The flocking sheep.
Gaggling geese
Gave their account,
And now Pinocchio knows.

Two days later, we had a visit from a rich American who lived in the village who had heard the rumour. He was Joseph Deliso, the husband of Liz the lady with the castrated dog, Tattoo. We invited him in to have a look at our abode which he said reminded him of a famous painting by Pierre Bonnard: Le dejuner dans la salle de bains and likened our conditions to that of the Dickens era.

He immediately offered us accommodation, free of charge, no strings attached, at his Chambre d'Hotes '*Les Olivettes*', just on the outskirts of Lourmarin.

It was winter season and he had one vacant apartment which he said we could have until March, when the influx of visitors began. We were touched by his generosity, it so resembled the actual Christmas story, it made our hardening hearts beat with a more joyous ring. Other offers came from the locals and we were invited to join them for the celebrations, but Mr Deliso's was the first, and by far the most generous, so we accepted.

A fax arrived from Cruella, stating that she was coming over for Christmas and could I weld a steel pole to the top of the terrace, so that she could fly the family crest, letting people know that she was in residence.

I hadn't yet told her of our departure but I felt like telling her where she could stick her flagpole.

The Flagpole
Dame in residence,
Raise the flag.
High beyond the Chateau,
Sans noblesse is in town
Time to cut the gateaux.
Lourmarin a village blest
Frequented by olde England's best.
But keep those peasants
Off the streets
They're not the kind
This lady meets.

With only one more day to go, I took great satisfaction in faxing Cruella with the following:

"Dear Cruella, due to the inclement weather conditions currently prevailing in the Luberon, I am unable to fulfil your request to weld on the flagpole and as we are moving to more favourable accommodation, we shall be vacating your house tomorrow, 21st December. We have done everything else you requested and, as arranged, I will collect our final payment from the bank in Cadenet."

This expression of independence must have been too much for her, it also ruined the end game, which she and Whispering Grass had planned for us and thus provoked an angry response.

When I went to collect our wages the following day, my name had only hours ago been removed from the account, leaving us without money for Christmas. Here we were, after 9 months of faithful, honest service and this was our thanks. She refused to answer our calls or faxes but I wasn't going to be beaten by her. I had a plan. Cruella had another account in the name of the gallery, of which I knew all the details, and with the use of my pre-Alcoholics Anonymous training as a street ruffian, extracting my wages from the bank did not pose too much of a problem. We moved to the Deliso residence as planned and the following morning we woke to find Lourmarin covered in the purity of snow. We felt so free to be away from the evil of Cruella and her lackey Whispering Grass. The village had fairytale innocence about it and after what we had been through it seemed like an omen for better things to come.

We met Whispering Grass in the street and his anger over the money which I drained out of the gallery account brought accusations of theft and threats of bringing the Gendarme to arrest us, it was comical.

"Accept it, Whispering Grass,» I said, «you have been outwitted by an Irishman and there is more to come!"

Cruella arrived for her Christmas *sejour* at Tora Bora but without the flag flying to announce that she was in residence.

Monsieur Mathieu, the plumber, who had no respect for her, called us on Christmas day and said that Cruella had contacted him saying that she had no water and that the house was freezing.

"Madame, we don't do house calls on Christmas Day."

"Vengeance is a dish that is best served cold" was what he added and we all had a great laugh at Cruella's expense.

CHAPTER 62

The snow and ice remained in the Vaucluse for three whole weeks and it caused chaos. It was so bad all over France that Jacques Chirac said:

"La France est blessée!"

We weren't too bothered by it as we had no work. Lourmarin was in hibernation. Other than our trips to the market, which although still operating provided a rather spartan display, we spent our days leisurely in the comfort of *Les Olivettes*, Joe Delisso's house. Our view of the village kept us informed of little else except the time, all commerce had been brought to a halt. Even the giant tower crane was frozen in time like a fossil and the only movement was the clock. A nationwide appeal to feed the birds brought people out from their cocoons and they could be seen everywhere throwing morsels of food like *semeuses d'hiver*. The stillness of the days permitted the blue smoke to rise vertically and Lourmarin enveloped by the mountains seemed suspended by a puppeteer's hand. It was the most beautiful sight I had ever encountered. Didier, an electrician we had met during the Cruella saga, rang and told us about a caravan site at Cucuron where we could stay right up until May, for very little rent, he had done so himself and said he knew the owners. But as Irish luck would have it, we received a call from Bernard, the Frenchman who had come to buy the Chateau in Auriol the previous year. He had found another building and wondered if we were interested in a few months work. It was situated in Aubagne, which, after Lourmarin, was a giant step backwards, but still, a gift horse. We were asked to come along for an interview though due to Cruella's bad attitude we were unable to use her as a reference. The house in Aubagne was the original home of the Bishop of Marseille and there was a little chapel attached to the house, not too dissimilar to the one we had restored in New Zealand. Two architects had been brought in to help with the conversion of this 900-square metre mansion to a *Chambre d'Hôtes*. When we produced the album and numerous newspaper articles pertaining to our labour of love on St Patrick's chapel in NZ, no further CVs or references were required and we got the job. Bernard was taking possession just about the time that Joe Delisso needed the apartment back. I told Joe that if not been for his act of generosity at Christmas, we would have gone back to Ireland where the drink would have killed me, AA or no AA. It was time once again to pack the two suitcases and the dog for a continuation of what was becoming an adventure in Provence.

We went to say goodbye to the wonderful friends we had made in Lourmarin and although we had signed a *compromis de vente* to buy the *cabanon*, we were beginning to feel that it would never materialise and therefore it could well be our last time in Lourmarin. Neither of us ever decided to go anywhere, we usually let fate decide for us, so after Aubagne, we could have ended up in the Algarve if the next client lived there. Mossy and I had our last walk around the village and at the statue of the Geminis, where many a time we saluted the Sun, it was time to cast our shadows.

CHAPTER 63

Our first day at La Royante and it was like a league of nations with Bernard being the only Frenchman on the team. The architects came from Italy and Slovenia, the electrician from Poland, Caron from New Zealand and I, the Irishman. The plans were discussed and it was discovered that Bernard had decided to do a number on the chapel by breaking a hole in the wall, making it part of another apartment. The architects were furious, as indeed were we, and it looked like we would be packing Mossy and the suitcases almost immediately as there was no way I was going to put a sledge hammer through such a wonderful building and even though we had nowhere else to live, this was an atrocity as far as we were concerned, besides, buildings are innocent. We were again asked to produce the album of our chapel in Wanaka, and after explaining the potential that could be achieved by saving the chapel as a tourist attraction, it was given a reprieve and the work was allowed to commence.

Nina, the Slovenian architect, told us that she refused work on a regular basis because of ethical questions regarding the demolition of some building or other. She was my kind of lady and I knew from the onset that this was going to be an o.k. job, despite Bernard's initial bull at the gate approach. Zenia, Bernard's lady had been made famous by Levi Strauss when they used her naked bottom (with pocket stitches painted on each cheek) for their world-wide poster advertisements back in the 70s and what a *derriere!* A sight to behold and it can still be viewed (the poster that is) at the Strauss advertising museum.

Mossy was in her element, with acres of ground to explore and two docile Labradors, who did little else except eat and sleep all day. The house was a hive of activity with two more crews joining us, one lot were building a swimming pool and the other drilling a well for water, which incidentally they found at sixty metres without one trace of a foreign body or chemical, it was pure as pure. I found this rather odd here in densely populated Europe. We were in the South Island of New Zealand with only 800,000 people, and when we had a well drilled our water was not even recommended for drinking, as it had so many pesticides in it !

To help with the work around the site, Bernard went to fetch a jeep, an old American one, known as a Willy, which he had bought some years previously in Morocco. It had been in storage near Aix-en-Provence and had no brakes. When he asked me to come along in my car I had no idea that I was going to be towed home. Yes, that's how he overcame the no-brake problem, he towed me with the jeep and I did the braking every time he put his hand up, yet another piece of the French manoeuvring that never ceases to amaze me.

Because we had moved from Lourmarin to Aubagne, we had, under French law, changed departments and therefore we were obliged yet again to change all our documentation, including the number plate on the car, such a stupid system.

This is where the French taxpayer's money goes, they designed a system to penalise themselves and pay one another to do it. Since coming here we had changed departments so many times that my documentation had become a victim of error, resulting in having three different dates of birth, on the driver's licence, *carte de sejour* and passport. As for the names, they never got it right. One day some officious bureaucrat is going to notice and I will end up in the stocks for not making him aware.

We had completed yet another move and we were settled for the time being in Aubagne, just across the road from the French Foreign Legion headquarters.

Bernard's mother came to visit, she was 86 and she spent most of the afternoon teaching her seven-year-old great grandson how to drive around the field. She was amazing for her age and full of *joie de vivre*. Provence seems eternally to host the oldest living person in the world, and a wonderful story I read in the New Zealand Herald in 1995 would support this phenomenon.

"Oldest Living Person Outlives Heir"

Marseille - the local French dignitary, who bought Mlle Jeanne Calment's apartment on an annuity arrangement 30 years ago, thought he was on to a good thing: at ninety, she was unlikely to live much longer, so he would be able to take over her property. But yesterday, Miss Calment remained hale and hearty at age 120, while relatives of Monsieur Andre-Francoise Raffray of Arles were preparing to bury him; he died on Christmas Day, aged a mere 77.

Under the life annuity scheme he was to pay her 2500 francs a month for however long she lived, after which he would become the owner of her first floor apartment. Mlle Calment earlier this year became the oldest living person known anywhere in the world.

AFP

Mlle Calment, who had been a personal friend of Van Gogh, went on to live another two years when she was replaced by another Provencal lady, Mme Germaine Haye, who was at the time 113 in becoming the oldest person in the world. It was such a coincidence, but the journalist who compiled that report, Francois Bringer, lives in Bonnieux not far from Lourmarin, and I eventually met up with him and he showed me video footage of his interview with Mlle Calment.

CHAPTER 64

Caron loses her *carte de sejour*. This is just about the most serious crime one can commit in France and the penalty would surely be the harshest since the offing of heads during the revolution. Every known document in one's repertoire has to be produced at the *Prefecture in Bouches du Rhone, Bureau des Etrangers*. One is definitely going to be made feel ostracised for this almost treasonable offence. For us who had been travelling light, we were not in the habit of retaining the French reams, so yet another nightmare began. A list of what she had to furnish was presented to us as well as being cautioned by article 161 of the penal code, should any information be falsified. But we had learned something in our time here about the French and their system.

1. Always present your documentation in a neat clip folder.
2. Turn up late for your first appointment. (Bureaucrats don't like being shown up.)
3. After every transaction say,"*Vous êtes très efficace Madame!*" as if you mean it.
4. Be prepared to wait for an eternity for a response.

Well, it was a bit of a struggle, eight weeks in fact, but she was successful although with a bit of French twist. Her new card had given her a sex change, Caron Patrick had become Patrick Caron! Understandably enough though, as Caron is a well known French surname and Patrick, a Christian name. She wasn't complaining, because a change of identity has a certain charm about it and besides, if she brought it to their attention she might well have had to contend with article 161 for fraudulently changing her name and ending up behind bars! The other advantage of course was that now we could say she lost her driving licence and using the *carte de sejour* as ID, they would issue a new one in the name Patrick Caron and I could use it, because nearly all the points were gone off my own licence. When a mistake is made in the French bureaucratic system, it is impossible to have it rectified and any attempts to do so would be seen as an insult to their sole purpose of being. They are infallible and every French person has total confidence in the system because just as in Ireland where no house is more than a mile from a pub, every French family has a relative in a state-run institution.

Nearly fifty per cent of the French workforce are *fonctionaires* or civil servants and the great tragedy of the French revolution is that they did not top the lot of them and leave the aristocrats alone. The *fonctionaires* are just one up from parasites and survive off the backs of the workers who pay huge charges in order to keep the whole outdated system afloat.

The Germans run a far more efficient country with only twelve per cent of the workforce being fonctionaires. If France was an island and if the French en masse did not holiday at home, this country would have been down the tubes years ago. The tourist industry is certainly enormous, but it is so largely because it can be accessed by car and train. Besides, it is the gateway to the Mediterranean. The French have rested on their laurels for too long and since the opening up of Eastern Europe, there is a noticeable decline in visitors and indeed in real estate purchases. Even the wine industry is suffering and everywhere one looks, the farmers are pulling up vines. Spain has recently out-paced France as a holiday destination and Michael O'Leary of Ryan Air has had a huge influence in that. My friend Holly who lives in Barcelona can fly direct to Cork and from Marseille, I can only go to Dublin from Marseille and that's only in summer. As far as I am concerned, France is in decline and the romanticism of living here ended when the last *deux chevaux* rolled off the line at the Citroen assembly plant. When the baguette can be bought in Cork City and Calvinist sheep farmers in the south Island of New Zealand are producing better wine than the French, then what is left to live for here?

The politics is all that's left. (No pun intended!)

CHAPTER 65

The Presidential elections in France had turned from:
"Oh non, pas une autre élection, nous en avons eu assez!" to
a seat-edge drama as Monsieur Jospin, the Socialist candidate
was eliminated in the first round, and the extreme right southern candidate, Jean-Marie le Pen was contesting the final heat
with Jacques Chirac.

Democracy was threatened and just like the elections in Al-
geria, some years previously which were annulled because they
didn't produce the desired result, such utterings could be heard
between the lines of the national journals if by any chance, Le
Pen did get in. The French media, under instruction, were asked
to come up with a marketing strategy to save La France from the
jaws of the world. Hollywood style tactics were embodied, and
on came the glitter brigade pledging their support for Chirac.

Football stars and singers were being quoted daily on the
dangers of Le Pen. Johnny Halliday was recruited for the job
and the whole affair provided a grand spectacle which proved
without doubt that democracy, like impressionist art, is not
about Monet, but about money. No expense is ever spared when
the populous is liable to make the correct decision. One only
need look at the Danes, who said no three times to the EEC, but
new referendums were thrown at them and they were eventually
forced to say yes. The subtle difference between democracy and
dictatorship is that in a democracy it takes four years to get rid
of the dictator. It was not my country, but nonetheless, I was
extremely interested in the outcome and being in the south, the
national front stronghold, it was fascinating to watch the procedure from Aubagne, a hot-bed for the extreme xenophobes.

Bernard had inherited a *pigeonnier* with La Royante but the
pigeons didn't like one bit of it and had moved on to the roof of
main house, much to Bernard's disgust. Their springtime coo-
ing and wooing bothered him enough to go and buy a box of
repellent, and also to block up all the access holes, leaving dis-

traught mothers unable to feed their young. We were not too pleased by this and aware as I am that our fourteen years of vegetarianism had given us a holier-than-thou attitude to nature, we were not amused by the French and their treatment of wildlife. Take the robin redbreast for example, its hunting was banned 20 years ago, yet in 1990, a hundred thousand were eaten in the Var alone.

We threatened to walk off the job, unless the pigeons were given access to their young, it was like the battle to save the chapel, but Bernard was a considerate man and he conceded. The pigeons were given a reprieve and our threat to walk off the job was withdrawn.

Mossy used up one of her nine lives while at La Royante, by falling into the pond which was about two feet lower than the wall. She must have been swimming around there for hours as when we finally found her her paws were all bloody from trying to claw her way out. She was very distraught, but a few hours wrapped in a blanket and she was back to her old self. There was at the time no regulation in France regarding fences around pools or ponds. What a way it would have been to lose her.

Before we left Bernard and Zenia, there was a party held in our honour and it coincided with my second anniversary of AA sobriety. At it, a presentation was made to me and it was the most incredible gift of a lifetime. During the time I worked alongside Bernard, we spoke of Ireland frequently and I once related to him that I had had a misspent youth and had never achieved anything in my life. I told him that our mantlepiece at home was full of prizes which were won by my two brothers, for all sorts of sporting events and there was not one item to represent me.

Bernard must have been touched by this and at the presentation he related that story. I had no idea what it was all leading up to, until he opened the box and pulled out a huge cup. Bigger than any on the shelf back in Ireland and on the side was a plaque which was dedicated to what he described as he biggest victory anyone could achieve. Because alcohol is not a competitor, it is an opponent.

There was not a dry eye in the house and it was I that led the procession of tears.

What Bernard and Zenia had done for us, was truly amazing and they restored our faith in humanity.

The Aubagne job got us through the spring and when we were finished there, we were again in a dilemma as to what we should do next. Ireland came close on several occasions, but as always, something came up and we got derailed. This time we decided to go back to the Luberon to the *cabanon* in Cucuron and camp out for the summer. It was May weekend, and we were more than happy to get away from Aubagne, which by now we had had enough of. Before going to set up our abode at the *cabanon* which we did not yet own but had the keys to, we decided to go and see what was happening in Lourmarin.

We were surprised to see 'The Dead Duck' still operating and an advertisement for another *vernissage* plastered to the window, but a look through the glass assured us that little had occurred since last year with virtually all the same paintings were on the wall.

It called for another poem.

Ouverture (second year)
Just another vernissage
Half cooked garlic
And cabbage
May Day! May Day!
Sounds distressed
Swan in trouble
Who'd have guessed
Oils on waters
Call it slick
Last year's choices
Take your pick.

Cruella was flogging a dead horse, but her alpha-ego would not let her admit that neither she nor her English gallery were wanted in Lourmarin.

I met the writer who first prompted me to keep an account of my time with Cruella and he informed me of a few other little gems that had occurred since our departure for Aubagne.

Tora Bora went on the market, as Cruella was in financial trouble over buying the 2.4 million house in St Tropez, the purchase which caused us to have to wait for our last months wages before Christmas. However the Dead Duck flagship was being retained for integration purposes. She strata titled the building, held on to the gallery and sold the house up top. The exhibiting artists were likening the gallery to a museum, with their works on permanent display behind closed doors and many had requested them back. I had yet to meet Frank, but it looked like his prophecy was coming true and maybe the Dead Duck Gallery was flapping with one wing.

We moved back to our hopefully-to-be land at Cucuron and after Aubagne it was like being in heaven, despite having no

running water or electricity or even a toilet. My first task was to dig out a long drop (outside toilet) and put a lime base to decompose our waste. They are usually about six feet deep with a box on top for sitting on. In Ireland, prior to septic tanks, they were quite common in the countryside and usually situated behind the house in a little field known as the haggart. There's an old story I once heard about an Irishman who had spent forty years in New York and returned to the old homestead, to be greeted by a young lady at the half-door.

"My name is Dermot Breen, are the family about?"

"Sure, they're all up at the haggart, having a barbecue Mr Breen."

"God damn it, when I lived around here, we ate in the house and shit in the haggart, now they're shitting in the house and eating in the haggart!"

CHAPTER 66

One of the local farmers in Cucuron, who was obviously upset that we were in the process of buying the *cabanon*, came by and tried to put the frighteners on us. He said that due to the land being agricultural, it would be impossible to get electricity or water, because one had to have a farming certificate. Effectively it would not be possible to turn the old mill into a residence. He also told us of the enormous rats that live in the stream that ran nearby. We could see a Jean de Florette type story unfolding and that was even before we had bought it. We weren't too worried by the rats, Mossy was more than capable of dealing with them and as for the power and water, for now we could use the stream for all our washing purposes and draw our drinking water from the village fountain. Electricity was no problem because the days were long and we had a gas burner for cooking. We had no fancy computer equipment, television or washing machine. So in other words Monsieur Shit Stirring Farmer, why don't you just fuck off and weed your turnips.

As we didn't want to ruffle anyone's feathers by assuming that the *cabanon* was ours, we declined putting up a post box and Caron went to enquire at the *Bureau de Poste* for a private box. There was such a waiting list, the lady advised her to go and buy a box and just stick it up and the *facteur* (Postie) would give us our address. Up until then, we had lived in some odd places but never before had we been somewhere that had yet to be given an address.

In France, all rural letter boxes are standard green rectangular, with an option of one or two doors, the door at the rear made no sense to me and when Caron arrived home with one, I could only say why didn't you get the cheaper version, the one without the tradesman's entrance. (Since I stopped drinking I had become as tight as the bark on a tree). With our pup-tent pitched and the long drop already christened, I made a clothes line and an area to hang out our solar shower bags. An old stainless steel sink which I found at the Lourmarin dump was mounted on a wooden base with a drum to catch the waste water for our vegetable patch. Cooking with gas, Caron made this humble abode into a paradise of culinary wonders, with her attaché case of Indian and Asian spices, (a must for interesting vegetarianism). It might have seemed rather odd, since we were living in what some would find hardship, but we were in our element. Drawing fresh water from the village became a daily chore, and it was soon common knowledge that we were *'Les étrangers avec une différence.'*

There was one thing a little impure about our Bohemian existence though, we had a cell phone which we charged from the cigarette lighter of the car, a necessity for work. One day Miss Poirier, an American lady, called us out of the blue and asked if we would renovate a little house she had bought in Peypin D'Aigues, a village not far away from Cucuron. We had met Holly while we were doing up Cruella's house and she was aware that we had been forced to live in the bathroom. She told us that stories of Cruella had become the topic of many a social get together in New York, and that some of her friends were eager to come to Provence to see her.. The job for Miss Poirier was only for two weeks and it was right up our street as we had come to realise that of all the people we had worked for since coming to France, the Americans were magic - normal, extremely generous, and up front.

While we worked for Miss Porrier, who incidentally was in New York, I became friendly with Robert, her next door neighbour in Peypin d'Aigues. He called me in one day to try and open his gas bottle which had been abused by an ill fitting spanner and the nut refused to turn. Robert was a hunter, retired, and in poor health. His whole house was wall-to-wall with taxidermy, reminders of his hey-day with the gun. Mossy found it strange and had to be put out because of her refusal to stop barking. What really upset me was when Robert told me he never like the taste of *'gibier'* (wild game) and that he only killed it for the fun of it!

"Tradition is born of necessity
Sport is contemptuous mirth."

Moi Meme.

CHAPTER 67

One day while I was sitting and enjoying the view of the Luberon Mountains from the long drop of our addressless abode, the *facteur* rolled up the avenue through the vineyard, leaving his van at the gate. He was calling:

"*Est-ce qu'il y a quelqu'un?*"

I was caught with my trousers down. He had a letter (from himself) telling us where we lived and as he opened it in our presence with a horse-shoe in one hand, he exclaimed:

"*Monsieur, madame, votre address est Fer a Cheval!*" and for good measure he handed us the horse-shoe because the woman at *la Poste* told him we were foreign and this was his best attempt at explaining what 'Fer a Cheval' actually meant ! They might have known I was dyslexic and the symbolism of the horse-shoe was the purest form of Steiner education, wonderfully humourous and a good luck omen for things to come.

With the customary:

"*Bonne chance!*" he made off to his van smiling at his genius and we thought that this place was getting better and better despite the fictitious rats.

We mounted our letter box on an old tree stump and I nailed the horse-shoe to it especially for the benefit of the *facteur* and waited for our first letter.

Getting up for work didn't require an alarm clock as our pup-tent walls kept out little except the mosquitoes. The bread delivery man was in the habit of giving his claxon two hoots at each of the bends on the road which we later discovered formed a horse-shoe, hence the name Fer a Cheval.

Caron (not I, due to my yeast infection) was still eating bread and decided to avail herself of the morning delivery with a croissant and a baguette. It was only then we discovered the purpose of the second door in the post box.

The *boulanger* had a master key and was able to open both doors of our letter box and the baguette protruded at both ends!

Our letter box didn't survive long though, one of the local farmers who wanted to buy Fer a Cheval smashed it to pieces while we were away. I took photos and reported the incident but there was little point. We bought a second one and the same thing happened. But whoever it was had no hope of ever buying it even if we were intimidated and left, because the owners said that they would never sell it to any of the surrounding farmers (Fucking Catholics the lot of them) in French of course.

The locals had been talking about us - word had spread and soon we were becoming a tourist destination with people coming by on the weekends to see *les étrangers* and our set-up at the old mill of Fer a Cheval.

We were even asked to pose in photographs for inquisitive people who could not fathom how or why anyone would or could live without running water or a proper toilet in this day and age. It all seemed so normal to us and we could not understand the interest nor all the fuss. But the French are not a rough-it nation and we were a bit of an enigma, especially as we went to work everyday and we were not drawing social security of any description. We were true Bohemians and in some ways people not only admired our lifestyle, they also envied it. Little did they know what hardship really was and this was a piece of cake after what we had gone through living in Lourmarin in Cruella's house.

After finishing the job in Peypin for Miss Porrier, we spent a few days wondering what was going to become of us. It was summer and living in the tent would not be an option over winter. We could not expect Joe Deliso to house us again, but we were sure if things didn't work out for us, he would no doubt oblige, or at a push we could have taken Didier's suggestion and move to the caravan site in Cucuron. In Provence, it is said that bad weather never stays long and in a way, one could apply it to everything in life. My cell phone rang.

"Finney, it's Frank, I'm in a restaurant in Lourmarin and guess what?" In a flash I went through a range of potential possibilities and the one that seemed to favour me most was that Cruella was lying on the floor while someone was trying to perform the Heimlich manoeuvre to remove a fish bone firmly stuck in her throat. No such luck, but what Frank had to report was better news than anything I could have imagined about Cruella. The couple who owned the well known shop in Lourmarin, *Mistouflon,* were friends of Frank, and they had just received a call from the people who were meant to look after their house while they went to Spain for two weeks holidays, saying that they were not able to fullfil their promise. Frank told them that he knew somebody who would love a proper house with a pool for a fortnight, and asked me, were we interested?

Of course we were interested, there was no question.

CHAPTER 68

Frank arranged an interview with the couple, George and Florence, who would show us the house and what we were required to do. It seemed that we had the job even before we met them, Frank's recommendation was enough. Florence was the daughter of Anne Marie Chapoulton, the writer of the children's cult book *Mistouflon about* a fictitious six-legged animal that lives in the Luberon mountains.

Our tasks were simple, feed the chickens and the doves, water the garden and take care of two dogs, Vanille, a black bitsa (it is of course entirely logical that a black dog be called Vanille because the vanilla bean is black, but from where I come from a white dog would be called Vanilla, after ice cream I suppose!) Vanille was stone deaf. There was also, Plume, an enormous mountain dog, who had the reputation of being a bit of a wanderer. This was the heartland of the Luberon, with our next door neighbours being Peter and Jenny Mayle, whom I almost met at the opening of the Dead Duck Galerie and here I was again looking into their back yard.

George and Florence took off and were happy that everything was going to be fine. We took advantage of the house and having no day jobs we made some trips to places we might otherwise never get to see. One such visit was to *Terre Vivante*, an organic farm complex in Istres. This is where all the information regarding Eco housing and biologique growing was to be found and what a display. It was a day well spent and with an organic vegetarian restaurant on site, it made it possible to spend the entire time being educated by the most dedicated team of naturalists we had come across. Our faith in France was restored, it seemed someone did care about the environment.

Terre Vivante was founded in 1990 by four people with a vision and today employs twenty people. Set in an old farm, like an oasis in the forest, this ten hectare wonderland proves without a doubt that pesticides, herbicides, and fungicides are not the necessary farming tools our governments encourage us to believe and I would challenge any Agricultural minister to prove otherwise. *Terre Vivante* as a farm was how we used to be before the avalanche of uneducated waste.

"Allez a la recherche de temps perdu avant que c'est trop tard!"

This motto should be adhered to, because we read at *Terre Vivante* that the bee population of the world was in decline. Einstein said if that the bees disappear, we will follow soon afterwards. Rachael Carson in her book 'The Silent Spring' said likewise, but France has a long way to go and *Terre Vivante* was a voice in the hills that spoke to itself. But the echo of doom was being picked up by the growing number of visitors annually and only a week before we went there, the French Agricultural Minister had paid a visit.

Chapter 69

Our day out at the organic farm was slightly spoilt by the state of Plume on our return, she was covered in blood - initially we thought it was the chickens, but on inspection we found nothing disturbed around the house. Vanille, in her deaf innocence, remained silent when we quizzed them both, but it didn't bode well for our first day on the job.

We were soon informed that a farmer from the other side of the Luberon had had thirteen of his sheep killed by a pack of marauding dogs and some days earlier Vanille was seen in the vicinity. I assured him that Vanille would not be agile enough to worry sheep as she was deaf and almost blind, but the police demanded that she go on an identity parade because someone had seen the pack. It was a bit of a dilemma for us especially since the owners were on holiday and we didn't want to ruin it for them but also, what if Vanille was picked out and put down wrongly! It was a risk, but I was convinced she wasn't involved, so I took her along. There were nine other dogs on parade but like identity parades for people, some of them may have been stand-ins and could have even belonged to the Gendarmes. Vanille looked the most likely suspect because she was blacker than black, but the man that was going to point the finger at the police station didn't give her a second look as he passed by and we were allowed to go, dog and all.

When George and Florence finally came back, we decided not to say anything about the identity parade but we did advise them of Plume's bloody face one evening when we came home.

We went back to our camping site at *Fer a Cheval*, we had received our first letter, from an American artist friend called Chris from Dieulefit in the Drome. He wrote a rather nice note saying that he was attracted to the village of Dieu Le Fit because it meant 'made by God' but it would take an Irishman to find an address like Fer a Cheval since luck is better than love. He was right, because the luck was with me - we got a call from

Florence and George regarding a little *maison de village* in the centre of Lourmarin, which they said we could have for a very nominal rent. Mossy knew by the tone of my voice that it was once again time for the suitcases as this was an offer we simply could not pass up. The house was at the *Place du Castellas*, just under the clock tower, giving us an excellent view into the back of Cruella's place. The locals, almost all of whom we knew after being in the village for so long, were delighted to see us back and although not contrived, it would give me an excellent chance to conclude the final chapter in my book from a grandstand view.

Florence and George were earthy people and they were concerned about us living at the *cabanon* with the weather changing, it was a timely gesture which we appreciated immensely. Joe Deliso, the American, came to see us when he heard we were back and he gave me the entire maintenance of his properties in and around Lourmarin. George and Florence also found us work and even though I was working on the black, we were at least surviving.

CHAPTER 70

Word of Robert's death (the hunter from Peypin d'Aigues) came as a shock and despite my aversion to his passion I was extremely upset to hear about it. It was only six months earlier that Mossy and I had sat in his chamber of horrors while he told me about the events surrounding the killing of the different animals on display. I was invited to the wake and as he lay there with two five-franc pieces covering his eyes, hiding from those eyes he had taken little notice of all these years, I tried to imagine what the stuffed animals were thinking as they looked down on his body. The talk from the other hunters made Robert out to be some sort of hero, as they recalled story after story about each of the beautiful creatures that looked over us from their parade, innocent of crimes never committed.

Once again, I felt an urge to record in poetry what I saw and the feeling that I was a judge between Robert, the animals and Robert's friends produced the following verdict.

The Hunter
Vacant eyes looked down
In an unforgiving stare
Innocence denied its freedom.
What now brave man, one
Must but see their pain.
Trophies from your violent past,
Art has no comparison.
Rusting fusils a symbiotic
Insult to the game of waste.
May the howling winds remind you,
Nor thoughts alone be left devoid of predators.
Tell-tale signs
Of hot and cold
On the roof tops told
Icicles transfused their droplets

From a weakened sun
But soon these veins of life solidified
And as the heart a resting place it found,
The longest hibernation had begun.
With weighted eyes,
Eternity became the face of inexpression.

Robert had taken his own life, with the same *fusil* he had used on the creatures hanging in the room and I sadly report, that he apparently also shot his dog.

CHAPTER 71

Before we left Cruis to go to look after the house for Claude in Auriol, Mrs Collis, the English lady who worked at the Manosque social security office, had told us about an organisation which helps people start their own businesses and having been working illegally for so long, we thought we'd give it a go.

The grant was for 70,000 Francs, an interest-free loan of 50,000 francs plus being tax free for one year. We were not too disheartened by the bureaucracy, so we filled in all the necessary forms and left it in the horse-shoe of God, which had been doing a reasonable job for us until now.

Our luck was an on-going miracle and all the bad that the Englishwoman and her lackey Whispering Grass had done to us, was being made up for by Joe Deliso and Florence Chapouton.

Florence came by to see us at Place du Castellas, with more good news. A neighbour of hers, who was a Parisian, was looking for guardians to mind his house as he was away most of the time and there was a free cottage going with it. Situated at the foot of the Luberon overlooking Lourmarin, we had said yes before she caught her second breath, and yes, Mossy did get a scent of what was going on when the two suitcases were pulled out from under the bed, and we were on the road again.

The weather had turned bad with the dark evenings making it even more dismal and Mossy became quite ill, refusing to eat for days. We took her to the veterinary surgeon in Pertuis and he said that her kidneys had failed. He put her on a machine over the weekend and said that some dogs recover and can go on for quite a while on a special diet, but Mossy did not respond and we were summoned to the surgery.

He assured us that there was no hope and as she lay there unconscious and smelling of urine and faeces I could have died with her. Fourteen years and only ever out of her company twice! We were in tears as they handed her to us in a plastic bag. There was no way I was going to bury her in something like that, so we went back to the house and I took one of the suitcases and laid her gently with her head facing south to New Zealand, her birth place. While we were digging her grave on the Luberon behind Peter Mayles house, Plume came by and sat silently as I closed the lid on one suitcase, and my dog.

Mossy
I drove through
The tears.
With my mind
In the rear view mirror,
Last night's thunder
Echoed all the fear
We knew existed
For a dog alone
And dying.
The time had come
To say goodbye
In silence.
Then, to the mystic mountain,
With hearts and hands
Already heavy
In the stony clay.
An Irish mist came
Softly down
And leafless trees
With water buds
Did weep.

Mossy dying and the move to our new abode on New Year's Day, into a house that had been lived in for the past ten years by two French chain smokers, was almost more than we could bear. The walls and wooden beams, even the keys were covered in a cancer-coloured veneer of tacky sap with a smell much like an early morning pub one finds in the docklands. The weather was grey and unrelenting, we were miserable.

Our *patron*, Monsieur Jean, was there to greet us with a *"bonne nouvelle annee!"* The grand house known as Mas des Poules was designed by Jean's father and it had all the hallmarks of a concept that was entirely executed in summer. It must surely be the most dismal house in Provence and looked like a miniature Masonic Lodge with an open atrium and dark marble tiles throughout. There was no double-glazing with the windowless living area at the north end. Jean sat in his ski-gear and mittens as he gave us our instructions. Our little cottage, on the other hand, was well insulated with double glazing and wood burning stove. We were required to do one day's work a week, each, for our rent and to be on the premises every night. This was an insurance requirement but I'm sure that any robber that might come by would be very disappointed due to the lack of anything worthwhile to steal and the house was more than likely on one of their lists as 'not worth the bother'! Jean was a Parisian bureaucrat and as one of the locals told us,

"Il est penible."

Every little detail had to be written down, how long we spent sweeping up the leaves, how long it took to cut the firewood and a stacking procedure of four different sizes was emphasised as being imperative. This list would be reviewed at the end of every month and any spelling mistakes got more attention that the actual work we had done. Early on in his employment we decided that in order to fiddle a little time, it would be necessary to continue with the coccinelle French and to accept his corrections with humility. He always homed in on our spelling errors and the occasional mathematical miscalculation, which we would put in on purpose, gave Jean good reason to keep an eye on our hours and not on the actual work which was meant to correspond with it.

We were in an excellent area at the foot of the Luberon only a few hundred yards from where we had buried Mossy. Our closest French speaking neighbours were George and Florence and our closest English neighbours were Jenny and Peter Mayle, who may as well have been in the Var or Invercargill as far as we were concerned.

CHAPTER 72

Another year in Provence was unfolding and a surprise visit from Frank and Olivier to see our new abode brought us a positive injection which we were lacking. They both agreed that we were extremely fortunate to have found such a good deal and so close to Lourmarin. We were in the process of washing down the whole house when they arrived and Frank said that the smell of smoke would never leave unless we repainted everything, using the traditional Provencal system of *chaux* with ochre from Roussillon to colour it. The *chaux* or whitewash, as we call it in Ireland (no matter what colour it is) is also meant to act as a disinfectant. The whole job of cleaning and painting took us a week and certainly helped, especially me, to keep my mind off Mossy's death. The move itself was an easy affair as we did not have a lot of furniture other than what I had found at the dump in Lourmarin. Living in a pine forest, we had access to all the firewood we wanted and as we lit our first fire, the snow began to fall. While Caron stuffed some food bags for the robins, I hung some of our artworks and a sense of home was soon chasing away the feeling of being in someone else's space.

Being winter when the Luberon seems to die due to lack of residents, we had little else to do except start the procedure to avail ourselves of the grant for our business concept, a multi-service, with the emphasis on the small stuff like renovations, garden maintenance and management of secondary homes which no-one else seemed to be doing. This was our intended niche market. If you thought getting a *carte de sejour* or changing number plates was a nightmare, you ain't seen nothing yet! This was the most challenging test to my sobriety I was ever to experience. Virtually every aspect of the French system had to be visited and one could write a book on the subject. But despite all the bureaucracy no-one noticed that the dates of birth on my passport, *carte de sejour* and driving licence were all different, and it proved that the vast majority of the French fonctionaires were not only inefficient but unnecessary.

We were obliged to do a week-long course in Avignon at the *Chambre de Metiers* (Chamber of Industry) to educate us on how the French system of paying taxes works and believe it or not, I managed to get a certificate at the end of it so I am now eligible to pay *les Impots*. From the time we first applied to the actual receiving of the grant, was to be 8 months. But the wait was worth it as we would be accepted into the circle of Artisans. In France, unlike other western countries, the Artisan is a respected member of society and to prove that I was qualified to do all the things I said I could do, all I needed was a piece of paper to say so. That was an easy task with all my connections in London and Ireland. There is no problem pulling the wool over the eyes of the French bureaucrats.

They do take you at your word and honour is still a code of practice here. While all this was being set up, we did the occasional job on the black but had to be vigilant, for if we were caught it would negate our chances of getting the grant and we could never trust Whispering Grass or Cruella, because they would have loved to see us fail in France.

But little did they know it, they were instrumental in my success, because I was determined to make a go of it and couldn't wait for the day when I would be sending them a signed copy of this book.

CHAPTER 73

On a dog-less walk up the Luberon, I heard the whimpering of an animal that sounded in distress and on further investigation, I found a lady lying dead with hedge-clippers still clasped in her right hand beside a chair which had fallen over. Her dog was at her side crying. It was my first time having to deal with death in this way, but years ago I had done a Red Cross First Aid course, which included CPR, although on further inspection, it was obvious she had been dead for sometime and any attempts to revive her would have been futile. The house was open and a glass of whiskey was on the table with the television flickering - it had all the ingredients for a setting in a 'who done it'. Alerting the authorities was all that could be done and while I waited, I wrote and dedicated a poem to her.

Intentions
The wild hedge
Of spring
Bothered her.
Though hardly enough
To scare away
The birds,
A quiet clip
In the afternoon
To pass the time,
But not for long.
The television flickered
As she lay there,
An almost horizontal Liberty
Shears in hand
And good intentions.

In memory of the lady
Who died in her garden
April 23, 2003

Caron had been visiting Mossy's grave regularly and like a mother who had lost a child, she wanted another dog, a Foxie. I was still in mourning and had no desire to replace the best, best, best, dog, but I was out-voted and the search for a breeder was on. We looked at some of the local litters and felt as though there was something odd about all those we had seen. So we contacted the home of their origin and spoke with the President of the English Foxie Association, who said he would contact us as soon as a pup was on the way.

Luberon Property Care

☘

It's by our service you'll decide

Nos services vous feront nous choisir

A multi-service, including the small stuff
The people who own the business
do the business

Les propriétaires de l'entreprise à votre service
Un multi-services comprenant les petits travaux

Luberon Property Care, our company, became a reality. A multi-service serving a neglected clientele, small jobs our speciality. Like any new enterprise, I expected launching it would be difficult and even more so after what Peter Mayle said about the undependability of the Irish workmen because of alcohol. The idea of putting a sign on my van saying I didn't drink, might in some strange way, get the French thinking that there might be something sinister about me. Weeks and even months went by and if it were not for George and Florence finding the occasional bits to do around the village, we would have gone under. So here I was at the foot of the Luberon with a van full of tools and despairing. In the middle of all this we had a call from the president of the Fox Terrier Association of Britain, saying that he had a pup ready to be collected, just what I didn't need, the expense of the dog, plus the drive up there. But Caron wanted a dog and that was that. We drove to England. The breeder, also president of the fox terrier club lived near Bristol and unaware that we were living in France at the time of our initial enquiry, he advised us on the day that the pup had to be injected if it was being taken out of the country. So instead of smuggling Mossy from France to England, we were now faced with doing it the opposite way round because it was Saturday and we weren't hanging around for a vet until Monday. I was depressed enough over my failing property care venture and England was adding to it. The little male Foxie, who was still nameless had to be hidden from the potential spot checks, which the customs still operate despite being in the EEC for the past 30 years. I couldn't think of any other way to put him to sleep, except the traditional Irish liquid lullaby of a drop of whiskey in some hot milk. The barman at the pub in Dover found it rather odd when I asked him to microwave some milk with a little whiskey in it. He made me pay for a full glass even though I only needed to put a tiny amount in the milk for the dog.

"What will I do with the rest of it sir?" he enquired, as I walked away from the bar.

"Throw it down the sink," I replied, and as I went out I heard him say:

"Bloody Irish are getting odder!"

I had made enquiries about the sailing times and dosed the dog accordingly and our smuggling attempt succeeded. A quick visit to Boulogne-sur-Mer while we were in the region seemed a good idea. My Anglo-Irish friend Chris rang me and asked how the smuggling procedure went and also asked if he could have naming rights for the dog to which I agreed.

Chris has a slight speech impediment, and when to our amusement he replied stammeringly:

"Bono ... *Bono*," and the dog was instantly christened as such.

Chapter 74

Since quarantine no longer existed, we were not going to be trapped in France by the dog if the business failed and that was looking more and more likely. I had tried everything in my power to launch Luberon Property Care but to no avail. Whilst in New Zealand we had experienced a similar problem with a café we had started, I came up with a marketing strategy which saved us from the jaws of our loan provider. They had given us one last month before deeming us bankrupt. I went to an artist friend and asked him to make us an award for the best café in Auckland. It was to be signed by the President of the 'Auckland Provenders Association', a fictitious organisation which I made up myself. We framed the award and hung it behind the cash register and within days we were visited by the press and television and not one person ever questioned what was the 'Auckland Provenders Association'. Lanigans Café took off and our bank manager said that he had never seen a business come off the life-support machine so quickly.

But what could I do in the Luberon to get our ailing company resurrected?

Think Yiddish, Dress British and Luck Irish did nothing to halt the inevitable.

I read an article in *La Provence* and it said that a 2000 year old Roman Bridge just outside Bonnieux known as the Pont Julian was to be closed down when the replacement bridge was finished. What if, I thought, I could manage to be the last person to drive over the Pont Julian in my Luberon Property Care van which was sign-written on both sides with a shamrock for good luck. But how, was the question, how would one organise a stunt like that? Go straight to the top, that's how and I wrote a letter to President Chirac explaining that I had started a business in the Luberon with the aid of a government grant and I could not manage to get it off the ground. I told him that the publicity of being the last person to cross the beautiful old bridge would certainly get us off to a great start. It was a long shot, but I still had the horse-shoe the postman had given me at *Fer a Cheval*.

As is often the case in Provence, the project was delayed and the contract to finish the new bridge went way over the time clause and my request to be the last person over Pont Julian was most likely in a bin at Fontainebleau.

I was not giving up though and another scheme which was even better had me thinking that I could save us from the privations of cloudy overcast Ireland. I was surprised I did not think of my second solution sooner and as they say in Ireland 'if it was a dog it would have bit me'! I couldn't see the wood for the trees. Peter Mayle was going to save our company and he was just down the road. He wrote a chapter in the April section of a 'Year in Provence' in which he introduces another Englishman, who makes a semi complimentary/derogatory remark about the Irish. It was a mere four words, but it would have been at least, at the minimum, better than nothing on the side of my van.

The rest of the chapter which was the authors own words, did little to enhance my job prospects in the Luberon.

So Mr Mayle, it was time to make amends for what you said about us and I wrote him a letter asking if I could use the quote '----- --- ------ ----'. This would look wonderful on the side of my van, on the website and on the printed fliers I was advised to do by the *Chambre de Metiers*. As the crow flies, Mayle was only a bird call away from where we lived, but there was no letter box at the end of his drive. So I went to the post office in Lourmarin for a stamp and addressed the letter to:

Peter Mayle
Lourmarin 84160

I passed the letter over the counter to Brigitte, the post lady, and on reading it she said that Peter Mayle was ex-directory and he did not want anyone to know where he lived. She said that he had a post office box and that I should use that. She handed me another envelope and under her instructions I wrote:

Peter Mayle
C/Z La Poste
Lourmarin 84160

And Brigitte said that that was *"Beaucoup mieux."*

Caron and I never used the village much because we were buying 100% organic and there was little in Lourmarin catering for our lifestyle. So I never met Mayle, although I did run into Jenny on occasion and after waiting weeks for a response to my letter, I took the liberty at the Friday market in the village to ask her if Peter had got my letter. She assured me that he had but he was too busy to respond. She said that he had just gone to America but that he advised her prior to his departure that Finney *(c'est moi!)* the Irishman could use the quote from the book. Bingo!!!!!!!!!!!!!!!!!!!!!!!

I was made and I could have kissed her feet with relief and joy at Peter's generosity. It would only be a matter of time and my business would be booming, I was sure of it. But first, I had to get a website set up, the van sign-written and the leaflets printed, it was so exciting:

"Luberon Property Care, '----- --- ------ ----' " Peter Mayle - what could be better!

I was so overjoyed that I was trying to think of something wonderfully different to give or do for Mr Mayle and his lady Jenny. It would have to wait until I was up and running because just then we were in debt and going further into it, but I was sure that it would only be a matter of time before our company would be known all over the Luberon.

I told all my friends, most of whom disbelieved me, but I was going to prove it very shortly and wipe the smirks off their faces. One of the AA people put me in contact with a printing company and a computer expert who would prepare all our advertising. We got a sign-writer to re-do the format and add the Mayle quote and we were ready for business.

Les. (L'escargot)
Les arrived today from Angleterre
Stow'd away in cargo, artifacts from
New Kings Road, Tunbridge, like
Wells Fargo. Hidden in an old French
Chest, behind a photo of Georgee Best,
Looking very frail and extremely pale.
I imagined what he thought, perhaps
Good fortune, to La France was brought.
So we decided to give him a treat, you know,
a chance for him to mate and meet !
Not far for us to go by van, to a little
Vineyard near Lourmarin. The grapes all
picked, we put him near a vine, Caron
counted at least another nine.
But alas, in Cafe Antiquarian,
Unfortunately not vegetarian,
All dressed in garlic went our snail
and ended up in Peter Mayle.

CHAPTER 75

I was at home doing a few jobs for Jean our patron when the *factrice* arrived with our mail- Caron was on her way down the drive with a face like a plate full of mortal sins and an open envelope in her hand. It was from Peter Mayle lui-meme and he said that I was not permitted to use the four word quote to launch my business.

All that money on the advertising and and now this, Fuck, Fuck Fuck!!!!!!!!!!!!!!!!!

What the fuck does he think Luberon Property Care is?

"Calm down, calm down," was Caron's reply.

"Go to an AA meeting or you will be drinking before you know it."

Jesus, does he think we are making fucking bombs or what?

"Think back" Caron said, " it was not so long ago that he did the same thing to Cruella. One minute he was opening the gallery and the next, we were out day and night pulling down and retrieving the posters because he changed his mind."

Yeah, that's what's said about the Treaty of Limerick, the English changed their minds before the ink was dry. Ah well, we will just have to come up with another idea or accept the consequences and go back to Ireland to a council house. Ned O'Keeffe, the Fianna Fail T.D. might be able to help me get one.

While we were talking and licking our wounds, Bono Bono in a fit of excitement ran down Jeans drive, out on to the road and got hit by a car. The driver was oblivious of her act- probably didn't even see this tiny 7 month old pup and had driven on. Bono Bono was sitting quite calmly in the middle of the road but wouldn't move – it was obvious he had broken his hind leg or worse, his spine.

I put my head in my hands and in the silence of the darkness, I surrendered.

There was no peace and the saying that 'God spends six months a year in heaven and three in Provence' seemed a joke and so was the shamrock and the horse-shoe from Fer a Cheval. I was finally beaten and what kept me from the bottle I will never know. It was off to Pertuis with Bono Bono to the same veterinary surgeon that put Mossy to sleep and all because of that fucking letter from Peter Mayle. I lost my concentration and neglected Bono Bono over that bollocks down the road.

Bono Bono had broken his leg- he couldn't be operated on for a few days because he was in shock so he was strapped up and sent home for the weekend. On arriving home he got out of the car and attempted to once again run down the drive, though this time on 3 legs- so much for the shock! Foxies are mad!

Things were going from bad to worse and I considered selling the van with all the tools and accepting the inevitable. I phoned Ireland and got Ned O'Keeffe's address from my mother and wrote him a letter explaining our situation.

It was at this time after the series of set backs over the dog and Mayles refusal to let me use the quote, that I got so depressed that I went to the Lourmarin dump and threw out my typewriter and the entire research and manuscript for Two Suitcases and A Dog. A whole week passed before the cloud lifted and then I got a panic attack over throwing everything out. Caron and I rushed down to Lourmarin in some half cocked hope that the skip would be still there. It hadn't rained, a skip was there and it was full. Whether it was the same one or not, I had no idea. But one thing was for sure, I knew that it was empty a week previous and if my manuscript was there, the skip would have to be emptied.

What a nightmare it was as there was all sorts of shite in it. But out it was coming and that was that. I resembled a fox terrier rooting and stuff was flying in all directions, but I got to the bottom of it and found my book. Your book !

In Alcoholics Anonymous there is a dictum:

Grant me the serenity to

Accept the things I cannot change.

Courage to change the things I can,

And the Wisdom to know the difference

I quoted this to myself several times as the days passed and other than our obligation to Jean and Joe Deliso's work, we had nothing and I came to the conclusion that the first line of the dictum was where I as at. So I accepted.

Joe Deliso heard about Bono Bono breaking his leg and I expect he knew that I was pulling my hair out and I think he invented another job for me. He had a house on Rue Camus and he asked me if I could fabricate a pergola for him. The house, *La Petite Maison* was just opposite the Catholic Church in Lourmarin and only one house away from the home of Albert Camus where Catherine his daughter still lived and she passed by several times a day as I was welding Joe's pergola. We got to know each other over a short period of time. She is a very down to earth lady, who on discovering that I was Irish (and not Murphy from Donegal) she enquired if I would be interested in looking after her garden. I very nearly said no as I had virtually made up my mind to go back to Ireland at that stage. But how could I refuse Albert Camus' daughter.

So I accepted and assured her that I would begin as soon as I had Joe Deliso's job finished. Caron was quietly delighted and no doubt relieved, Ireland was on hold yet again.

Outbacks
Here I am at the foot of The Luberon
hiding from the sun.
I saw an Irish car today, with a pair of
Micks, anaemics, my wife said.
Flourescent like a pair of corpses, with
an O' Thule coffin on the roof.
Dubliners they were, Bram Stoker
country and possibly vampires down
for the tomato picking season.
It's the same every year, we go there
and they come here.
Ryan Air white outs they're known as
on the Riviera, burnt as toast in a day
and cursing the French.

CHAPTER 76

When I went home there was a letter from Ned O'Keeffe with all the information regarding a new council scheme of houses in my home town and he advised me to get my name on the list as soon as possible. I was in a right quandary and if Catherine Camus had not asked me to work for her, I would have gone straight to Mallow on Ryan Air and registered for a house, but I felt as though my luck was changing so we procrastinated on the Mallow idea.

Working for Catherine Camus was in some ways as good as Peter Mayle endorsing our enterprise, and Catherine, unlike Mayle, had no problem with me stating on my literature that I was the gardener to Camus. Unfortunately at that stage I had gone to press once too often and been forced to destroy everything in case someone sued me. Now I was totally broke and Albert Camus would have to wait before he appeared beside the shamrock on my van.

It was a pleasure to work for Catherine because she had the same philosophy as we had, and she was particularly impressed by what she read on our advertisement about the chapel we had left behind in NZ. My wife refused to sell it because she was not sure about Ireland and it would have been her home to return to. So we let someone else pay our mortgage on St Patrick's while we took the chance with our two suitcases and Mossy. This is how I marketed our company after Peter Mayle's refusal to let us use the quote from his book.

"12,000 miles away in the South Island of New Zealand is a little stone chapel which we restored as our home. Due to the distance, visits are infrequent therefore it's important for our peace of mind that we have a reliable company to look after our interests. So here in the Luberon we offer you a similar service and whether it's

*your castle or your cabanon, we will treat it as a sanctu-
ary, because we know what it feels like."*

This little quote was accompanied by a photograph of the
chapel and a list of our services which were mainly cleaning and
organic gardening.

Between Joe Deliso and Camus's garden we were surviving
and with the occasional odd job that Florence Chapouton found
for us, we were hanging in there.

Catherine Camus permitted us to have any produce her garden yielded and she never bothered us other than to tell us to
pick up all the snails before we cut the lawns. She was truly a
naturalist and so rare especially here in the Luberon as we were
to discover.

CHAPTER 77

A letter arrived from the Conseiller General regarding the closure of *L'Ancien Pont Julien*, the bridge I had written to President Jacques Chirac about and my wish had been granted! I was to be the last person to drive over this 2000 year old Roman Bridge. The letter came from Avignon which is the capital of the Vaucluse department and there was I having totally forgotten that I had even written to Mr Chirac. But it was not my first letter to him and the last one had been answered also, although not bearing his signature. Nevertheless, my humble request had not been tossed in the *poubelle* and I had no idea where this event was going to lead me. On the morning of the official closure, the bridge was alive with journalists, photographers and cameramen and across the way was the new bridge with a red white and blue ribbon ready to be cut just after I made my crossing. Crates of Champagne were stacked around the reception table as the cameras flashed like lightning and history was being recorded with the same enthusiasm as the final stages of the *Tour de France*.

After crossing to the other side of Pont Julien, the municipal workers were placing huge boulders with a JCB and from that day forward it was to be used solely for cycling, walking or horses.

Only two of the stone bridges built by the Romans still exist in the Vaucluse. One is in Vaison, the second being Pont Julien, located in the township of Bonnieux, eight kilometres from Apt and three from Lacoste. The Pont Julien is where the Via Domitia, the ancient Roman road linking northern Italy to Spain, crossed the Calavon River. The river narrowed here and the rocky outcrop provided a natural base from which to build such a bridge.

The name Pont Julien refers to the Imperial family, the Julii and the city of Apt originally called Apta Julia, built during the reign of the Emperor Augustus.

The bridge was built in a course of large stones and spans sixty-eight metres, with three semi-circular arches of unequal size. The two end arches are smaller than the middle arch and the top has a distinctive hump-backed shape at the point of the keystone. The Pont Julien is the best preserved example of Roman bridge construction in Europe and the Luberon National Park was wise to build another crossing over the Calavon River.

On the day of my final pass over, I was somewhat ashamed of my countrymen and the state they have left the river in. Just up the N100 in the direction of Apt, is the biggest fruit factory in the EEC, owned by Kerry Gold Ireland. They process all the regional produce and the cherry orchards of Provence are now known as 'Kerry Orchards'.

Last person to cross the 2000 year old Roman bridge known as
Pont Julien

The river was green with their silted pulp waste and an in-quisitive journalist asked what was causing it. I told him that it was just a harmless vegetable dye like the stuff they use in the Hudson on St Patrick's Day in America and because an Irish-man was the last person to cross over the Calavon using the Pont Julien, they dyed it in my honour. His next question was:

"How did an Irishman manage to achieve this?"

I quoted a line from the Alchemist, a magical fable about fol-lowing your dream by Paulo Coelho.

"When you want something, all the universe conspires to help you achieve it."

A plaque was placed on the bridge in English and French and it says:*"We don't know who was first to cross this bridge, but Finn Mac Eoin of Ireland was the last."*

CHAPTER 78

During the celebrations which followed, I got talking to an American who had a Masters in historical preservation. He had been sent over from the US to oversee one of the biggest renovation projects ever undertaken in the Luberon. It was in the village of Lacoste, ancestral home of the Marquis de Sade. His name was Bob Dickensheets and he became as fascinated as everyone else, as to how I managed to get into the history books and I not even living north of the Luberon. When I told him that I was about to go under with a business I had only recently started and was using the crossing as a publicity stunt, he offered me a couple of weeks work, just to boost my confidence, I expect. Well, he succeeded in that and with the excitement of the day's events and the prospects of work from Bob at the American College in Lacoste, we decided to celebrate.

Living in the Luberon is in some ways, a Hillbilly lifestyle and one tends to get cabin fever from the incestuous monotony and claustrophobic attitudes which are village life.

Everyone gossips from dawn to dark and the constant character assassinations are reminiscent of putting people in the stocks. So it is necessary to get away from it as often as possible and for us the therapy was Aix-en-Provence which was just a thirty minute drive from Lourmarin. Aix is an old Roman settlement and claims some of the finest fountains in France. One in particular is on the famous *Cour Mirabeau*, the main street of the city. Aix is a student city and along the *Cour* in summer they parade themselves like the prostitutes in Amsterdam. It is the biggest brothel in France and it is said that if you can't find a woman in Aix, your chair's the wrong way round!

We went to the movies and then to *La Grillon* where all the intellectuals of the city congregate. Inside is a life-size painting of Fredrick Mistral, the Nobel literature winner and while I was waiting for Caron to come back from window shopping, the sound of thunder brought on the inspiration to write the following poem.

Sound Barriers
Invisible fault lines in the sky,
Where noise is discriminated
Against, behind pales of silence.
Thunder lives there.

Just as I was about to put my fountain pen in my pocket, a man at the next table said:

"It's not often one sees people using fountain pens these days."

I was writing with a Mont Blanc pen, a wedding present and constant companion, I never went out without it and people were constantly fascinated by its elegance. The gentleman was English and it is a rare day that they will initiate a conversation. I got to talking and he told me that he had a place in the region and he offered me a job at his house in St Maxime doing maintenance and guardianship. It was nice enough of him, but after working for Cruella and Whispering Grass, I had enough of the Brits and there was no way I would ever again go within a donkey's roar of them in a working capacity. So I declined his offer. He finished his coffee and left. Just then a Frenchman rushed over to my table and asked:

"*Puis-je emprunter votre plume, monsieur?*"

Thinking that he was just going to write some young lady's telephone number, I had no problem but he ran off down the *Cour Mirabeau* and for a minute I thought he had nicked my pen. But the woman at his table assured me not to worry. I kept my eye on him nevertheless. He caught up with and stopped the Englishman I had just been talking to. No doubt he was after the guardian job at St Maxime, he must have overheard our conversation.

They spoke for a while and the Frenchman handed the man my pen and he appeared to write down his details. Arriving back with my Mont Blanc and a big smile on his face, he went first to the lady at his table and showed her the inside flier of a book he was carrying and she said, "Bravo!" so I assumed he had got the job.

He brought back the pen and showed me also what was written in his book. It was Eric Clapton's signature, with a fish hook scroll underneath and in my green ink!

When Caron came back and I related the story she said that I was telling porkies and how could I not recognise Eric Clapton, everyone knows him.

It is true no doubt, but like they say about Woodstock:

'If you can remember it you weren't there,' I had missed Clapton during my thirty years of darkness which was brought to me by Guinness. I have related this story many times to people and am always asked the same question;

"If you had known it was Clapton, would you have taken the job?"

The answer to that is, If I had known it was Eric Clapton, I would not have been offered the job.

I suppose I can wonder for eternity where my life would have gone had I said yes to Clapton. I resisted the peer pressure on me to contact him and accept his offer after discovering his identity. There are always choices and just as the one I had to make regarding the job at the nudist colony near Forcalquier or looking after the bastide in Auriol, it all comes down to having... 'the wisdom to know the difference.'

All I can say is Clapton gave me an opportunity to work for him without any references or CV's. But after our experience with Cruella and Whispering Grass, I decided, from then on, it is I would be requesting references from my employers if they were English!

So instead of St Maxime chez Clapton, we would have to be content with being guardian for Jean in Lourmarin and working in Lacoste.

CHAPTER 79

Neither of us had ever been to Lacoste and having thought that Lourmarin was the most beautiful village in Provence, we were pleasantly surprised to discover that there could even be one better!

Lacoste made Lourmarin look like a wet kitten by comparison and one would work there for nothing it was so incredibly beautiful. In fact, the locals say that the village has so much charm, that Bonnieux was built as a spectator's platform simply to admire the village across the valley. Pierre Cardin had only recently bought Chateau de Sade stating on his website that Lacoste was the most beautiful village in Provence and added, 'possibly the world.'

Well, it was here that we landed and it was our first job north of the Luberon, which seemed far more classy than the south. The Luberon Mountains separated Lacoste from the constant influx of 'Techno Type' day-trippers from Marseilles who crossed from Bouche du Rhone to the Vaucluse at the bridge outside Cadenet, not far from Lourmarin. These criminal classes have in many ways changed Lourmarin from what was an idyllic village, to a crass caterer to the masses and its soul has migrated across the mountains. While we lived in Lourmarin we had come to accept that this was all there was, but Lacoste because of its geography had escaped the Costa del Sol mentality we had been enduring. The drive north out of Lourmarin to Lacoste is through a gorge and it had bandits operating freely up until 1920. It was the winding road which kept the hooligan element within the confines of Lourmarin where not a day went by but incidents of theft, burglary or grievous bodily harm were reported at the local Gendarme. They even spoke of having vigilantes on patrol there, or 24 hour CCT all around the village. We were fortunate not to be living in the actual village of Lourmarin.

Lacoste was a totally different story and the more well-heeled tourists who could afford the time, could be seen meandering through the cobbled streets in a carefree environment.

Lacoste or *La Costa* which is the original Provencal name for the village is a safely guarded secret and little is ever mentioned about it in the tourist brochures. This is the village policy and keeping it undiscovered is not a difficult task. When it became common knowledge that I was writing a book about our life in France since coming here, I was asked by several of the villagers not to write about Lacoste. I assured them that my writing was not likely to cause them any reason to be distressed as I had come to accept what my wife had said about the book.

Pierre Cardin and Finn Mac Eoin. The text on the T-shirt in French and English is a quote from Einstein and reads *"Great Spirits have always encountered violent opposition from mediocre minds"*

CHAPTER 80

Most people coming to Lacoste expect to find an industrial zone fabricating clothing for the Lacoste range and this misconception is exaggerated by the presence of Pierre Cardin, whom many assume owns the crocodile brand.

Crocodile Tears
Creases on the mountain
Bonne Coiffe, Cardin-ated
With Parisian flair
Pompiers comb the hills,
Summer heat and pestilence
Is rife. The Marquis de Sade
Enjoys the view, Bonnieux in
Full sun swelters. Hell fires, ha-ha!
From Lacoste in evening shade

Rene Lacoste was the worlds top ranked tennis player in the years 1926/7. He was a very tenacious player and once he got his teeth in the game, there was no letting go hence his nickname, 'le crocodile.' A friend of his drew a crocodile that was embroidered on his blazer which he wore on the courts - it became a focal point for all the newspaper photographs which went worldwide. Monsieur Lacoste was approached by a Parisian couturier seeking permission to use both the name Lacoste and the crocodile logo. This was to be the first time in history that a brand name was to appear on the outside of a garment and so, Lacoste was born.

It is rather ironic though, that Pierre Cardin, (the Lacoste brand's biggest opposition) ends up owning the most prestigious building in the village of Lacoste!

I had a *coup de foudre* when I saw Lacoste for the first time and as much as I loved Lourmarin, my affection for the place proved superficial and the desire to leave it became all the more acute. But I would have to continue with the humble pie, because Lacoste was not available, and even if it was, we would never be able to afford it. All the upper half of the village was belonging to S.C.A.D., the Savannah College of Art and Design. This college, which is based in Savannah South Georgia is the biggest art college in the world, hosting 9,000 full time students. Lacoste is their European campus where between 60 and 80 students come on 10 week semesters four times a year.

Again, people wonder how on earth did an American College end up in the Luberon, owning virtually half of the most picturesque village in France. I asked myself that very same question.

After the war, many a Provencal village was abandoned and in Lacoste there were only ten *Lacostoises* on the Register of Electors in 1950. A lack of work had driven people away to Avignon, Marseille and Paris. The houses were stripped of their roofs to avoid taxes and in the years that followed, they became ruins. Many of them were gifted away and many more sold for as little as the price of a fridge in America at the time. An American with vision came in the seventies and bought up the upper half of Lacoste. His name was Bernard Pfreim and he had a dream to fulfil which was to start a college for underprivileged American children where they could study art and experience French culture in what he described as 'the last step to Heaven.'

Pfreim ran the college until the late nineties and after his death it changed hands several times before being taken over by S.C.A.D. Bob Dickensheets was the man who pitched the idea to Paula Wallace, the President of SCAD. President Wallace created an empire in the city of Savannah and it was as a result of her dream that SCAD has grown from only four students to nine thousand in less than thirty years. The village of Lacoste was currently going through a renaissance and hence an opportunity arose for Caron and I to work there.

I will never forget our first day on the job when Bob gave us a whole bathroom to plumb in.

"But Bob," I said weakly, "I'm not really a plumber."

To which Bob replied:

"I'm off to America for two weeks and when I come back you will be!"

At the onset he said two weeks, so no matter what we did we were going to get paid, but the idea of plumbing in a complete bathroom and toilet in that time was asking a bit much of us.

We worked every available minute and what we found most confusing was the fittings and which ones to use, but we managed it and by the time Bob got back we were on to other things around the campus. From then on we were appointed as the resident fixer-uppers and gardeners. I had been under the illusion that gardening was just about weeding and watering and when I was being asked on a regular basis the names of different plants, I had no other option than to say that I had learned all my Horticulture in Latin. My most favoured name, when I was stuck, was *"tricuspideria-lanciolata"*, not only did it cover for my lack of knowledge, it made me seem highly intelligent. I often heard people say:

"He is truly amazing, that Finney, he even knows Latin!"

If they only knew, I couldn't tell a daisy from a dandelion. But the Lacoste gardens were established and our task was mainly the upkeep. Going home every night to Lourmarin after a day in north Luberon was like going back to school after the holidays and we lusted after a house in Lacoste but nothing much ever came on the market there and if it did, it was quickly snapped up by the American College which was expanding its portfolio.

CHAPTER 81

Maitre Manet, our notaire from Cucuron contacted us and advised us of a definite date for the elusive *Acte de Vente* for the old mill at Fer a Cheval.

Our dream of owning a place was becoming a reality and even though we had changed our affections from south to the north Luberon, beggars can't be choosers. The three-year wait for the cabanon would be worth it. Living with Jean was becoming tiresome and contrary to our initial assumption that he would have been more often in Paris, this was not the case. We were forever at his beck and call and after nine months with Cruella and Whispering Grass, then 3 years with Jean we had had just about enough of being treated like serfs.

The morning of the signing at Cucuron, we were approached by a local farmer who asked us if we were interested in selling the *Compromis de Vente* before signing the *Acte*. In other words, we would be selling our right to buy and he would continue with the purchase in his own name. This seemingly was a practice in France and apparently quite often in Paris people just sign for properties and sell on their rights before the three-month period is up. Why the sudden interest in our land had us wondering but as it was Frank who had found it for us we would not have liked to let him down. So we declined.

Maitre Manet had some bad news for us and we felt stupid for not selling our title to the farmer only a half hour before. As the three owners of the Cabanon were under psychiatric care, they all had to have a judge sign on their behalf in case they fell victim to swindlers.

Two of the judges turned up, but the third could not show because the young lady (one of the three owners) had gone missing. So, Maitre Manet said that the *Acte* could not be signed. Is this Irish luck or what I said. A nation-wide search was launched for the young lady and posters were placed in every Gendarmerie across the land.

We had been naive to think that things happened at a similar pace as they did in some of the other countries we had lived in, so we decided to just let nature take its course regarding the whole affair.

CHAPTER 82

North of the Luberon was becoming more and more our source of survival and even though Lacoste was lacking in the commerce of Lourmarin, it had that certain charm about it. It was for a start, a south facing perched village which gives every house the morning sunlight.

Across the valley lies the village of Bonnieux, another perched village, but unfortunately it is north facing and takes the full force of the Mistral. It was the Romans who named this wind *Magistralus* (Majestic) and they, who bowed to nobody, were often forced to remove their head-gear in its presence.

It is not commonly known, but Lacoste is the only village in the Luberon that doesn't suffer from the Mistral. In fact, there is an area in Lacoste on the famous rue Basse known as *'petit Nice'*, and on a day when the Mistral blows, one can leave a candle alight on the street without seeing a flicker.

Down in the valley between Lacoste and Bonnieux, lies a rather large old farm with *dependances* which is known as the *Maison Basse*. This was once the stables of the Marquis de Sade and had just been purchased by the American College.

One day while dumping some materials there, I found a book by an English author named James Cleugh, entitled 'The Marquis and the Chevalier'. The Marquis was of course, de Sade and Leopold Von Sacher-Masoch, the Chevalier. The book, which was published in 1951, had a hard back black cover and must have been used as a candle holder by its last owner, Bernard Pfreim, the original founder of the college at Lacoste. Pfreim had written on the inside flier, *Professor Bernard Pfreim, Lacoste, Vaucluse, France.* It was the candle grease, which covered one complete side of the book, that had saved it from the elements, how long it had lain in the long grass was a mystery. My discovery seemed fated and an obligation to read it was without question. Up until then, my knowledge of the Marquis de Sade was no different to that of the masses. I knew his name had created an adjective, as indeed had his friend Masoch(ism), just as Plato(nic), Machiavelli(ian) and another Frenchman, Chauvin(ism), are some of the more common name-adjectives. If one were to ask a hundred people on the street what they knew of de Sade, ninety-nine per cent will all tell you the same thing, he was a murderer and a sadist. Incidentally, according to my Roget's Thesaurus, the synonum given for sadist is 'non-conformist'. Being a sadist may not be such a bad thing if one is to look at it in the following context.

The Masochist said to the Sadist:

"Hit me!" and what did the Sadist say?

"No!"

That makes him a pacifist does it not!

So, there I was at the *Maison Basse* where, it is said, lies a body of one of de Sade's victims and on the hill top in front of me the half-restored Chateau with a tower crane pivoting an accusing finger in a 360 degree direction at the world. I saw it as an omen and my quest to pursue the life of this maligned man had just been given a green light. Setting about reading immediately, away from the eye of my managers, I sat in the shade and commenced to discover the truth of De Sade.

It was a sentence on the last page which invited me to read the book again and also to persist in my studies further than simply reading Cleugh's book. James Cleugh had succeeded where everyone else had failed and I, for the first time in my life, overcame my inability to finish a book.

The sentence which captured my attention went as follows:

'The Marquis de Sade did not lead a 'good' life, nor was he a 'good' man; he was, perhaps, nearly a great one.'

So Cleugh, whom I have come to admire, created an unquenchable thirst within me and I genuinely felt and still feel that it was my destiny to pursue without fail, as much information as I could about de Sade. Before I left my bower at the

Maison Basse, I was inspired to write the first of many poems which I attributed to de Sade and indeed to Cardin, who in my mind was doing his bit to vindicate de Sade, though remaining discreet about it. The poem titled Resurrection, speaks of history though still pertinent today in Lacoste; the jealousy across the valley from Bonnieux. Under the guidance of Cardin and Paula Wallace, the President of the Savannah College of Art and Design, who were in the process of regenerating this once ruined hilltop, Lacoste was becoming the gem of the Luberon.

Resurrection
Up from ancient ruins
In phoenix flight
Domaine de Sade
Appeared before my
Very eyes. Stone by
Stone, their Titan feat,
Rose and rose beyond
A dream, where lark and
Passing clouds can meet.
Now, a beacon, on this once
Lacoste'd hill.
Has far off Bonnieux put to
Shame and soon the moon it will.

Dedicated to Paula Wallace and Pierre Cardin

CHAPTER 83

Yes, Lacoste was being rebuilt and no expense spared as both Wallace and Cardin in harmony with the regional architects and historic places trust, were carefully and painstakingly taking on a huge historic preservation contract.

S.C.A.D. even created a specific course on stone preservation and sent their experts over from South Georgia to oversee this mammoth task. Students eager to see Provence and of course Lacoste, were soon flocking here and this previously dead village was being resuscitated with a new energy. The villagers were also benefiting from the employment being generated. Some lucky locals hit the jackpot, because when they put their properties on the market at Parisian prices, there seemed to be no questions asked and even old ruins were being snapped up. I was watching all of this and thought it would be a wise move to try and find something there before the bubble burst completely and so I contacted Pascal Danneau who is a real estate agent in Gordes.

Cardin's Note to Finn

I had previously met him at a college *vernissage* and he had a good aura about him, not like some of the agents I had met in other countries; the tyre-kicking, failed car salesmen types who had no scruples whatsoever. Danneau impressed me and as I was a novice in a foreign market, I needed a dependable agent. For us, there could be no error of judgement, because the slightest mistake and we would be moving back to Ireland with cap in hand and going on a council list for at least two years, while in the meantime living in some poxy damp flat and lamenting Provence or even New Zealand, at a push.

So we asked Monsieur Danneau if he could find us a property with a garden in the village, everyone's aspiration. He was positive and told us,

"Everything is possible in Provence."

Our dream of owning the old cabanon in Cucuron was slowly fading although Maitre Manet our *notaire* said that the owners were tied into a binding agreement and could not sell to anyone else but us. Not a very reassuring proposition, but at least we didn't have much money invested in it other than the ten per cent deposit.

Remaining guardians for Jean might well be our lot and despite not approving of his practices, it was an idyllic setting. George and Florence, who had found us the place, came by frequently walking the donkeys en route to collecting firewood and in summer, if we were not there, they'd often leave a bag of vegetables by the door or an invitation to their home for lunch.

We could never leave the estate empty overnight because our contract with Jean stated that we had to be permanent residents and as we were working for our keep, it was extremely inhibiting to be working full time plus fulfilling our guardian obligations. Jean had the house valued for rent by an agent and we were basically paying market rates, plus being confined to barracks on top of it. As guardian positions went, it was pretty hopeless, but we were in a difficult situation when we took it on and were happy to be avoiding paying an actual monthly rent.

Caron was the *femme de ménage* (cleaning lady) and that in itself was a pain especially over the dead flies, because Jean hated them, and of course the mice. Now this was a serious problem and there was an infestation of field mice. Jean bought some traps and every time before going back to Paris, he filled and set the traps, but as he was going out the gate I would go over to the house and free them all. He could never understand how the mice were doing it, but he continued and the mouse population was increasing.

As summer approached we were obliged to fill Jean's swimming pool and this was another part of the job which infuriated us. It took a full month with the tap open to the maximum to fill the gigantic pool and here we were in the Luberon of Pagnol's Jean de Florette, where people had died over water shortages. It was disgusting and I had no respect for Jean's decisions and why we had to empty it in September, I will never know.

Caron was getting fed up with living in tents, building sites and now being a bell-hop for Jean so when a ruin came up for sale in the village of Cucuron, we decided to take a punt as getting a place in Lacoste was unlikely and the cabanon purchase at Fer a Cheval had gone on for years. The ruin was affordable though with only 3 walls standing, needed lots of work. Going through the motions of getting a *permit de construire* is a nightmare in France and despite being assured at the point of purchase that this building was eligible to be rebuilt, there were still a lot of loose ends to be tidied up. It appeared that there was a cave under the ruin and it belonged to a neighbour, therefore an engineer's report was necessary before we could even consider moving forward. It looked like we were never going to get out of Jean's and at the same time, just as Claude regretted buying the house in Tuscany, we regretted buying the ruin in Cucuron. But, like everything else that was occurring in our lives, yet another divine intervention came to pass.

The phone rang. It was the agent in Cucuron and she said the landowner behind our ruin was thinking of expanding his house and was interested in buying our acquisition. We arranged to meet him at the Café Ormay in Lourmarin. His proposal was interesting and the offer of considerably more than we had purchased it for seemed too good to refuse, so we accepted. We were speculators at last!

But the luck did not end there, Pascal Danneau called only days later and said he had found a *maison de village* in Lacoste with exceptional views, lots of light and a garden to die for. The price was 200,000 euros. Could we manage such a sum, our total capital being a mere 40,000 euros, after paying back the loan on the ruin?

We spoke with Pascal and he said he would explore every avenue of possibility to help us achieve our dream home. It was on the Rue Basse, in the area known as *petit Nice* where the Mistral has never ever huffed or puffed.

Pascal made a rendezvous for us and the house was indeed a charming proposition. It was an old *epicerie* and therefore purpose-built with generous windows and looking virtually due south with a car park on the east side giving it even more light than any village house we had seen. There was a woman renting it who had been there for the previous eighteen years who was apparently looking for money to get out as the owner refused to sell it to her. She was there when we visited and her presence and the general filth in which she lived, were doing the sale no justice. The house had been totally neglected and virtually everything needed to be re-done but at least it had 4 walls. Pascal brought us to the window and pointed to the valley at what must surely be the most fantastic garden in Provence and he jokingly said:

"Finn and Caron, this is the garden I was referring to!"

The garden was belonging to Alex Dingwall Main the author of 'The Luberon Garden' and even though it was a ways off, it was certainly a sight to behold and believe it or not, the garden had a big influence in our decision. So we signed subject to finance, and once again the Americans came to the rescue.

After going to the first bank we were told that due to being self employed as a gardener / handyman, our chances of a loan were nil. The manager explained that if I had a regular contract with some company we would be better placed. I spoke with my American College people and they said that they would write me a letter stating that I would have permanent work as long as the college existed and this is what achieved the loan for us.

CHAPTER 84

It was springtime, and the last chapter in our south Luberon life story, since we were moving over the mountain to Lacoste, was at last a reality.

Jean was in the process of looking for a replacement and the French couple he accepted stated emphatically that under no circumstances would they work on Saturday or Sunday. This of course is par for the course with the French and yet they are forever complaining about the foreigners buying out houses from under them. I have worked seven days a week all my life, and it is many a time and oft I have been berated by the French for my disregard of the holy day.

Nicholas Sarkozy in his election campaign stated that he wanted to see every French person owning their own homes and he implied that he was going to stop the wholesale exodus of natives from the beautiful villages of France.

How would he go about that, one might ask, because as long as the French were under the illusion of living in Utopia and working as little as possible, then the statistic of one of the lowest home ownership countries in Europe would continue to exist.

Des étrangers, sont contents de voir les Francais en profitent de la joie de vivre and while they are out there doing it, they will continue to buy up their villages! This is the price they pay for Socialism.

" Socialism can be cured
Prescriptions are for sale
At your nearest Lottery outlet ".

Not long after we moved to Lacoste, I met an Englishman who was adamant that there were too many French in the village and he envisaged another Dordogne in The Luberon.

Moving out of Jean's was an easy task, as we only had a one-bedroom apartment and all our furniture had been acquired or found in the Lourmarin *déchetterie* (dump). Our only client on the south of the Luberon was Catherine Camus and she presented Caron with a wonderful going-away present, the original prayer stool *(prie-dieu)* which her father Albert brought back in the fifties and she gave me Camus' Bicycle which is hanging on my bedroom wall. Every day as we went to work in Lacoste, we were also taking a load of furniture across the mountain and one day, we never returned.

We even took Ziggy, our in-house mouse who had lost the bottom half of his right rear leg in one of Jean's traps. He would certainly have been killed if we had left him behind and even though he could not climb anymore, he was not such a pest, but Jean had no nature. Releasing him north of the Luberon was a humane act and I hope he is still there zig-zagging around Lacoste.

The house on Rue Basse needed a full make over but we had plans and the end product was vivid in our minds. The day we had come to look at the house originally, there were plenty of others toying with the idea of purchasing it, but the filth and dirt of the resident put many potential buyers off. We had no idea that people could have lived in such unhygienic conditions. The toilet pan was leaking into the basement and years of silt had built up in the evacuation pipes of the kitchen and bathroom. There was no heating and the fireplace was back-venting and unusable. A health inspector would have closed it down and our early days were spent cleaning the grime off door handles and ceilings, just to make it habitable. Are the French a filthy lot, or, were we just misfortunate to have found three houses in succession that were only suitable for horror scenes in Calcutta? Bono Bono, who had only ever lived at Jean's property, refused to come into the house on Rue Basse and took to sulking and wanting to sleep on the doorstep and he had to be forced indoors every night for a week until his spirit was broken. Foxies are strange and it is only people who have had one who can understand the complexities and sensitivities of their minds. You can command most dogs, but one has to negotiate with a Foxie!

Living and working in the village had its advantages, but living in and renovating a house at the same time is a virtual impossibility, especially when it was going to be a major conversion. Three walls to be removed on the ground floor, one to be relocated and four walls to be removed on the top floor. The basement also had to be totally gutted. Our plan was to continue to live in the upper house and finish the basement so we could move down there and then attack the top two floors. Fortunately one does not, as yet anyway, need permission for interior work in France. So we were able to get on with it as soon as we moved in. Frank from Lourmarin came over frequently by bicycle to help me with the heavy work like demolition and if it were not for our neighbours, the job would have been finished in double quick time.

We had the misfortune of living next door to some angry amphibian xenophobes and they were making our lives a misery. We were told that they wanted to buy the house, but the owner refused to sell it to them and so, we were seen as not only foreigners, but the people who deprived them of this spectacular location. So I had to try to be mister nice guy because I wanted to get planning for a balcony on the exterior of the house, which needed the consent of the regional architect, since the Luberon is a national park. This was paramount to making the house one of the finest in the village after Sir Tom Stoppard's and Pierre Cardin's Chateau de Sade.

Unexpectedly, Caron was asked if she would join Pascal and his real estate team.

Pascal was an up-front agent, young and dynamic, a man going places. So much was it apparent, that not long after Caron joined his company, he was approached by Sotheby's of London, they had chosen his agency out of all in the Luberon to represent them in the region.

It meant a huge lifestyle change for Caron and of course there was a lot of expense to get set up. Our 1980 Volkswagen Golf which smelt like a moblie kennel after Mossy and Bono Bono, would have to be got rid of and her gardening clothes upgraded along with a new laptop and the usual extras one needs to become an agent.

She said yes without even thinking and within a week I was doing the work of two people.

Working seven days a week had to be extended to eight and one day on the street outside the house, a neighbour's child said to me:

"Is it true that you never sleep?"

It had become that for sure and with our whacking great mortgage I had no alternative or the "For Sale" sign would be for real. I was like Napoleon, a war on the border and manoeuvring around the Luberon at all hours of day and night trying to keep my clients happy. I had far too much work and as a result of the publicity which followed my crossing of the Pont Julien, my business had rocketed out of control.

There is an old saying, 'If you want a job done, ask a busy man', and amid all the turmoil of moving and renovating, I came up with an invention which I patented.

The Puppet Bucket, a device for the construction industry which would enable *maçons* to discharge rubble from any floor height to a container or skip on the street without the use of a second person to empty it on the ground. It is a very simple idea and the patent attorney in Marseille said he was surprised that it had not been thought of before. Working for the American college permitted access to a creative invention course and the professor used my idea as a work study program for the students. Their task was to find the most intelligent way to present my patent. All the permutations were explored until the ultimate design was found and finally, I was after achieving a lifetime ambition, that of becoming an inventor. It was while I was renovating the house and being on my own most of the time that the concept of the Puppet Bucket was born out of necessity, as are most good inventions.

Not a day passed when somebody wouldn't ask:

"Where did you buy that?" and up until then I assumed it was just another practical device that would be dumped after the job was over.

But would the job ever be over was the question.

CHAPTER 85

BonoBono our impediment-ed dog was becoming as well known as myself in the village and some of the locals maintained that, *"Le chien est comme son maitre, un peu bizarre."*

Someone even posted a metal plate one night on our door, ATTENTION, CHIEN BIZARRE and it remains there to this day.

He is certainly a character and everytime I stop the van he runs off up the street barking his head off and on returning he jumps up and tries to savage my boots so I am forced to climb the ladder attached to the back door of the van for accessing the roof. This occurs fifty times a day if I stop that often. I have no idea what it all means, but after a couple of minutes it all calms down and he hops back in the van and plays with his balls.

Dan Adel, our resident village artist decided that Lacoste needed a magazine or journal, to record the eccentric behaviour of some locals and BonoBono was the first dog to be featured. The magazine would be known as 'The Fig Bone'. It is bilingual, the French title being 'L'Os de Figue'. The expression derives from the game of *boules*, when after a day of solid *Pastis*-drinking, a player's ball goes off in some unexplained tangent, the mishap is accounted for by saying:

"Ah, il a frappé un os de figue!" that is, he hit a fig bone.

True, in autumn when the leaves fall the fig leaf has a rather sinewy skeleton which lies around the *boules* courts, but in fact it is a tongue-in-cheek expression and basically means that Pierre or Philippe or whoever was as pissed as a fart and lost sight of the marker and sent the *boule* on an orbital route around the target.

CHAPTER 86

Dan Adel in the initial copy of the FigBone featured a few of my poems. My reputation for writing poetry crossed the Luberon with me and soon after arriving here, I was declared 'Poet Laureate' of Lacoste. To some it might sound a very prestigious title, but when one considers that there are only 470 people on the register to vote, it's not exactly a Ted Hughes type Laureateship. But nevertheless, there was a knight of the British Empire living here at the time and he was by no means an average writer. Sir Tom Stoppard had not even been considered for the position and in some ways I felt as though I was an impostor. Mister Tom had been living here some 12 years when I arrived, but we did eventually co-write a poem together.

It was an inspiration from Mister Tom's garden which was just under the Chateau de Sade, looking out across the Luberon Valley to Bonnieux. On a winter's day when we had a fall of snow, I was seduced by the silence and the vast blanket of pure white snow under a blue blue frosty Provencal sky. The sun at this time of year only came up for a brief inspection. Lacoste and the Luberon Mountain lay undisturbed in the foetal position with erotic curves pronounced by the contours and ravines of this optically attractive hillside that even De Sade wrote about. My poem was a metaphorical serenade to this ice lady who for the previous year summoned my attention on many an occasion. But no matter how I tried, I never managed to title the poem and as I was working for Sir Tom as his security man, I thought, why not ask him if he could read it and see if he could unlock my stalemate

Here is the poem with Mister Tom's suggested title, which I duly accepted.

The International Library of Poetry

Virgin Bride

White frocked virgin earth,
conceal your imperfections
before the light of sun
demands to see within the

chastity of your gartered lace.
Toss your snow dropped bouquet
to the blizzard wind and mock
the innocence of its confettied waste.
Then smile mischievously at all
the season's suitors you have graced.

Finn Mac Eoin (Title by Sir Tom Stoppard)

So I gave him the poem and he perused over it for a couple of days and decided that it could well be called 'Virgin Bride'. Sometime later, I entered the poem in a competition and it won first prize. Mister Tom and I shared the copyright, but one could never truly ascertain if Sir Tom Stoppard's name had not been associated with it, would it have done as well ?

Chapter 87

There appeared an article in the Fig Bone entitled: "Bono-bono to go into Therapy".

This was the headline which launched our dog into stardom and even though the content of what the editor wrote about him was true, it was a light-humoured article and not to be taken seriously.

But as Omar Khayyam so wisely said about the written word:

'Nor all your piety or wit can lure it back to cancel half a line, nor all your tears wash out a word of it.'

Give a dog a bad name, yes, Bono Bono was typecast and not long after the Fig Bone was launched, on the front page of 'La Provence', the regional paper, the Mayor's office sent out a dog warning all around the village.

"*Avis des Chiens. All dogs from now on to be tethered and free roaming is outlawed.*" Raymond, our village Gendarme would be enforcing the law and any dog caught in disobeyance would be taken to the pound with a fine of 100 euros. Also, all dogs had to have a contact number on their collars, and it was all because of this following article.

'Bono-bono, of the Rue Basse has let it be known through a spokesperson that he will be undertaking both anger management and a behavioural modification course of psychotherapy beginning in the fall. His frequent and unprovoked outbursts of barking and his particularly violent reactions to sounds such as clapping or laughing have led him and his owners to acknowledge the possibility of either substance-abuse or unresolved issues from puppyhood, both of which will be addressed in the therapeutic context'.

The humour of this piece must have been lost on who ever translated it for the Mayor's office and as a result, not only did Bono Bono become a local to be viewed with suspicion, it also brought *le maitre* (myself) into the limelight.

Even The Gladiator, the great Russell Crowe who was featured on the same page of *La Provence*, had reservations about Bono Bono.

He was in Lacoste filming 'A Good Year' directed by Ridley Scott who lives just over the hill in Menerbes or 'Men Are Bees' as the American tourists call it. I met Crowe on the street while I was watching the Equinox through a welders helmet and a tap on the shoulder asking if he could also take a look was our introduction. A conversation ensued and it transpired that he was from the same part of Wellington in New Zealand as my wife. He invited us to his concert and to a behind-stage private party later on. I brought him a bottle of *'Poteen'*, illicit Irish whiskey which I had smuggled through customs as Holy Water from Knock where the last Irish Virgin appeared. Crowe was no stranger to Ireland and was a personal friend of Richard Harris, whom in many ways he resembles as a character.

Between filming and hanging out in Bonnieux where he was living during the shoot, we met him in Gordes with his child and of course, we had Bono Bono who was off his lead.

Bono Bono got into one of his rages and Russell Crowe decided that without Gladiator armour, this psychopathic canine was best left in the arena alone. Perhaps he read or heard about the Fig Bone article and thus his cautious retreat.

Imagine the headlines if Bono Bono attacked the child:

"Irish Fox Terrier-ist attacks Baby Crowe", just what we needed to be run out of Lacoste.

The Mayor of Bonnieux was quick off the mark when he heard that Russell Crowe's wife had conceived in the Priory, (a hotel in Bonnieux) and the foetus was given the keys of the village. Yet, the proprietor of the Priory was overheard one night telling Crowe to go find a pizza if he was not satisfied with his dinner. Crowe apparently had made a complaint about what he had been served and the hostess was having no bar of The Gladiator's remarks.

Chateau Carnogue, where the film A Good Year is set, is an organic vineyard and the publicity was certainly going to make a big impact on sales of this apparently wonderful wine. I had occasion to take a tour there once and at the tasting, I was asked why I was not participating. The French have no concept of alcoholism and one may as well be telling them that you are suffering from 'Slapadictomy'. Most people in France think that alcoholism is an Anglo-Saxon disorder and that the French are exempt or immune. It is like being a vegetarian, when you go into a restaurant and tell them you are one they will bring you fish or chicken. Same with alcohol.

"Je ne bois pas d'alcool, madame." And they will pour you a glass of wine as they don't consider it alcohol. The only thing they understand is diabetes and that works every time, but it means no dessert!

CHAPTER 88

As Laureate of Lacoste, I had the occasional request for a poem in French, but as the region was becoming more and more Anglophone, most poems were in English and here is one I was asked to write for the label of the Chateau La Canorgue.

Wine
And as the gaiety of
Life is spilled,
Our inhibitions are at
Once unwilled
Then what of morn, should
All of night be chaste!
The wine has gone and
But the hourglass filled.

'Assimilating into Provencal life is not to be recommended and the least one has to do with the locals, the better.' Anon.

This is written on the wall of the quarry behind the Chateau.

What I can add to this quote is, one would certainly be better off not letting locals into too many aspects of one's private life, and the poorer they think you are the better they will like you. The French love their Socialism and poverty becomes them.

But I took no notice of the message on the rocks and got right into the hearts and minds of the *Lacostoises* so much so that apparently, not long after arriving I had become a prime-time topic of conversation. Being Irish helps of course and once the French have sifted one out from the Brits, it's plain sailing. My friend Joe Patch from Ireland used to say:

"I'd rather be black than British!" and Joe lived in South Africa for years.

Being Irish is a carte blanche for almost anything, and anyone Irish will have noticed that all we need to succeed in life is our humour and of course 'the Blarney.'

Druid Chefs
Where west, each wind is born
Mischievous 'Gaels' with pots
Of vapoured broth, disperse it's
Brew and laced with ancient portents,
Concoct a drape to cloak the Saxon horde.

The wind is with us and even here in France, the French have not forgotten the Irish regiments that wiped out the Brits at the Battle of Fontenoy. And as one of the latter day 'Wild Geese' I never miss an opportunity to remind the French that the greatest tragedy in their history is the Channel Tunnel. Sarkozy was over in England recently trying to improve relations and basically offered them the olive branch for history, while Carla Cosy was employed to try and get the Poms to smarten themselves up.

CHAPTER 89

Every summer in all the French villages there are festivals of differing origins, but fertility, growth and harvest are the basis of them all.

In Lacoste we have a week-long celebration that includes a wheelbarrow race, which incidentally starts outside my house on Rue Basse to the Place de L'Eglise. One is obliged to push somebody and there are two contestants in each heat. In last year's one, as I was the winner, I had had to run five times and I was the oldest contestant. At 55, I was twice the age of any other individual so I was given a reduction in weight due to this. Instead of having somebody in the barrow, I was permitted Bono Bono and an anvil. I sometimes think I was actually penalized as the anvil plus the dog was as heavy as those anaemic French teenagers the others opted for. Bono Bono had to be strapped in due to the article in the previous years Fig Bone where the editor character assassinated him and gave him a bad name. One of the judges even asked to have him muzzled and advised the other contestants to wear elbow length gloves in case of close encounters en route! The street was lined with enthusiastic crowds and as it was the first time that an Irishman and a Terrier-ist were taking part. It attracted even more than previous years.

Bono Bono was fitted with a pair of builder's ear-muffs and sunglasses to isolate his vision in the hope of reducing the barking, but this theory of the three monkeys was quickly disproved. As we rounded the bend for the uphill push past Café de Sade to an applauding mass of spectators, Bono Bono went ape-shit and totally lost the plot, playing into the hands of the editor who said that he was mad and should be put down. For me it was only the start of the drama as I had to contend with it another four times. Caron suggested giving Bono Bono half a Passeflora (a mild organic sleeping pill) to make him drowsy. This was a disaster because someone saw me with the bottle of pills and just as Lance Armstrong was accused of taking drugs, so was I .

On page 6 of *La Provence* dated mercredi le 2 aout 2006, I was hailed as the outright winner with the following inscription under the photo of Bono Bono crossing the line in the fifth and final heat.

'Le pilote et son chien Bono Bono, bien attaché, ont fait un parcours sans faute ni faille!' ran the headline – the driver and his dog Bono Bono well tied in, finished the course without fault.

Before the prizes were given out, I was called into question and accused of using performance-enhancing drugs. Bono Bono had been on his best behaviour for the last three heats and as the reporter observed, he was not even interested in the several cats which we had passed on the way. The journalist was under the impression that the two leads holding him into the barrow, were there to stop him worrying the felines.

Bono Bono has been accused of everything in Lacoste, they even said he was a *pédé*, pronounced paddy (Mutt O'Sexual) as he had been seen on tow by another dog, four-by-two-ing around the Place de La Mairie with a confused grin on his snout.

In the August 2007 edition of the Fig Bone, the editor had a field day reporting the ongoing controversy surrounding our victory.

Here is the headline and article.

Doping Charges Continue to Plague Fête du Village

Nearly a year after the controversial events of the 2006 *Fête du village*, charges of illegal doping continue to work their way through the courts. Finn MacEoin, inventor of the Puppet Bucket, and winner of the *Course de Brouette* has been one target of these enquiries. It is alleged by the *Commission du Doppage dans les fêtes du village*, that:

"There is no conceivable way a 55 year-old man could possibly have wheel-barrowed an anvil and a short-haired

Foxy terrier 200 metres in 34 seconds, out-manoeuvring opponents half his age, without substantial chemical assistance."

A spokesperson for Mr Mac Eoin's legal team of fifteen Parisian attorneys responded to the charges:

First off, the Committee members fail to recognize the extraordinary degree of physical strength and endurance that our client has attained through years of gardening and poetry. But most important, whatever foreign substances may have been in our client's bloodstream at the time of the pre-and post Brouette blood and urine tests, they were only there to enhance his poetic and not his athletic abilities".

It was a dark day when this publication hit the Luberon and not solely due to the embarrassment of the findings, but because on the next column was an article about Bono Bono, which headlined:

Bono Bono Still Bonkers After a Year in Therapy

Bono Bono of the Rue Basse has recently been determined by a panel of canine psychologists to be just as demented as he was at this time last year when they began the first in a series of therapeutic interventions. According to his owner, Finn Mac Eoin, inventor of the Puppet Bucket, he continues to bark wildly at nothing and growl at cute little girls. He's even taken to sending unprovoked hate-mail in which he threatens to file frivolous lawsuits. This comes after spending the last year in and out of a variety of mental health remediation programs, such as Meditation for Mutts, Music Therapy, Canine Cognitive Therapy, Gestalt Therapy, Bark Therapy and even Electro-convulsive Therapy, which though ineffective, did have the side benefit of providing certain neighbours with some measure of Sadistic satisfaction.

Says Mac Eoin: "We haven't given up. There's a program that's just been started in Zurich, called Aromatherapy for Terriers which has been getting rabid reviews. If it doesn't work we will be sending BonoBono to an all dog Ashram near Bombay. There's a very angry puppy lurking deep within Bono Bono's bite-sized brain and we need to soothe and comfort it. Otherwise we'll have to have it surgically removed."

Some people in Lacoste became highly upset that Bono Bono was getting so much publicity. One such family were the owners of Romeo, the black Labrador who lies with his paws facing east just outside Café de France, waiting for short female drivers to run over them. When he is not wearing a lampshade around his neck after being head butted by a bumper, he's seen hobbling around Rue Basse after yet another Jay driver de-gloved him. Personally, I have always felt that Romeo has suicidal tendencies and is a far bigger threat to the villagers than BonoBono, but they seem to have it in for both my dog and I.

Across the road from me lives Titti Truphemus, an anaemic looking Jack Russell whose urine and shite are identical from eating *croquettes*. The family of Truphemus are another lot who complained to the editor of the Fig Bone over the rising status of this *étranger* Bono Bono.

I remember one day when a group of Parisians passed by Rue Basse, and Titti Truphemus (or Blas-phemous as he is often called) attacked their poodle and the Parisians said to Monsieur Truphemus that his dog should be tied up (and thrown over the wall I added under my breath.)

Jacky Truphemus came to Titti's defense saying:

"Mon chien habite ici plein temps et il n'est pas en vacances comme votre chien, il n'est pas un touriste!"

In other words, resident dogs can do what they like, resident French dogs that is and not Bono Bono. It was true, the locals felt that they had some divine right because of their history in the village but were not yet aware that the EEC had not only given our dogs equal rights, they had also been given passports. Titti was never further away than Menerbes and that was when he was a pup and he got lost.

It wasn't until then that I realized the dogs were as parochial as their owners and Bono Bono's well travelled attitudes were being viewed with a jealous suspicion.

But it was not only the handful of Provencaux left in Lacoste who were of this mentality, there were also a lot of Scandanavian, Lutheran and Canadian Calvinists who were afraid of change. One of those was a lady called Marie and she and her followers only lived here part time, never voted here, paid no taxes, and yet they wanted the village to stand still so that they could come and enjoy the peace and patronize the locals. I was in the opposite camp with a mortgage, a business and therefore doing everything in my power to make Lacoste accessible to the tourists. Something that the anti-Christs of the village were totally against. Even the foreigners here are xenophobic of their own kind.

The Village of Lacoste

CHAPTER 90

It was looking more and more like we had finally struck gold and what was about to occur in Lacoste was nothing short of a miracle for us. The American College was still buying property but at a slower rate than that of Pierre Cardin, with his incredible acquisition of virtually anything with commercial potential on the Rue Basse. I contacted my friend Patrick from Dublin and told him to get on down as quickly as possible before the bargains were all snapped up.

Patrick, a businessman to the core, took my advice and bought two houses on Rue Basse and no more than four hours later, Monsieur Cardin was ringing Sotheby's expressing an interest in both of them. He bought one which he is currently converting into a hotel and Patrick's second house which Monsieur Cardin leased, is currently the temporary *Boulangerie* while a new one is being refurbished. Again, Monsieur Cardin bought the old *Boulangerie* and the houses either side of it plus the one across the road apparently offering three times market value for one of them. People were asking why was Monsieur Cardin doing all this at the age of 87?

They are such a jealous and uncompromising lot in Lacoste, what right do they think they have to ask why Monsieur Cardin is buying up the village.

What is going to happen after he dies they asked?

What happened when Henri Ford died- Lee Lacocco took over and made the company even more successful, was my response !.

What happened when Walt Disney died? One could go on ad infinitum.

There was even an element here who accused anyone who sold to Cardin as being traitors. I was at war with virtually everyone in the village and I refused to back down. Napoleon said he never got a soldier from Provence and I was beginning to understand why. The Provencals are not French in the real sense of the word and like their Italian ancestors, an element of 'the Womans blouse.' syndrome exists here.

It was election year and a group of villagers set up a organization to contest the Mayoral elections in order to, as the wife of one of them said to me ; ".... stop Cardin."

A business woman of the village has been quoted on the Slate Magazine as saying,

" I've bought a nice bottle of Champagne to open when I get the news. Cardin is 86. He'll die before I do."

Her remark was supported by the vast majority of the bitter left socialists - marxists - fascists, who contested the local elections.

I was having none of their narrowmindedness and struck back with a poster campaign based on Ned Ludd.

After preparing the text, I hand delivered one to every house in the commune and also posted them around the village. But every morning when I looked, they had been torn down. I persisted as it was obvious that I had struck a raw nerve .

Our car and my van fell victim to their anger and it did not stop there either. All our windows in the basement were smashed. We feared for Bono Bono.

Luddites a Lacoste

Dans le nord d'Angleterre, en 1812, il y eut une revolte tres impopulaire contre le concept de progrés. Ce mouvement était dirigé par un certain Ned Ludd.

Il s'opposait à l'arrivée des métiers à tisser, inventés par Philippe de Girard, un français de Lourmarin (1745 - 1845)

Les members de ce mouvement se firent appeler Les Luddites.

Leur seul but avoué était d'empecher le plus natural des phenomenes, le Changement.

A Lacoste nous avons un groupe de la même facture et dont le seul programme est la chute de Monsieur Cardin et du College Amêrican qui sont tous deux,à mon avis, une force de vie pour notre village.

Ces Luddites Lacostois oublient facilement que notre village est mort une fois déjà.

Aprés la seconde guerre mondiale, par manqué d'emplois L'histoire a l'habitude désagréable de se répeter souvent.

Je ne peux rester là à regarder ces gens a l'esprit étroit, essayer de s'emparer de mon village pour les 6 années évenir.

Ned Ludd était un ignare.

Merci d'avoir lu ce texte.

Finn Mac Eoin - L'Irlandais

The article speaks of Ned Ludd and likens the anti Cardin group to them.

It speaks of Phillipe Girard a Frenchman from Lourmarin who invented the linen machine. The one Ludd and his lunatic followers were smashing.

I also brought attention to the previous decline of Lacoste after the second world war and how without Pierre Cardin and the Savannah College, this village would be dead and possibly abandoned for a second time.

Within days I knew who was who and the funny thing is, I had had my suspicions about a lot of those who had stopped talking to me because we have a saying in Ireland about socialists, they are known as the unhappies.

Some of those who were fit to kill me were the ones who had never achieved anything in their lives nor had they mortgages as they had simply inherited their houses. They were not in the real world.

One of the village *maçons* who is retired and spends most of his life waiting to tell the tourists how evil 'Cardang' is, was outside his house one Sunday during summer and he quoted the following to a group of passers by.

" *Moi! j'étais un maçon pendant toute ma vie. J'ai travaillé dans la pluie, la neige.... cinq jours par semaine pour gagne ma vie. Et Cardang! qu' est-ce qu'il a fait dans sa vie ?*

This is the Provencal mentality, if you are not earning your living by breaking your back and filling your lungs with lime and cement, you are not worthy.

Anyone suspected of using their brains are deemed unfit to live amongst them and Cardang, who at 86 has no right to exercise his *cerveau*. He should have been retired since he was 65 according to their mathemathics.

The foreigners who were opposed to Monsieur Cardin had second homes here and were making their livings in other European capitals. My wife and I were the only étrangers in Lacoste that lived here permanently. Lacoste is a ghost town and in winter everything closes, even the two cafés. I sometimes felt that I had committed another act of self-mutilation and repeated the New Zealand experience. If it was not for the American College, this village could have put up a sign:

'Would the last person to leave please turn off the light!'

While I was in New Zealand I had encountered the Scottish Calvinists and ended up in a long battle there also.

I single-handedly changed the alcohol dry status in an Auckland suburb in 1996, after nearly a hundred years of prohibition and the first liquor outlet in the former dry half of Auckland is called after me. So jazzing up Lacoste was not going to be such a difficult task. Monsieur Cardin's buying spree was creating a media boom, he had an agenda and I was right there beside him, The Pied Piper ridding the rats from the streets seemed to me the only solution to achieving a harmonius atmosphere in "Sinisterville."

259

One family sold their house, which had a market value of 350,000 euros, for 1,100,000 euros and the Luddite Leader called them traitors. Well, the traitors are now living in a wonderful house in the country with two acres of land and they will be smiling ten years after they are dead.

I would sell to Cardin without a thought for patriotism (the final resting place of a scoundrel according to Churchill) but apart from loving my job at the college, I am most interested in vindicating the Marquis de Sade on or before the 200th aniversary of his death in 1814. On the night of the election after we ousted the Luddites, the new Maire, Madame Louche asked me if I would launch this objective on behalf of the village.

Pierre Cardin had already expressed his support and wrote something to that effect on the inside flier of on my book 'The Marquis and the Chevallier', so he knows where I'm at, and Lacoste will have to open its gates and hearts to the memory of de Sade whose last wish to be buried on his own land, which was ignored.

I am planning an exhumation of his remains and a re-burial here at the Chateau in Lacoste and Monsieur Cardin will be fully supportive of my venture.

I was particularly impressed by what Charles Baudelaire said about de Sade:

"The day and century will come when statues will be erected to him in the walls of every city, and when at the base of every statue, sacrifices will be offered unto him."

Could Lacoste be the first city? And just as changing the prohibition laws in New Zealand was perhaps my reason for going there, am I now to assume that de Sade is my latest calling? It certainly seems that way and winning the election was preparing the ground for this eventuality.

There is a lot about de Sade which needs to be set right and one victory already achieved was the removal of an article from a BBC website which had been posted for six years.

A journalist came to Lacoste in the year 2000 and booked into the Café de France where he wrote the following article:

"Here I am in Lacoste, famous for its Chateau and of course the infamous Marquis de Sade. As I look across the valley to Bonnieux, I can see cows making their way to the pastures and on a day when the Mistral blows from the south I can hear their bells chiming in the distance. The Marquis de Sade was executed in Marseilles for murdering prostitutes."

Now, the thing about this article is, number one, there aren't and never were, cows in the Luberon because there is simply no grass here for them. Lyon is the cow line, olive oil from there down and butter from there up. The other thing is, the Mistral blows from the north. But the most damaging statement of all was that de Sade was executed in Marseille. De Sade died at Charenton Mental institution of pneumonia aged 74 in 1814. I wrote a letter to the BBC and said I was a student of de Sade and that I was prepared to take a legal action on his behalf if the article was not rectified.

An apology was received not long after and I was invited to post the current article.

But what one must accept from this is, if in the year 2000 a journalist could be so misinformed and his story go unchallenged during 6 years, then what hope was there for de Sade in the 18th and 19th centuries.

At a concert in the carriere behind the Chateau, which is now an annual summer month long event in Lacoste hosted by Pierre Cardin, I was, by an incredible coincidence, seated beside the current Comte de Sade, Xavier de Sade who now lives in Richelieu. Imagine, nine hundred people allocated seats and I, perhaps the only person in the audience researching de Sade and by some stroke of faith I get placed beside Xavier Comte De Sade.

At the time I was reading 'Sade' by Maurice Lever, who was the most informed of all the biographers of The Divine Marquis. Xavier de Sade was in no doubt of my passion for his ancestor and offered me every possible assistance, including an invitation to his home where he has original copies of de Sade's letters which were literally written in blood due to the authorities prohibiting him ink.

It was ironic really, here I was in Lacoste and only four years earlier I had spent six months working for a museum researching French history and one of my subjects was Napoleon. And now it transpired that it was Napoleon who had de Sade incarcerated at Charenton. De Sade was far saner than Napoleon ever was. But Bonaparte was afraid of de Sade's pen and it was he who denied him ink and thus induced de Sade's self-bleeding to pursue his great passion of writing.

Just along from where I live on the Rue Basse, is a grand Bourgeoise house which was owned until recently by Andre Bouer.

Bouer is as fascinating a character as de Sade and obviously had a lot of respect for him, because Andre Bouer spent almost 40 years restoring the Chateau after he bought it back in the sixties. It was a labour of love and a book published in 1984 by Edisud and written by Henri Fauville, gives an account of the mammoth task which Bouer, a school teacher, undertook. Of course we all know that Pierre Cardin came on the scene and put the finishing touches to Bouer's work, but when one considers the state of the Chateau back in the sixties, it is amazing that anybody had the will to even contemplate restoring it. Most people would have sold it for scrap as was almost the case with the Chateau in Lourmarin back in 1920 before Laurent Vibert came to the rescue. There is always someone to pick up the pieces and I have the greatest admiration for them and having restored an old stone chapel in New Zealand, I suppose I am more sympathetic than many and I can appreciate the passion which motivates these so-called eccentrics who become obsessed by the impossible. The Bouers are decendants of the Vaudois, a Protestant sect which was based in this region. They were hard working and clever people who despite their initial difficulties with being accepted into what was a dominantly Catholic population, made it to the top and ended up being huge landowners. When de Sade lost favour with his fellow aristocrats, he socialized with the Bouers, the Appy's , the Sambuc's and the Pauletts all of whom are still well got in the region.

My friend Patrick bought the Bouer house and with it came an interesting story. On page 73 of the book 'Sade en Provence' there is a photograph of a door, a door which came from the Chateau. Andre Bouer wrote an article entitled 'The Pillage of the Chateau'. Apparently, after the revolution the villagers helped themselves to virtually everything at the chateau including the stones, which they pushed aside and rolled down the side of this perched village. They built houses and furnished them with some of de Sade's private collections. The finer pieces were carried off to Aix and sold. During my research, I found the original bathtub of Donatien de Sade, the Marquis, which had made its way to Paris and is now in a house on Rue de Dames, as ironic as it sounds! But the door of the Chateau escaped the auctioneer's hammer and was fitted to this grand house on Rue Basse. The original key which, de Sade used was still in the lock after all those years.

The door itself has had many interested souvenir hunters and one in particular, a Japanese business man, offered 200,000 francs for it in 1998.

Patrick eventually sold the house to Cardin and as he was more often than not away from France, he made me guardian until Cardin took possession. My wife was acting as interpeter for Patrick who spoke no French and on the day of the signing between Cardin and Patrick at Maitre Bomels, the *notaire* in Bonnieux, I was in Ireland and I forget to tell Caron that the original key was in the safe of Patricks house in Dublin. So the deal was signed and Cardin got the replica key by accidental ommission! What was I to do - I could hardly walk up to the Chateau where Cardin is now living and say:

"Monsieur Cardin, Patrick forgot to give you the original key of de Sade's door!"

But what Patrick did'nt know, was when he asked me to have a duplicate made up, I actually ordered two and the one Patrick had in his safe was a burned and beaten version which looked quite similar to the original.

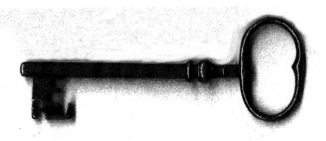

Key of Chateau de Sade

So I said nothing and I still have the original here in the house and I plan to have a museum here one day with all the bits and pieces I have acquired from such people as Albert Camus, Sir Tom Stoppard, Peter Mayle, John Berger, Russell Crowe, John Berger, Lawernce Durell and various other people who have contributed to the collection.

As time passed, Cardin's Lacoste portfolio increased to 35 premises and I only wished he was 30 years younger so that he could have bought up the rest of the village and got rid of the negatives who still remained. There was no doubting it, but Lacoste has a sinister shadow and it was being expressed through some of the residents here. A book published in 1988 entitled 'A Guide to Provence' by Michael Jacobs describes Lacoste with this opening sentence.

'My own experience of Provencal village life is derived mainly from lengthy stays at Lacoste.' He goes on to say:

'The atmosphere was on the whole unwelcoming and slightly sinister.'

This is still very obvious here twenty years on and the *Lacostois* are a jealous and bitter lot who detest anyone who has money or is progressive. By standing still they can hide like trees in the forest. But the octogenarian entrepreneur from Paris has come and shaken them, roots and all and I watch with glee as their little *cul-de-sac* minds are given a long overdue shock treatment. The recent Mayor's election brought everyone's innermost thoughts to the surface. What is it about this place that produces such anger and hatred? Frank who lives in Lourmarin maintains that even the swallows have deserted Lacoste. In some ways what is happening here is just natural evolution and a day will come when it will be soley owned by The Savannah College Of Art and Design and Pierre Cardin and I would contribute to this end by then selling my house to either. For the moment I feel as though I need to be here especially to help in the vindication of de Sade and who knows, perhaps after the Divine Marquis has had his history addressed, then Lacoste might be liberated from the curse that is very obviously engrained even in the mortar that keeps the village perched above the warm Provencal landscape.

Other than Stoppard, de Sade, John Malkovich, Laurence Durell and a one night stand by Picasso, there have not been many famous people here with the exception of Louis Malachier who was a miller and stone mason. Malachier operated the windmill just behind the Chateau. He discovered that there were 28 different winds affecting Lacoste and all were named and positioned inside the mill around the wall. Malachier also custom-made all the chimney pots for Lacoste and apparently not one chimney back-vented. Today, there are none to be seen on the rooftops, but I found a wonderful specimen while gardening and it has been identified by Monsieur Linfors, who is also a stone worker, as an original Malachier.

Louis Malachier was unlike the rest of the villagers and had many interests other than the idle gossip practiced by virtually everyone that lives here. When the Eiffel Tower opened in 1890, Malachier walked from Lacoste to Paris to see it. Long after his death, his work remained in the quarry but one day a professor from the Bard College of Art, who were the owners prior to the Savannah group, took his class to the quarry and they smashed everything in sight. The professor apparently said that demolition makes way for new art. So in effect, I have one of the only known pieces of Malachier's work which avoided the hammers.

Today in Lacoste there are no real characters and the only one who could qualify is an Algerian known as Aristide. He lives a gypsy life-style and has no fixed abode, but works every-day with farmers from spring to autumn. In the village itself he is not recognized as a local and in some ways he is ostracized. Admittedly he has a short fuse when it comes to alcohol, he is one of the only villagers who is able to speak English so he has the advantage of being able to tell them to fuck off without repercussions.

Occasionally when I am going over to Bonnieux I take him and his dog and the proprietor of La Flambe serves Aristide drink, since he is now banned from both the cafes in Lacoste. Recently his dog had twelve pups and for convenience Aristide called them after the twelve apostles, regardless of sex.

Since the litter of pups were born, Caron has become a sur-rogate mother of Aristides dog and buys a large bag of Tuckin Futters once a month though we often wonder if the is dog getting her fair share, because her rib cage is visible both sides. Aristide lives ' Belle Etoile ' (under the stars) but as he is a rag head, I presume that his status does not entitle him to municipal accommodation.

Over the hill in Menerbes I became friendly with Joe Down-ing, a famous artist who came to Europe originally during the Second World War, but like many GI's, he never went back. Joe had pieces hanging in the Louvre and was recognized world-wide. A more understated man you could not meet. He had lived in the house in Menerbes for forty years and one day he took me down to his cellar which had no furniture, nothing except corks on the floor, thousands and thousands of them.

He told me that every wine bottle cork that was ever opened in the house for the past forty years was thrown into that room and they were a half a metre high. Joe said that one day he was going to count them and look for the first one he threw in because he had put the date and time on it. He died just before

Christmas 2008 and when I heard the news I rushed over to see what was becoming of his personal belongings. But a man at the house said that everything was being taken to his native home in America called Horse Cave. So we may never know how many bottles Joe was involved in, but I have made a rough estimate from the area and height of the corks and I would say approximately 40,000. Before he died we visited him and he had an old old dog who was blind, deaf and full of arthritis and everyone said that he should get the dog put down. Joe, who let the dog sleep on his bed said:

'More than heat passes between us and as long as his tail can wag as he sniffs his dinner, there will be no need for such talk as putting him down.'

If it was not for Joe Downing, I would never have known that the painting I discovered in the attic of my house was the work of a famous French artist. When we decided to take the ceilings down in order to give the rooms a more spacious feeling, I found a copy of 'Art Style' by Dunoyer de Segonzac which had an entry by the artist in black fountain pen ink and also signed by him. Joe, who was keen to see our house, came by one day and saw the book on my rubbish bin and he alerted my attention to what he described as the find of the century.

CHAPTER 91

Our house is on three levels, and the lower floor being an old stables, we decided to make it a separate apartment. Because the village is perched our house has entrances on 2 levels, giving the apartment its independence. In France one only needs planning for external work and anything that goes on inside is no business to either the Mairie nor the Parc de Luberon. Personally I think it is the daftest of all French laws, because people take out load bearing walls and put in steel beams which are not nearly as large as they should be. Over a few years they get what is known as metal fatigue and begin to sag, just as those big old wooden beams one sees in country pubs in England. Also, the welded joints can resemble pigeon shit when done by D.I.Y. week-enders who hire machines and learn the art of arc-welding on their first job. The beams are then covered with Gibraltar board and nobody is the wiser. Buying one of these buildings could cost you dearly and believe me I have seen a fair few since coming to France.

But the authorities here make up for their lack of internal control as regards planning by getting one at every corner on the outside. There are ways to beat the system and just as I had to use my initiative to keep my hours up for Jean, I used the same tactics to achieve what I wanted regarding the external renovations of my house here in Lacoste.

Here's how you get around the French Curve without ending up wanting to smack some fossil-faced old fart who should have been sacked a week after taking the job. Let's say you want to put a Velux window on your roof and from experience of other people who have asked, the council will say 'non.' Non is what made Edith Piaf famous, because it was what the people wanted to hear. If she had sung, "Oui, je regrette tous" she would have been thrown back in the gutter she emerged from. Non, is a palindrome and even dyslexic friendly. It is the ultimate word and it requires no imagination to use it. You can say non after oui, but never oui après non and this is what the French excel at. Non is the ultimate negative, just as Socialism is the politics of depression and if you look at the consumption of Prozac in France, then there is NON need to elaborate. It is only those French who are adventurous enough to accept that France is not an island and therefore risk crossing her borders and visiting the *Oui* countries beyond her frontiers, that ever truly comprehend why their national symbol, the Rooster, can stand in the shit and crow about it.

CHAPTER 92

Regarding the Velux, here is what I did. I got up on my roof and glued on an old wooden window that I had picked up in the dump and photographed it. Then I applied to the council to place a Velux and gave the dimension of the existing one. The planning advisor visited and took some photographs and as there was an existing window on the roof, no more questions were asked. You must make things simple for them and remembering that they are only there to complicate your life makes dealing with them easier. They must be made to feel important. A full stop in the place of a comma can cause a hernia to most French *fonctionaires* and the result of such blatant neglect could cause you a three-month stand down period while the said person is treated and returns to work. Dossiers are not interchangeable in France and if a bureaucrat dies while on your case, you can kiss your ass good bye. So it is important not to jump to the first available desk even if your number is called. Make sure you chose someone that looks healthy enough to live three months, because this is the average time it takes a French government agent to say "Oui!" You might have noticed when practicing your French at the mirror that you nearly have to smile to say *OUI* . The French associate smiling with lunacy and by continuously saying *NON*, they convince themselves that despite taking prozac with their saccherine, they are saner than you - you being the foreigner who bought a ruin and everybody knows without doubt that you are a mad bastard who drives on the wrong side of the road.

If you apply for planning for a balcony or terrace, find out what is permitted and ask for more and when they discover that you made an error they will get great joy in telling you off. You must at all costs put in a defect that is easy to find, because if you do everything to norm, they will spend months looking to see if there is anything they can get you on. Misspellings are also an advantage, because that makes them feel superior and they will get great pleasure in giving you a French lesson next time you are summoned to the Mayor's office. Turning up a day before your appointed time will gain you a whole lot of brownie points because the thicker they think you are the less worried they become about you. They love simpletons, especially foreign ones, the ones who buy old mills and pigeonniers, barns and stables. The French have a disdain for anything that is not being used for what it was designed and a recent article I read on " Anal Intercourse " would testify to that.

I managed to get all my planning through and my house on Rue Basse is only a bird call away from the Mayor's office. But as always, the safest place to hide from a spotlight is to sit on top of it.

Or in the case of the tree which has been obstructing our view across the valley, it meant turning the spotlight off. Just in front of our house is a Municipal lamp standard which has a screw in bulb and controlled by a photo electric cell. It comes on when the hens go to roost and goes off automatically at dawn.

For the third consecutive New Year's Eve, I disabled the light by unscrewing the bulb and climbed into the tree equipped with hand saw and a large pruning shears.

This exercise is best performed at midnight and a jar of wet mud to cover the fresh cuts is imperative. Also, clearing away the debris before morning is just as important. The main thing is not to be too excessive or the gaps would be noticed.

These are just some of the subdifuges one has to resort to, in order to make things happen in Provence if one is an étranger. The locals are virtually exempt from any form of permits. There is even a house here on the brow of the mountain and it was allowed by the Mairie because the man that built it was a cronie.

Yes, there is no doubting it, a Mafia style life exists here and the sooner we are rid of the Mayoral system in France, the better for everyone.

Lacoste has become more and more a mecca for travelling artists in search of the perfect landscape and with both Cardin, who is a patron of the arts, plus the Savannah College, who are constantly putting the village on the map, it looks like becoming the art capital of the Provence. At a recent press conference, Cardin stated that he was going to turn the village into the cultural St Tropez of the Luberon

. As I am around the village everyday there is not much goes by without my noticing it and just recently I overheard two English visitors who were looking for a high point to do a painting of the Luberon Valley between Lacoste and Bonnieux.

The highest point in the village is Chateau de Sade, but it is not accessible just yet because of on-going renovations inside. The next best point of panoramic vision is from Sir Tom Stoppard's garden, to which I have a key. The new owners, the Dunns, are frequently away from the property, so I offered the garden to this English artist and let him have the key and asked him to pop it in the letter box when he was finished. Two days later I just checked to see if he was still using the garden and to my surprise, he had left me a letter-box size painting which he obviously created expressively for that purpose and he signed it Alan Cotton. The name meant nothing to me, but Dan Adel who himself is no mean artist, said that Alan Cotton is as famous as God in England. So I looked him up and discovered that he was a travelling artist companion of Prince Charles.

Watercolour of a Greek Urn in Sir Tom Stoppard's Garden

He has invited me to his exhibition at Messum's Studios in London where if I am lucky, I might get to meet the Prince because we have such a lot in common. Organics and historic preservation being both our passions!

David Messum requested a brief account of my life including a photograph as well as the poem I co-wrote with Sir Tom for Alan Cotton's forthcoming album in the fall. This was a golden opportunity to launch my book of poems, titled 'Art Verse and Yarn'. Forty pieces of artwork, forty poems and forty short stories all connected and the idea for this came from an encounter I had with the author John Berger, again here in Lacoste when I was invited to his book launch. A week previously, I was re-planting an olive tree for the Savannah College and while digging the hole, I found a most beautiful old soup ladle and having once read the wonderful poem which Berger wrote about a ladle, I asked him to sign the one I had found. The concept of 'Art Verse and Yarn' evolved from his poem, the ladle and the story of its discovery.

Chapter 93

Meanwhile in Lacoste scaffolding has sprouted like forests of steel. In Bonnieux, the locals prayed for a similar miracle and hoped like anything that Cardin might one day decide that their village was more beautiful and that he might come and invest. A wish in vain I might add. Bonnieux is like a boiled-over pot of milk, it makes no sense as a village and besides it is north facing and acts as a shield for the Mistral.

Almost weekly, Lacoste was being visited by journalists who were all flocking to see what Cardin was doing to the village and one such reporter, Catherine Simone from Le Monde, called by my house to see me. Rather odd, I thought, wondering how she had obtained my address. It appeared that she had spent all day in the village and could not find anyone who was pro-Cardin and the Mayor sent her along to me. We had an hour-long interview and I was expecting that the consequences of the article would certainly have me in the stocks. The villagers were angry and the xenophobia had raised its ugly head. Cardin was offering tenders for the work and the non drinking Arab *maçons*, were winning all the contracts from the French. The local *maçons* were operating a smear campaign and telling everyone that the Arabs were putting inferior materials into the projects and thus being able to quote lower prices.

It was comical to watch and was a similar story with the locals who were renting. They too needed a scapegoat and Cardin was being blamed for everything that was wrong in their lives. They proclaimed that rents would go up so that they could not afford to live here anymore. They could not ever imagine that moving would solve their problems or perhaps that if they just waited to see what was going to transpire and they might even end up working for Cardin and living in one of his properties. They could not see the wonderful changes which were occurring.

A new *boulangerie* was opened by an *artisan Boulanger* and the wafting aroma of fresh bread pervaded the village. Up until then, our bread was being taxied over from Bonnieux and it was utter crap. We were soon to have two hotels and a state of the art café, but nothing would suit the Luddite anti-Christs. They complained that there was not enough parking in the village for the locals. It was the incestuous gossip that was poisoning them and their little lives which went no further than Apt, Coustellet and Bonnieux, had been breached by the outside world and they were not able to cope with it.

They spoke of their discontent to the reporters in the hope that their whingeing might be listened to and that Sarkozy might pass a law which made progress illegal. They were being pathetic and just like the New Zealanders who threatened my life for changing the prohibition laws, I had neither sympathy nor respect for the selfishness of the *Lacostoises* who tried to keep the village elite and whatever Catherine Simone was to write about me didn't matter, because I was in the stocks anyway. We waited for the publication of Le Monde and there was not one positive word in it. It was a totally anti-Cardin article which was obviously the purpose of her visit , why she wasted my time I will never know.

Cardin was not fazed and only days later we had a television crew from TF1 and a more positive twist was being aired to the French public. On this live interview I was asked to go back to Ireland by an irate mini minded Lacoste female resident after I expressed my opinions. Hours later I was invited to do a live transmission direct to America on a radio station in Georgia 1690 AM WMLB with Larry Lawson, and the journalist Joe Webber invited me to go to the US for a full length interview regarding my time since coming to France. There is no doubting it, but Uncle Sam has been my saviour in France and to show my appreciation for everything good that has happened as a result of meeting Bill my AA sponsor, Bob Dickensheets who got me started with the Savannah College and Paula Wallace who helped my buy my house in Lacoste, I was going to take up

Larry Lawson's offer and bring my "Two Suitcases and a Dog" to America.

> " *The thing about America is that there*
> *are so many people who want you to*
> *do well. They will you to do well.*
> *They encourage you and they rejoice*
> *In your success. That's a great virtue".*

The above is a quote from the 'Irish Tenor' Doctor Ronan Tynan, an old friend of mine, who was selected as the only soloist to sing at Ronald Reagan's funeral.

THE END

P.S.

> *I have felt ashamed of having spent my life*
> *trying to please sitters and make friends,*
> *instead of telling the truth and making enemies.*

> *Sir John Lavery (1856-1941)*
> *Irish portrait artist .*

List of Characters

Here are some of the key characters who influenced the book, which began almost 10 years ago. In all, there are 90 people mentioned, but not all are worthy of inclusion as their roles were often only of an en passant cameo in silhouette.
Six are deceased.

AMANDA FRY, who is mentioned in the opening scene at Boulogne Sur Mer, is the only one of the cast who never made an appearance and I have no idea who she is or where she has gone. Perhaps a reader might locate her and put us in contact.

BOY LINGUS is still working for the tourist board of Nord Pas De Calais, but apparently refuses to speak English after the annoyance we gave him.

EMANUELLE LAGA, our fairy godmother and the biggest player of all, is marketing manager for Nausicaa. Recently she met a Frenchman and from her years of experience at the marine aquarium, proved without doubt, that only frogs can be turned into princes.

FRANCOISE AND MARC PETERLONGO sold their house in Cruis after they found 50 of Monsieur Giraud's sheep in their swimming pool, Baathing !

BILL, my AA sponsor lives between Paris and Naples Florida. I keep meaning to ask him where that is exactly.

MADAME CLAUDE sold at Auriol and lives in Tuscany where she studies angst.

MICHAEL, The Master has a Chambre d'Hôtes near Salon, where the soap is made. He once remarked that it was not a noble way to make a fortune.

MADAME FERLIN lives on Rue du Temple, Lourmarin and still wonders what Montgomery did with all the bananas she served him at the chateau after the war.

FRANK. Frank has a better story than any to tell and why perhaps he featured so much in our lives. Without his generosity of spirit, Two Suitcases and a dog might not have materialized

CRUELLA, who is incognito and often wears camouflage, can be seen walking sideways along the beach at St Tropez.

WHISPERING GRASS, when he is not at the Pizza Place in Cadenet, will be at the end of Cruella's extension lead and responding in repetitious threesomes of yes, yes, yes, to every tug on the line.

BERNARD AND ZENIA are currently selling La Royante after a successful five years in business.

SUPER TAF is still operating his shop in Lourmarin and no doubt wiping his doughnuts with his butchers apron.

MONSIEUR JEAN, our patron is still reclusing in the mausoleum his father built in the shade.

BOB DICKENSHEETS has moved to manage another department of the SCAD college in the US.

ERIC CLAPTON can be seen on the Cours Mirabeau in Aix en Provence scratching his head and wondering why the Irishman failed to recognize him.

PIERRE CARDIN has bought a property next door to us and the neighbours seem to think that he is going to leave his entire fortune to me.

DAN ADEL is hoping my book will be a success and that the fame will rub off on him.

TOM STOPPARD moved back to London, after losing the poet laureate of Lacoste bid, to a dyslexic schizophrenic Paddy who was the only boy in Ireland to fail the primary certificate.

PETER MAYLE only barely made the list. Not because he refused me the right to use the 4 word quote, nor was it due to his derogatory remark about Mr Murphy and the Irish.

No! It was because he ate LES.

Two suitcases and a dog